D1009857

CHICAGO STUDIES IN THE HISTORY OF AMERICAN RELIGION

Editors

JERALD C. BRAUER
AND MARTIN E. MARTY

A CARLSON PUBLISHING SERIES

For a complete listing of the titles in this series,
please see the back of this book.

Fall from Grace

RELIGION AND THE COMMUNAL IDEAL IN TWO SUBURBAN VILLAGES, 1870-1917

James F. Bundy

PREFACE BY MARTIN E. MARTY

CARLSON
Publishing Inc

BROOKLYN, NEW YORK, 1991

BR
560
.015
B86

Please see the end of this volume for a listing of all the titles in the Carlson Publishing Series *Chicago Studies in the History of American Religion*, edited by Jerald C. Brauer and Martin E. Marty, of which this is Volume 2.

Copyright © 1991 by James F. Bundy

Library of Congress Cataloging-in-Publication Data

Bundy, James F., 1942-
    Fall from grace : religion and the communal ideal in two suburban
villages, 1870-1917 / James F. Bundy ; preface by Martin E. Marty.
        p.   cm. — (Chicago studies in the history of American
religion ; 2)
    Includes bibliographical references and index.
    ISBN 0-926019-40-6
    1. Oak Park (Ill.)—Religion. 2. Evanston (Ill.)—Religion.
3. Sociology, Christian—Illinois—Oak Park. 4. Sociology,
Christian—Illinois—Evanston.   I. Title.   II. Series.
BR560.015B86   1991
306.6'09773'1—dc20   91-27973

Typographic design: Julian Waters

Typeface: Bitstream ITC Galliard

Case design: Alison Lew

Index prepared by Scholars Editorial Services, Inc., Madison, Wisconsin, using NL Cindex, a scholarly indexing program from the Newberry Library.

Printed on acid-free, 250-year-life paper.

Manufactured in the United States of America.

Contents

An Introduction
to the Series

The *Chicago Studies in the History of American Religion* is a series of books that deal with topics ranging from the time of Jonathan Edwards to the 1970s. Three or four deal with colonial topics and three or four treat the very recent past. About half of them focus on the decades just before and after 1900. One deals with blacks; two concentrate on women. Revivalists, fundamentalists, theologians, life in the suburbs and life in heaven and hell, the Beecher family of old and a monk of new times, Catholics adapting to America and Protestants fighting one another—all these subjects assure that the series has scope. People of every kind of taste and curiosity about American religion will find some books to suit them. Does anything serve to characterize the series as a whole? What does the stamp of "Chicago studies" mean?

Yale historian Sydney Ahlstrom in *A Religious History of the American People*, as influential as any twentieth-century work in its field, pays respect to the "Chicago School" of American religious historians. William Warren Sweet, the pioneer in such studies (beginning in 1927) at Chicago and, in many ways, in America at large represented the culmination of "the Protestant synthesis" in this field. Ahlstrom went on to name two later generations of Chicagoans, including the seminal Sidney E. Mead and major figures like Robert T. Handy and Winthrop Hudson and ending with the two editors of this series. He saw them as often "openly rebellious" in respect to Sweet and his synthesis.

If, as Ahlstrom says, "a disproportionate number" of historians have some connection with the Chicago School, it must be said that the new generation represented in these twenty-one books carries on both the lineage of Sweet and something of the "openly rebellious" character that scholars at Chicago are encouraged to pursue. This means, for one thing, that the "Protestant synthesis" does not characterize their work. These historians question the canon of historical writing produced in the Protestant era even as many of them continue to pursue themes shaped in a Protestant culture. Few of them concentrate on the old "frontier thesis" that marked the early years of the school. The shift for most has been toward the urban and pluralist scene. They call into question, not in devastating rage but in steady patterns of inquiry, the received wisdom about who matters, and why, in American religion.

So it is that this series of books focuses on blacks, women, dispensationalists, suburbanites, members of "marginal" denominations, "ethnics" and immigrants as readily as it does on white men of progressive urban bent in mainstream denominations and of long standing in America. The authors relish religious diversity and enjoy discovering the power of people once considered weak, the centrality to the American plot of those once regarded as peripheral, and the potency of losers who were once disdained by winners. Thus this series enhances an understanding of an America overlooked by the people of Sweet's era two-thirds of a century ago when it all, or most of it, began.

Rebellion for its own sake would not long hold interest; it might tell more about the psychology of rebels and revisers than about their subject matter. Revision, better than rebellion, characterizes the scholars. Re + vision: that's it. There was an original vision that characterized the Chicago School. This was the contention that in secular America and its universities religion mattered, as a theme in the national past and as a presence in the present. Second, it argued that the study of religious history belonged not only in the seminaries and archives of denominations, but also in the rough-and-tumble of the secular university, where no religious meanings were privileged and where each historian had to make a case for the value of his or her story.

Other assumptions from the earliest days pervade the books in this series. They are uncommonly alert to the environment in which expressions of faith occur. That is, they do not take for granted that religion comes protected in self-evidently important and hermetically sealed packages. Churches and denominations are porous, even when they would be sealed off; they cannot be understood apart from the ways the social environs effect them, but their power to effect change in the environment demands equal and truly unapologetic treatment. These writers do not shuffle and mumble and make excuses for their existence or for the choice of apparently arcane subject matter. They try to present their narrative in such ways that they compel attention.

A fourth characteristic that colors these works is a refusal in most cases to be typed in a fashionable slot labeled, variously, "intellectual" or "institutional" history, "cultural" or "social" history, or whatever. While those which concentrate on magisterial thinkers such as Jonathan Edwards are necessarily busy with and devoted to his intellectual achievement, most of the books deal with figures who cannot be understood only as exemplars in a sequence of studies of "the life of the mind." Instead, their biographies and circumstances come very much into play. On the other hand, none of these writers is a reductionist who sees religion as "nothing but" this or that—"nothing but" the working out of believers' Oedipal urges or expressing the economic and class interests of the subjects. Social history becomes in its way intellectual history, even if the intellects are focused on something other than the theologians in the traditions might like to see.

Some years ago *Look* magazine interviewed leaders in various denominations. One was asked if his fellow believers considered that theirs was the only true faith. Yes, he said, but they did not believe that they were the only ones who held it. The editors of this series of studies and the contributors to it do not believe that the "Chicago School," whenever and whatever it was, is the only true approach to American religious history. And, if they did, they would not hold that Chicagoans alone held it. To do so would imply a strange solipsistic or narcissistic impulse that would be the death of collegiality in the historical field. They have welcomed the chance to be in a climate where their inquiries are given such encouragement, where they find a company of fellow scholars in the Divinity School, the History Department, and the Committee on the History of Culture, whence these studies first emerged, and elsewhere in a university that provides a congenial home for massed and massive concentration of a special sort on American religious history.

While the undersigned have been consistently involved, most often together, in all twenty-one books, we want to single out a third person mentioned in so many acknowledgment sections, historian Arthur Mann. He has been a partner in two or three dozen religious history dissertation projects through the years and has been an influential and decisive contributor to the results. We stand in his debt.

Jerald C. Brauer
Martin E. Marty

Editor's Preface

Two American suburbs, Oak Park and Evanston, Illinois, "fell from grace," argues James F. Bundy in this close-up view of two communities. Why should anyone care? Why should people in Florida or Alaska, Hawaii or Maine, bother about a close-up of communities in the heartland of the United States, so far from them and their ways? Aside from the fact that Bundy's account makes for good reading, and is rich with stories of interesting, noble, and foolish people doing interesting, noble, and foolish things, why give notice to these two villages and not others?

Answers to such questions will unfold in the mind of readers as they encounter Bundy's chapters, but we can anticipate some of them here. First of all, the suburb has been given too little attention by historians. There are histories of small towns and great cities, but the suburb, home of so many millions of Americans today, has been neglected. Sociologists, of course, have discovered such communities and discussed their contemporary workings. Rarely have they paid attention to pre-World War I experiments, however. Social prophets look quickly, gasp in horror, and scorn suburbs as banal perversions of Jeffersonian agrarian or utopian urban ideals. What we have lacked is chronicles of how such suburbs were founded and what happened to the ideals of the founders. Bundy's is an original work that throws light on two foundings and, by indirection, on many more.

Why a close-up? Of course, one can learn something from integrative histories that correlate the foundings and unfoldings of suburbs everywhere. It is possible to compare charters, statistics, and other "falls from grace." But there is also no substitute for the immediacy that a work like this one offers. There is a certain sense of smell, sight, and sound a reader gets from coming across newspaper accounts, letters, and arguments from the people who lived on the scene, who most cared. Just as we learned about many "middletowns" from the famous studies of *Middletown* in the 1920s and 1930s and about many colonial villages from a host of close-ups of New England villages, so we can begin to learn more about suburbs from *Fall from Grace*.

Why Oak Park and Evanston? There are good "objective" reasons for the choice. Bundy does not claim they are unique, but that they are distinctive. Both were founded by white Protestants who had very clarified ideas about community formation. They all but re-created what they thought New England villages were about. They talked about classic concepts like "covenant" and "morality," and they put their actions where their mouths were. When newcomers arrived who did not find such concepts congenial, the founders began to complain in the best American "there goes the neighborhood" tones that a fall from grace had begun.

In the hands of a sneering, condescending, or impatient historian, this tale would suffer. Bundy knows that the righteous could be self-righteous, that those with lofty ideals often looked down on others, that they sometimes tried to effect through law—for example, prohibition—what they could not attain by persuasion. Yet he shows a small measure of awe and large portion of empathy for people who at least had some idea of how community should look. He also spends creative energies seeing how and why the twin satellites of Chicago took somewhat different courses, chiefly because Evanston had a major university and thus an earlier, wider window on pluralism. There are lessons for other communities here, but before one tries to draw lessons it is valid simply to enjoy a story, and this one, with its version of aspirations and frustrations, is a good one.

Martin E. Marty

Acknowledgments

I wish first of all to express my appreciation to Martin Marty, whose guidance has been invaluable throughout the project and whose encouragement has been an important motivation for me to bring the work to completion. I would also like to thank Arthur Mann and Jerald Brauer. I am grateful for the assistance and courtesy extended to me by members of the staffs of the Oak Park Public Library, the Evanston Historical Society, and the Northwestern University Library. Finally, at an entirely different level, I am grateful to my wife, Jo Carole, for her support and ideas, and to my parents, Fred and Kate Bundy, for a lifetime of support.

Fall from Grace

Introduction

Between the Civil War and World War I a number of forces connected with urbanization and industrialization came increasingly and rapidly to dominate American life. In one sense these developments were encouraging to people who had experienced the devastations of war. A great fratricidal conflict had ended and the way was open to make some new beginnings. The growth of cities and industrial enterprises did much to create an atmosphere of renewed belief in the seemingly limitless possibilities of the American experiment. A new age brought forth new hopes. Progress was once again the order of the day. Immense energy and vitality could be seen in the burgeoning activity of city life. A time of unprecedented prosperity was at hand, and although the benefits of prosperity were distributed unequally, industrial leaders such as Andrew Carnegie and religious leaders such as Henry Ward Beecher alike expressed the conviction that material growth would go hand in hand with moral and spiritual advance. The nation was perhaps once again on its way toward fulfilling a divinely appointed mission.

Yet as cities grew, a new set of realities began to be exposed that cast doubt on some of the traditional assumptions about what should characterize the life of American communities. Increasingly, the realities of the industrial city troubled people, not alone because of the magnitude of new social problems that had to be confronted, but also because of what urban realities might portend for the future integrity and uniqueness of American life. Immigrants, settling largely in cities, seemed to band together and resist being assimilated into what others believed should be the prevailing standards and dominant values of the culture. The growing strength of Roman Catholicism disturbed those who felt implicitly that Protestant Christianity was the spiritual foundation for the republic or, more broadly, those who felt that Roman Catholicism was inconsistent with patriotism. Extremes of wealth and poverty pointed toward an increasing class-consciousness and hardening of class divisions such as many Americans had believed the nation could avoid. Conflicts between labor and management, sometimes breaking into violence, obviously threatened the peace and further accentuated class divisions. Many forms of vice visibly flourished in the cities, and gradually the evidence mounted that corruption was just as prevalent, though more clandestine, in government and business.

For these reasons, and many others, the city might mean not only great prosperity and vitality but also impending chaos. It presented people with conflicting "signs of the times." Josiah Strong, a Congregational minister and best-selling author whose books sought to interpret contemporary trends, put the matter this way:

> A tale of two cities comes down to us from an ancient book. In its opening pages we see the first city built by the first murderer; and it would seem as if vice and crime had festered in the city ever since. In the closing pages of the book we find a glorious city as a fitting type of civilization perfected—a vision of the kingdom of God come fully in the earth.[1]

The Bible anticipated and confirmed contemporary experience. The city could at once foster the meanest human passions and express the noblest human aspirations.

Historians have treated many phases of urban growth and the responses to it. General histories of urban and industrial development as well as histories of specific cities have been produced. Agrarian panic and revolt and a host of urban reform movements have been understood as responses to the new world that the city was coming to dominate in both concrete and symbolic ways. On the national scene, the Populist and Progressive movements have been treated as, in part, responses to the problems posed by the city. A number of authors have recognized that the city presented problems of identity and meaning as well as specific social and economic problems. Those who have studied the churches' responses to change in this period have noted shifts in theological and sociological thinking among church leaders and have analyzed the varieties of church activity and organization within the city.

Thus, in general, the problems arising out of urbanization and industrialization have been approached either from the standpoint of the struggles going on within the geographical confines of the city itself or from the standpoint of the effects the city had on the small towns and rural areas that had been thought to provide the social, economic, and spiritual foundation of the nation. Largely ignored have been the towns that began to spring up on the urban fringe. These towns were not firmly embedded in a rural environment, but neither were they yet wholly suburban, that is, defined as an integral part of an urban-metropolitan network. When, in the post-World War II era, suburban communities began to receive a great deal of attention, the literature generally lacked historical perspective and was often polemical in nature.

In the Chicago area, two suburban communities that came to prominence during the late nineteenth and early twentieth centuries were Oak Park and Evanston. This book attempts to tell a portion of their story. The story is, in part, a story of people involved in and responding to the changes wrought by urbanization and industrialization. By interpreting these communities in this light, it is hoped that a dimension may be added to our understanding of the impact of the city on people and the ways people tried to deal with, or failed to deal with, the various disruptions in social life and ways of thinking and feeling. Though no claim is made that Oak Park and Evanston should be considered "typical" suburbs, their story may help to create a fuller, more diverse understanding of suburbs as a part of urbanization. I draw a portrait of people in Oak Park and Evanston: Who were they? What were the assumptions, beliefs, and cherished values that caused them to be troubled by the city? How did these beliefs and values guide the way they responded to the city and the ways they attempted to shape their own communities? What was the nature of the hopes that people invested in these communities?

The story of Oak Park and Evanston is not, of course, one-dimensional. The people involved traveled in an already heterogeneous society. Though, as we shall see, consciousness of a New England heritage was evident among the native born residents of Evanston and Oak Park, they might nevertheless bring with them a wide range of backgrounds, experiences, and attitudes. The combination of conscious motives and circumstances that could bring people to live in Evanston or Oak Park were many-faceted and complex. Attitudes and actions once there were naturally not uniform. Though many of the differences found in the communities are discussed, it cannot be assumed that all residents fell within the range of the descriptive terms and categories employed in this study. Of necessity, many people and events of interest and importance to the communities do not receive the attention they might deserve in a different context.

Nevertheless, even a passing acquaintance with the history and characteristics of the two suburbs ought to be sufficient to convince one that Oak Park and Evanston command attention as something more than aggregates of diverse individuals held together only by a desire to live in suburban surroundings, near to but apart from the city. Both Oak Parkers and Evanstonians believed

3

that a special sense of community characterized their suburbs, and there were frequent attempts to express precisely what constituted their distinctiveness and what they stood for amid the confusion and disarray of contemporary society. Both communities were temperance communities and remained so until quite recently. This was an important, though by no means the only, identifying characteristic that might be pointed to by residents and nonresidents alike. It is thus the primary purpose of this discussion to understand those who shaped, articulated, supported, and defended a special sense of community in Oak Park and Evanston and to follow them as they encountered various kinds of challenges to their vision in the period prior to 1917.

The theme explored is that these people drew heavily on and were inspired by an idea of an American covenanted community in which religion was to provide the foundation, the socially and spiritually unifying force that could endow not only personal but also corporate life with transcendent significance. Born and finding its archetypal expression in seventeenth-century New England, the idea and practice of the covenanted community was carried, in part consciously and in part by virtue of unexamined assumption, first to western New England and New York and then into the Northwest Territory. Though modified significantly by its successive environments and the course of events over several centuries, the tradition of the New England village was kept alive and continued to exert its hold on the imagination of people at varying times and under differing circumstances. Therefore, this is also a story of how this ideal fared when brought into a metropolitan context and when faced with the encroachment of urban and pluralistic patterns of thought and social organization.

Evanston and Oak Park were the most prestigious and best-known of Chicago suburbs during a period when the city itself was experiencing phenomenal growth, undergoing great turmoil, taking on the characteristics of a major urban center, and establishing its own particular identity as a city. The two suburbs were contiguous to Chicago, Oak Park on the west and Evanston on the north, and their relationship to the city was thus neither abstract nor remote. Residents of the two communities were themselves aware of a common bond between them, while at the same time they engaged in a friendly rivalry. They were sufficiently similar to invite that they be studied together, while at the same time they were sufficiently different as to invite comparison, a major difference being that Evanston's history was influenced, as Oak Park's was not, by the establishment of a major institution of higher learning, Northwestern University. Their stature as important suburbs of

Chicago asks that they receive the attention of those concerned with the past, present, and future of American cities and that their story become part of the record of urbanization. Their particular way of setting themselves apart from the city, involving as I believe it did the ideal of the covenanted community, asks that they receive the attention of those concerned with the social role of religion in American life. In any case these have been the concerns that have informed the study.

ONE

The Covenanted Community and the City in a Garden

We must be knit together in this work as one man.
Governor John Winthrop, 1630

We should aim at unity of spirit and unity of action.
Joseph Balestier, Chicago, 1840

In the latter part of the nineteenth century Chicago underwent a transformation. What had once been a frontier boom town became, in the space of just several decades, a giant commercial and industrial metropolis. The population, which had been only 30,000 in 1850, climbed to 300,000 in 1870, and by 1900 it had reached almost 1,700,000. Much of the increase was accounted for by immigrants who flooded into the city. By 1890 more than three-quarters of Chicago's population were immigrants or the children of immigrants.[1] Another reason for the growth was geographical expansion. One community after another during this period found itself unable to resist annexation. In almost every respect the city assumed proportions of an awesome character. It generated enormous activity and enormous social problems. It also generated wonder, fascination, and fear. What was happening in Chicago staggered the imagination. The implications of what was happening were perhaps even more staggering, though difficult to comprehend.

An additional aspect of Chicago's transformation was the growth of suburbs, and the two most prominent of these were Oak Park, located about eight miles inland directly west of center city, and Evanston, along the lake shore to the north. As these communities took shape toward the end of the century, they would have appeared to the naked eye as modern suburbs of a modern city. They had grown up alongside of Chicago. Their growth in size and importance largely paralleled and depended on the growth of Chicago. Many of their residents made their living in the city and in many other ways availed themselves of what the city had to offer. Within the communities, population growth and the addition of new homes and public improvements bespoke success, and the architecture of homes and businesses and churches was at least in keeping with the times, if not ahead of the times.[2] There was nothing about these communities that was anachronistic, little on the surface that would have immediately reminded one of an earlier day.

Yet Oak Park and Evanston were undeniably different from Chicago, too. That the residents felt their communities to be different was evidenced by the determined and successful efforts to avoid annexation. For some people that difference was merely snobbery and elitism. Oak Park and Evanston represented a social exclusiveness and moral self-righteousness that indicated that the residents of these places had turned their backs on the city while still taking advantage of the benefits they might selfishly derive from it. Oak Parkers and Evanstonians were not unaware of this negative image, nor were they insensitive to the charges that might be leveled against them on such grounds. Nevertheless, viewed from the inside the issues were cast in different terms. For many Oak Parkers and Evanstonians what inspired loyalty to their respective communities and what caused them to resist annexation with such passion was not merely a distaste for the city, its ways, and its people. It was rather a belief in and commitment to a distinct form of community life wherein resided the unique qualities of American life. While many people perhaps did not understand or attach much importance to where their notions of community life came from, the word "Puritan" surfaced not infrequently in efforts to describe what the communities stood for. If the intent was often to distinguish the communities as being more modern and enlightened than the image of Puritan communities, the very use of the word and the apparent need to confront the image was still a strong indication that Chicago was not the only point of reference for these modern suburbs. They were to measure themselves also by the precedents established by the original Puritan settlements in the New World. Thus, although it is hard to imagine that the seventeenth-century Puritan village was much more than a dim ancestral memory to the people of Oak Park and Evanston, their story must still be allowed to begin at that distant point.

The Covenanted Community

The keynote for the covenanted community in New England had been sounded by Gov. John Winthrop in his now famous lay sermon aboard the *Arbella* while still en route to the New World. Winthrop set out to remind people in no uncertain terms of the purposes of their journey, which were not to pursue selfish motives or satisfy "carnal intentions." They were to establish a "due form of government, both civil and ecclesiastical," the end of which, Winthrop said, was

> to improve our lives, to do more service to the Lord . . . that our selves and posterity may be the better preserved from the common corruptions of this evil world, to serve the Lord and work out our salvation under the power and purity of his holy ordinances.

Winthrop sought to impress on people that they had embarked on a divinely appointed mission. "Thus stands the cause between God and us. We are entered into a covenant with Him for this work." This, Winthrop believed, would require a strict fidelity. "That which the most in their churches maintain as a truth in profession only, we must bring into familiar and constant practice. . . . When God gives a special commission, he looks to have it strictly observed in every article." As the people were bound collectively to God, so were they bound to one another.

> . . . We must be knit together in this work as one man, we must entertain each other in brotherly affection, we must be willing to abridge ourselves of our superfluities for the supply of others' necessities . . . we must delight in each other, make others' conditions our own, rejoice together, mourn together, labor and suffer together, always having before our eyes our Commission and community.

In all of this, the people were to recognize that the importance of their work far transcended themselves.

> For we must consider that we shall be as a city upon a hill. The eyes of all people are upon us, so that if we shall deal falsely with our God in this work we have undertaken, and so cause Him to withdraw His present help from us, we shall be made a story and a by-word through the world.[3]

Thus Winthrop had laid out the broad rhetorical foundation for Puritan community life in the New World and had initiated the tradition of the "covenanted community."

The Puritan covenant, however, was much more than a theological construct articulated on significant occasions by spokesmen such as John Winthrop and leaving people free to struggle with its implications as they might will or desire. It came to be at the "constitutional" center of existence of each individual town or village, a written covenant being formally subscribed to by all who would become citizens of the community. Further, the covenant was enacted and its implications worked out in countless day-to-day activities and decisions. The covenant not only expressed a vision; it also functioned to guide concretely the policies and decisions that were meant, as fully as was humanly possible, to make that vision a living reality.

Still, as the Puritans knew better than anyone, there was inevitably a gulf between the covenant as vision and the covenant as reality. Thus while the term "utopian," which has been used by several historians to describe the covenanted community, may be useful in understanding the spirit of the Puritan village, several differences between the consciousness of the Puritans and the consciousness often associated with utopian experiments must be noted as a precaution.[4]

In the first place, whatever historians may perceive as the fact of the matter, the Puritans themselves were not conscious of making a radical break with their past or with the society with which they were familiar. The New World environment made possible some adaptations of English precedents and required others. Nevertheless, the Puritans conceived of themselves as bringing to fruition, in a way impossible in England, commitments, values, and aspirations already implicit in English Protestantism and English culture in general.[5] Such an attitude continued to be a part of American towns. The communities that later attempted to reproduce in their own way the covenanted community did not propound their radical opposition to the culture but saw themselves as embodying the highest ideals and deepest commitments of that culture. The difference was, of course, that the cultural reference point had become America.

Second, Puritans had a well-developed consciousness of human frailty and sinfulness. No illusions were harbored about the innate perfectibility of individual men. Consequently, the burden of perfection fell heavily on the community as a social organism as opposed to the aggregate of its individuals. This situation conferred a dual status on the idea of the covenant. On the one hand, aware that fallen individuals would inevitably sin or fail to live up to the full responsibility of their calling, the covenant functioned concretely to suggest proper means by which disputes could be settled, sins be forgiven, and policies be instituted that furthered communal rather than selfish ends.

At the same time the covenant performed a "mythological" function. It stood as a standard against which all forms of human community could be measured. Thus, each town's specific written covenant was only a particular expression of the more inclusive covenant that God had made with his people. If a community fell away from its covenantal obligations, if it failed in the terms of the covenant, it did not therefore mean that the experiment was doomed.[6] God could find a remnant. A new promised land could be designated. The idea of the covenanted community could no more be invalidated by the failure of specific communities than could the authority of holy scripture be questioned as a result of the shortcomings of a Bible commonwealth. Out of this perhaps grew a stubborn resistance to change that was so often a characteristic of covenanted communities. But the dual nature of the covenant is also responsible for a peculiar resiliency that allowed the covenanted community to be continually re-formed and to constitute itself as a tradition in a way that utopian communities are generally unable to do.

With these reservations duly noted, however, it is still possible to say that it was a utopian impulse that provided the enormous energy, psychic as well as physical, with which the Puritans approached the task of community building. Individually and together the communities were to constitute a holy commonwealth, bound by covenant to God and knit together as a unified, purposeful, organic society by a covenant with each other. A drive for purity in all phases of human affairs was central and unmistakable in these communities.

The Puritan covenant in whatever form, town covenant or church covenant or generalized covenant, was first of all a covenant with God. From this all other manifestations and characteristics of the covenanted community flowed. To be as "a city upon a hill" meant that God had chosen this people to reveal his will for human society. The covenanted community was above all a missionary community, and this only secondarily in the sense that it was given the task of enlarging the sphere of Christendom by converting the heathen natives to the true faith. Primarily, its task was to demonstrate to the civilized world the possibility of a holy commonwealth, and for this purpose it had been given a virgin soil, a promised land, where a truly new beginning could be made.[7] It had been sent on "an errand into the wilderness." Thus its success was to be measured not only by the quality of life it produced within itself but also by the extent to which it was looked to for example and inspiration by a fallen world.[8]

A necessary corollary to this consciousness of having been sent on a holy "errand" was the idea that a common purpose and clarity of intent must characterize the covenanted community. These must not be towns where some came to get rich, some came to escape personal difficulties, while still others came out of sacred duty. Secondary benefits might well accrue to individuals, but there must be unanimous agreement (a more realistic word would be acquiescence) on the foundations for the community's life and its fundamental reason for existence. The Dedham town covenant drawn up in 1636 included the following as part of its fourth provision:

> That every man that . . . shall have lots in our said town shall pay his share in all such . . . charges as shall be imposed on him . . . as also become freely subject unto all such orders and constitutions as shall be . . . made now or at any time here after from this day forward, as well for loving and comfortable society in our said town as also for the prosperous and thriving condition of our said fellowship, especially respecting the fear of God, in which we desire to begin and continue whatsoever we shall by his loving favor take into hand.[9]

Whatever material prosperity or adversity Dedham encountered, it was not to lose sight of the fact that the town was founded on the "fear of God." Circumstances might change, but not the shared sense of purpose that had brought the community into being and that continued to provide the meaning of its corporate existence.

The unity thought necessary for the covenanted community extended beyond a diffuse sense of purpose, however. More concrete manifestations of faith and purpose were required if the community were not to dissolve into a morass of uncertainty, mistrust, and misunderstanding. Such unity might be evidenced in several ways.

One way of attempting to ensure that everyone understood that the community fundamentally existed only to fulfill its divinely appointed task was to make clear the need for a common profession of belief. Thus article one of the Dedham covenant stated:

> We whose names are here unto subscribed do, in the fear and reverence of our Almighty God, mutually and severally promise amongst ourselves and each other to profess and practice one truth according to that most perfect rule, the foundation whereof is everlasting love.[10]

12

The town covenant could set forth the ideal of the profession and practice of one truth and require that everyone carry out his daily business in the spirit of Christian love and brotherly affection. But there was a difficulty hidden both in what the town covenant said and in what it did not say. For while all might agree "to profess and practice one truth," it was not the business of the town to set down specifically what that truth exactly was. This was reserved to the church.

The close relationship between the church and civil society in Puritan communities is well known. These were, after all, religious colonies, and the Christian faith was to illumine every aspect of secular activity. In addition to the sense of being engaged in God's work, the Puritans consulted the Bible for guidance both in the implementation of specific ordinances and in the effort to understand their situation as a chosen people. Thus the church could clearly be considered not just one among many institutions of the society; it stood, literally as well as figuratively, at the center of the town's life. From it flowed both the spirit of a resurrected Christianity and the more specific commandments, affirmations, and beliefs that were to give substance to the entire experiment. Thus attendance at religious services was required of all townspeople, the church was supported by public monies, ministers were called on to deliver sermons on important public occasions such as elections, and church membership in the early years was required for voting privileges. For the Puritans there was no "sphere" of religion; the entire enterprise was religious.

What is less understood, perhaps, is that there was a kind of "division of labor" between the church and civil institutions that if it was not rigid was nonetheless real. In his study of Dedham, Kenneth Lockridge alluded to the special role the church played:

> Founding a church was more difficult than founding a town. For the town, it had been enough to write down the skeletal social ordinances of the Covenant, whereupon admissions and allotments had gone forward, but months of painstaking discussion had to pass before a church covenant could be agreed upon. The basic principles were probably clear from the beginning, since they were largely the principles already written into the town Covenant. But in seeking to establish a true church the townsmen were trying to discover the exact means of salvation, a task whose implications were of the utmost importance.[11]

It was not that the founding of the town and the wording of its covenant had been unimportant. But the purity of the town and the purity of the church were of slightly different orders.

The church required of its members a testimony to the effect that they had experienced a conversion and thus were able freely and naturally to make a confession of faith, submit to all ordinances flowing from the covenant, and care for one another in a spirit of love and affection, not merely out of a sense of obligation. Church members thus constituted a fellowship of saints who adhered to the covenant as an outward sign of an inward and spiritual grace. In a sense they were an eschatological community even with God's chosen; they prefigured the end toward which all of society was moving. Unity in the church was guaranteed by and was a natural result of the fact that all members had personally received grace.

The role of the church then was to "point the way" for society at large. If the town covenant had to be content with the oath "to profess and practice one truth according to that most perfect rule, the foundation whereof is everlasting love," the church had the responsibility of going beyond this to define the characteristics of a worshiping community consisting only of "saints." The Dedham church created a sort of catechism to define the doctrinal basis of the proposed church. Question three asked "whether having these privileges of Christian communion and being bound by such duties [of Christian love] we may not rest in such a condition and look no further?" And the answer was:

> Negatively, we may not, but must seek for a further union even such as may . . . convey unto us all the ordinances of Christ's instituted worship, both because it is the command of God . . . and also because the spiritual condition of every Christian is such as stand in need of all instituted ordinances for the repair of the spirit.[12]

In the remainder of the catechism, in the church covenant, and in the church bylaws the "ordinances of Christ's instituted worship" were spelled out. The church reminded the community at large of its past and pulled it toward the future, proclaiming and, wherever possible, embodying the ends for which it had been established.

Speaking on behalf of the congregation of saints, the minister acted as interpreter and prophet. He was by law prohibited from holding civil positions. It was thought necessary that he be well educated. While he performed pastoral duties and was responsible for educating people in the faith, he commonly did not perform marriages or preside at funerals; these functions were handled by a civil officer. Such laws and customs reinforced the expectation that he preach the Word of God and stand somewhat apart from the routine of community life so that he could interpret to the community the meaning of things. Such meaning could be found everywhere. By carefully examining scripture, parallel patterns could be discerned between the story of the chosen people of old and the present-day story. Natural events were seen as signs from God. Wars and internal conflicts were likewise interpreted as evidence of God's displeasure. If the community was straying off its given course, the minister was obliged to prophesy, elucidating the nature of and reasons for the apostasy and exhorting the community to restore itself to the purpose for which it has been ordained. The minister told the town "how it was doing," where it had been and where it was heading. He was never fundamentally at odds with the society for he did not question the basic presuppositions on which it was founded; on the contrary, he continually resanctified those presuppositions and recalled the society to them.

By contrast to the church, the town was a covenanted community "in process." Its unity could not be precisely that of the saints, for even during periods when church membership included most residents of the town, a substantial number remained outside the covenant of the church.[13] Occasionally men were even elected to civil office without being members of the church. From the standpoint of absolutes and ultimate ends, the town contained imperfections. Nevertheless, it could aim at purity by so constituting itself that it might be a perfect vehicle for God's gradual and inexorable work in history to lead human society and individuals to salvation. In order to be this, the covenanted community had to be an orderly, smoothly functioning organism, united in will and intent if not in accomplished fact.

Two kinds of unity, going beyond mutual love and respect, were thus still necessary for the town if God and the church were to work effectively in and through it. Absolute obedience both to town ordinances and to an orderly process of settling disputes must be insisted on. Dissent and disorderliness would result in a breach of the covenant, gradual erosion of the community's singleness of purpose, and loss of the power to command the attention of those presumed to be looking to the Puritans for demonstrations of a new hope. More pragmatically, it would increase the possibility of English intervention in colonial affairs. Second, steps must be taken to ensure that all residents of the town at least desired and willed to grow into communion with God and the church, if they had not already had the experience of conversion.

Thus the community must be exclusive, accepting to the town covenant only those who they had reason to believe sincerely aimed at both their personal inclusion among the fellowship of saints and the ultimate accomplishing of God's intention through the covenants he had established. All of this was written into the town covenant.[14]

Perhaps paradoxically to the modern mind, it was the policy of exclusiveness that aimed at making repression unnecessary. This is not to say that there were scruples against the rigid exercise of authority when needed; the protection of civil liberties was not high on the list of Puritan values. Nevertheless, it was unity rather than repression that was the goal. Indeed, the very need for repressive action was considered a sign that something had gone wrong. Either applicants for admission to the town had been misjudged or something had happened to cause a breakdown in the singleness of purpose of the community.

The policy of exclusiveness necessarily produced a certain homogeneity in Puritan communities, but caution should be exercised in extrapolating from this either extreme intolerance of all differences or a tendency toward economic or political democracy. Evidence can be marshaled on both sides of such issues because Puritans accepted on the one hand the givenness of social and class differences and on the other hand worked to ameliorate the more extreme effects of radical differences in class and status that might be productive of disunity and discord. Neither pride nor exploitation on the part of "superior" classes nor resentment or rebellion on the part of "inferior" classes could be tolerated. The homogeneity intended was explicitly expressed as spiritual. "Only such . . . as may probably be of one heart with us" was the phrase used in Dedham. The problem, of course, was how to read the heart of a prospective citizen. The Puritans, living in a small face-to-face society, could engage in a rigorous process of testimony from the applicant and from all others who might have information bearing on his character in order to make the decision. In other communities under different circumstances it might be necessary to accept more superficial evidences of being "of one heart," and homogeneity might take on a different cast altogether.

To summarize, the Puritan archetype of the covenanted community was held, both ideologically and by written covenant, to be in special relationship to God. It had been given a special role to carry out in God's overall plan for the world. For this purpose the Puritans had been given a charter and safe passage to a new land where the principles of a reformed Christianity and a society based on love could be brought to fruition. The success of the mission and its integrity depended on all members abiding by God's ordinances, agreeing to resolve disputes peaceably and amicably, and sharing common beliefs and goals. The symbol of the community's faith and intent was the church. It served to place the process of everyday life within a frame of meaning, to interpret the significance of events, and to remind the community of its fundamental purpose. Each community was a separate and equal experiment in the life of the covenant. It was a microcosm of what God expected from his people as a whole. Thus each community functioned largely independently while feeling itself spiritually allied to like communities elsewhere. Out of a world fraught with compromise, disintegration, and worldliness would arise a new kind of community life based on order, love, and reverence.

Once the Puritan "synthesis" began to break down, its fullness could never be recovered. The unique and delicate blend of democracy and hierarchy, learning and piety, practicality and idealism, to mention just a few, could not be precisely reproduced. Thus Unitarians as well as fervent revivalists, aggressive entrepreneurs as well as "sturdy yeomen," utopian experimenters as well as aristocratic public servants could, with justification, claim a part of the Yankee heritage. In spite of this process of "splintering," however, attempts to reproduce the covenanted community were made again and again and constituted an important, if often ignored, part of the story of how the vast American wilderness was occupied and subdued. Such attempts were made with a conservatism, which was testimony to the power of the original vision, and at the same time with a willingness to adapt the model to circumstance, which would have made later versions of the covenanted community unrecognizable to the Puritans.

The essential conservatism of pioneer community builders in western New England, the Northwest Territory, and even the trans-Mississippi West has been emphasized by Page Smith in his suggestive study, *As a City Upon a Hill: The Town in American History*. Surveying a wide variety of literature relating to the small town in America, Smith sought to correct the idea that all people who went west either were when they started or, under the influence of the forest, became adventurers, individualists, heretics, liberals, or democrats. On the contrary, Smith argued, many of the people responsible for establishing society in the West were reacting not to the rigid orthodoxy of eastern settlements but to the breakdown of the covenanted community, the steady growth of a commercial and pluralistic society that made the simple life of the covenant impossible.[15]

Smith distinguishes two basic types of settlement: the colonial town and the cumulative.[16] The cumulative community was one in which the economic motive and spirit were predominant, in which there was no preexisting plan or model to define the nature of the community, and in which growth occurred by the gradual accretion of heterogeneous individuals. Specific and commonly agreed on principles of order that could define in advance what behavior would be acceptable, what kinds of people welcome, and the like were therefore absent in the cumulative community. Such characteristics as might give the cumulative town a unique corporate flavor or atmosphere emerged only gradually and as if by accident.

The colonized town, on the other hand, is so designated by Smith because it had built into it from the outset a principle of unity. Thus "some version of the covenant" would exist in all such towns. There were many forms that the colonized town might take, and there were many that had no relation to New England communities. Religious or ethnic colonies of European origin, towns established by railroads or land companies, and secular utopian ventures were the most common in this category.[17] The communal ideal might arise from a variety of sources, but it perhaps derived its most powerful hold on the imagination in America from the tradition growing out of the New England covenant.

Smith's contention is most easily demonstrated in the initial phase of New England expansion in the seventeenth and early eighteenth century. The promulgation of the Half-Way Covenant in 1662 and the loss of the charter and the imposition of a measure of religious toleration in 1664 and 1692 were events that signaled to all of New England that the covenant was dissolving. The effects of these events were naturally first and most deeply felt in well-established towns and centers of populations and government. Outlying towns might find it possible to resist for a time. But as more and more communities submitted to the processes of change, those who wanted to maintain the original intention of the covenanted community had little choice but to remove to the frontier. On a local level, of course, the dynamics of discontent might vary widely from place to place. A loss of piety, growth of a commercial spirit, personality disputes, shortages of land, dispersal of population, or the fact of growth: any combination of such factors might lead a group of people to split from the established community and seek to form a new town. But while motives might vary and while there was inevitably some reaction against established authority, an authority that probably considered itself as attempting to preserve the covenant, still the newly formed towns most often thought of themselves as attempting to recover the covenanted community and give it a new birth.[18]

This story is not so easy to follow outside the geographical boundaries of New England and beyond the relatively contained and coherent world of the seventeenth-century Puritans. New England influence in the settlement of western New York, parts of Pennsylvania, and the Northwest Territory has not gone unnoticed in either primary or secondary sources, but when specific evidences of such have been articulated, they have been treated in piecemeal fashion. New England ideas of order were written into the various ordinances relating to the Northwest Territory. Missionary enterprises originating in New England played a large part in churching the frontier. Village greens and New England architecture dotted the landscape. Interests in education and various kinds of reform such as temperance and antislavery have been assumed to be primarily New England in origin. Character traits varying from a high sense of calling and industriousness to shrewdness and stiff-necked rigidity, not to mention spiritual qualities inhering in Anglo-Saxon blood have been ascribed to the Yankee settlers. All these and other evidences of New England influence in westward expansion, more or less tangible and more or less debatable, have been duly noted.

The picture that most often emerges from such an approach is one in which New England contributions have blended with those of immigrants and settlers from the middle and southern colonies and all have been stirred in the cleansing and purifying environment of the frontier to produce a new kind of man and a new structure of society that was uniquely American. For example:

> This diversity of population, true of no other section of the nation in the nineteenth century, gave Midwestern culture a distinctive flavor. New York Staters rubbed elbows with Virginians. Maine down-Easters with Pennsylvania Dutchmen, later with Germans, Norse, Irish, Scotch and Holland Dutch, and still later with Poles and Italians, Finns, Czechs, and Hungarians. The end product was the Midwesterner, who owed some thing to Williamsburg and Boston, to William Byrd and Cotton Mather, William Penn and John Winthrop, to Count Zinzendorf and Martin Luther and Jonathan Edwards and Peter Cartwright, to Canterbury and Rome, and to a thousand other places and people and traditions.[19]

Something was owed to a variety of traditions, but what was produced was not a mere amalgam but a new thing. And whether the new thing was regional in character, as above, or national, it was basically traditionless

19

(despite all the traditions that had contributed to it), free from established prejudice, and democratic in style and sentiment, if not always in substance. One of the more encyclopedic historians of westward expansion exemplifies the attitude:

> In the Lake Plains they met and mingled, blending the social mannerism and economic habits of their homeland to create a unique society, distinct from those contributing to it and modified by the impact of the frontier. . . . The task was formidable; to conquer the grasslands pioneers must discard their prejudices, shatter past traditions, and develop an entirely new frontier technique.[20]

Page Smith's argument that the story of the covenanted community is not restricted to New England and does not end in the early eighteenth century cannot, of course, be taken to mean that no such mingling occurred or that changes did not occur as people, institutions, and ideas moved west. Nor, on a different level, should it be considered an attempt to reassert the cultural dominion of New England as against the historians who, following the lead of Frederick Jackson Turner, had sought to counter the overemphasis on the influence of New England advanced by previous generations of historians. But Smith does supply an added dimension to the story of westward movement and in so doing complicates the picture somewhat. The mood of settlers was often not adventuristic or opportunist and the ideal was often quite the opposite of those of pluralism, the melting pot, or hearty individualism. In the West, as in the East, it was, in general, urban centers that provided the setting for such values. But along with New England-style architecture and cultural institutions came a much broader and deeper commitment to a model of community that had its roots in the Puritan covenant. This was never fully assimilated into a frontier or midwestern style or type, though it might be and was adapted to varying circumstances and environments.

On the institutional level, the growth of denominations and the emergence of religious pluralism made it impossible for a single organizational focal point to act as the symbol of unity for a community. A single creed could not be held as a goal. The covenant of any individual church could not play a decisive role in community life. Articulations of the terms of the covenant, interpretations of its purpose, and judgments on success or failure could no longer flow from a single source. Upon what religious foundation could such communities exist? Where was the quintessential expression of the religious goals of the community to be found? Upon what basis could a town covenant exist where religious allegiance was fractured? Such questions had to be confronted if the covenant were not to be lost entirely and with it the very meaning and purpose of corporate life.

A potential for disunity had existed, as we have seen in Puritan communities, because not all residents of the town were members of the church. But in those instances there was at least a single institutional embodiment of the religious principles on which the town was founded and toward which it aimed, and steps were taken to ensure not only that all town members would attend religious services but also that they would sincerely desire to have that kind of religious experience that would enable them one day to affirm the church covenant and be accepted into the congregation of saints. A slightly more serious problem was raised, however, by the outbreak of revivals in the eighteenth century known as the Great Awakening. The Puritan phase of this widespread movement has been seen as an attempt to recover the spirit of the covenant. But in the process of attempting to restore orthodox religious belief and sentiment to its rightful place in personal and social life, the awakening produced several important side effects. For one thing the authority and policies of ministerial leadership had been challenged, if not seriously undermined. Leadership had been forced to take sides as being in favor of or opposed to the revivals. Contending parties brought an end to any pretense of unity. Furthermore, the principle of voluntarism began to establish itself as people were asked on their own to affirm the covenant. No longer was a policy of exclusion based on rigorous procedures of examination and formal acceptance by the congregation necessary or possible. The last concerted attempt to salvage the Puritan covenant had in effect made a return to previous forms of the covenant impossible.[21]

But if revivalism helped to fan sectarian flames within and across denominations and contributed to an attitude of voluntarism, it also helped to suggest ways the covenantal ideal might nevertheless be given new life. The idea that revivalism produced a personalistic rather than corporate style of religious life tells only one side of the story. By the time of the second wave of revivals in the nineteenth century, the new forms and attitudes that the covenanted community would have to assume were more or less clear. "The churches" had replaced "the church" as symbols of the covenant. Revivals provided the occasion for town to affirm the belief that a unified Christian spirit might prevail even if it had to be somewhat vague and lacked the explicit theological foundation that had once prevailed. Rarely did major denominations fail to support a revival.

The "ecumenical covenant" was necessarily more pragmatic than the Puritan covenant. For if agreement could not be reached on crucial questions of theology, church polity, efficacious ritual, and the like it could at least prevail on what behavior was consistent with a Christian spirit. Thus a temperance covenant became a common way of attempting to recover the covenant, and where this occurred it became a symbol of unity that was presumed to go much deeper than the agreement not to use alcohol. It is perhaps this that caused Page Smith to comment that the frontier town settled by New Englanders "was if anything more repressive than its parent community."[22] Codes of behavior had to sustain the heaviest burden in the preservation of the covenant. Furthermore, the mechanisms by which a sinner might be redeemed, forgiven, and brought back into the fold had broken down somewhat so that a breach in accepted standards of conduct was much more of a threat to the covenant than it had been previously. Here again, however, revivals served a function, for it was through revivals that the process of being received back into the covenant was carried on in full public view.

In addition to all this, revivals strengthened the covenant by providing the ritual drama for the entire community in much the same way that the Puritan sermon had once done. The community was reminded of what was at stake in the everyday choices that were made. The small town in the wilderness was made to feel that it played an important part in the universal drama of salvation. It is perhaps no wonder that those who carried the communal ideal to Oak Park and Evanston were so often products of revivals.[23]

The City in a Garden

By the time the Erie Canal and the ending of the Black Hawk War opened the Chicago area to emigrants from New England, more than two hundred years had passed since the first Puritan settlements in New England. Moreover, the physical and cultural environment of Chicago was, of course, quite far removed from seventeenth-century New England. If, as Page Smith suggests, there were many communities that could be seen as nineteenth-century versions of the covenanted community, Chicago was not one of them. Far from being a relatively tightly knit and controlled community, Chicago was extravagant in practically every respect. Its founders and builders seemed to recognize no limits in what they envisioned and respected no obstacles in what they set out to accomplish. As time went on more and more people were to observe that Chicagoans did not even seem to be limited by considerations of decency and morality. In any case, a spirit of individual enterprise and determination was everywhere. It could be seen in public efforts such as jacking the city out of the mud or rebuilding after the fire of 1871. It could be seen equally in everyday life and received succinct expression in the slogan so often associated with Chicago: "I will."

The official motto of the city, however, is "*urbs in horto*," the city in a garden. This motto may connote more of idyllic innocence than one is accustomed to associate with Chicago. The idea of the American West as a garden was itself an extravagant image and one that supported a number of different, if not contradictory themes. For example:

> The Land of Promise, the Canaan of our time, is the region which, commencing on the slope of the Alleghanies, broadens grandly over the vast prairies and mighty rivers, over queenly lakes and lofty mountains, until the ebb and flow of the Pacific tide kisses the golden shores of El Dorado.[24]

The author of these ecstatic words, written in 1856 as part of an introduction to a book entitled *The Garden of the World*, apparently felt no hesitation and saw no contradiction or inconsistency in proclaiming that the West was both a "Land of Promise" and an "El Dorado." While both metaphors involved visions of plenty and abundance, El Dorado was an image of empire signifying glittering wealth, splendor, magnificence. The Promised Land was, of course, a biblical image whose plenty produced not so much wealth and magnificence as innocence, harmony, and contentment.[25]

Still the author goes on to build on both of these images. The farmer of New England, he says, burdened by unrewarded toil because of scarcity and bleakness of the land, will find the West fertile beyond comparison and will see it as a "land flowing with milk and honey." Out of the West will grow a "virgin civilization" to bless mankind.

> The old world, cursed with despotism, is pouring out its oppressed millions into the lap of the West, and they will furnish the hardy sinews which, directed by New England minds [the author was, by the way, himself a New Englander], shall lay the untold bounties of nature under contribution and swell the tide of wealth.

Already, he said, the cities of the West, Chicago, Cincinnati, and St. Louis, were surpassing the established cities of the seaboard in wealth and population and demonstrating that they were to lead the march of empire and progress. As the cities continued to prosper, wealth would increase, and "the wildest dreamer on the future of our race may one day see actualized a destiny far outreaching in splendor his most gorgeous visions."[26]

> When a Pacific railway shall connect the farthest east and the farthest west within a few days' travel, and the now almost limitless deserts shall "blossom as the rose" inhabited by teeming millions pursuing their avocations peacefully, and each contributing his part to the good of all, it will be a consummation which the mind is lost in contemplating, and of which the imagination is powerless to form an adequate conception.

Such an overall interpretation of the significance of the West dovetailed nicely with the contentions of Chicago's own boosters that Chicago was, in effect, a city of destiny and would one day be the center of American commerce and civilization. Such boosterism was common in cities and towns throughout the West,[27] but in Chicago as nowhere else the predictions of boosters were vindicated by the course of events. As early as the 1840s the shift had begun from an economy based on handicrafts and shops to one based on the factory system, division of labor, and the use of steam power. In the 1850s the railroads revolutionized transportation, making Chicago a center of commerce. In the 1860s the Union stockyards were organized, industry was given a boost by wartime production needs, the political machine became a force, and manufacturers imported cheap labor from foreign countries. After the fire in 1871 Chicago, it was said, rose like a phoenix from the ashes, and it was clear that Chicago was a power to be reckoned with. By the 1880s it had surpassed Philadelphia in population, thus becoming the nation's second largest city. The city in the garden had demonstrated many times over that it was not content to rest in semirural contentment.

Nevertheless, it had not been impossible for some people to view Chicago as a village, even though it had been a village in name for only four years between its founding in 1833 and its incorporation as a city in 1837. The *Chicago Tribune* pointed to this in an editorial of 1873.

> It is a common remark that Chicago was set forward ten years by the fire. The mingled town and village aspects are gone, with the buildings of the early day that held the latter character in the center of the city. The tendency is to see the metropolitan in everything—buildings and their uses, stores and their occupants. And village notions are passing away with them. Even advertisers cease to insist on locations at easy distance from the post office, and a mile of our present area

seems less than four or five blocks a few seasons ago. We are getting to be a community of strangers. No one expects to know . . . half the audience at the church or theatre, and as to knowing one's neighbors, that has become a lost art.[28]

And commenting about the same period in Chicago's history the novelist Theodore Dreiser later wrote:

There were, at this time, several elements in Chicago—those who, having grown suddenly rich from dull poverty, could not so easily forget the village church and the village social standards; those who, having inherited wealth, or migrated from the East where wealth was old, understood more of the savoir faire of the game; and those who, being newly born into wealth and seeing the drift toward a smarter American life were beginning to wish they might shine in it—these last the very young people.[29]

What is interesting in these comments is that in a city that had been characterized from the beginning by speculative economic activities and had never had the stable family characteristics of village life[30] should nonetheless contain a significant number of people who "could not so easily forget the village church and village social standards" and who with the *Tribune* might mourn the passing of village aspects.

Neither Dreiser nor the *Tribune* referred specifically to New Englanders or the New England village. New England influence was, however, unmistakably present in early Chicago. In 1833 it is estimated that about 100,000 people left from Buffalo for the West. Of these about one-fifth eventually landed in Chicago, many of them to continue on to other places, of course.[31] Many, however, stayed, and although immigrants from foreign countries and other parts of the United States also came quite early to Chicago, the early leadership was dominated by men from New England.[32] The prediction that New Englanders would provide the leadership for society in the West in this instance proved quite accurate.

Nor did these people leave their values and convictions behind. Almost immediately upon the arrival of New Englanders an antigambling crusade was organized, and by the end of the year two gambling "nests" had been shut down and their proprietors jailed.[33] During Chicago's boom period in 1843, when the recovery from the panic of 1837 was in full swing and speculation was rife, Chicago also boasted four active temperance societies with a total membership of 2,000, more than a quarter of the entire population of the city, which was 7,500.[34] New Englanders were also concerned to see the Sabbath observed and in the view of an observer in 1856 had been largely successful.

> Sunday in Chicago, though not observed as it is in New England, is, I think, more respected than in any town of 20,000 inhabitants, or upwards, south of Philadelphia. Some few stores are seen open, but not of a prominent class. The movement for the people is generally churchward, and the churches are well-filled.

This prompted the observer to say that in spite of the frontier character of the city, the spirit of speculation, and the varying population, "yet the Puritan element so far predominates in the population of the place, that wickedness is neither popular nor respectable."[35] As late as 1867 James Parton was to make a similar observation about Chicago's Sabbath.[36]

This is not to say that Chicago's early leaders from New England necessarily envisioned their city as a transplanted New England village. Among them could be found some of Chicago's biggest boosters. One of these, for instance, was William Butler Ogden. He had been born in New York State, part of a leading family in a small town in the Catskills. He had come to Chicago to handle his brother-in-law's real estate investments. Once there Ogden saw the immense possibilities of Chicago and became an enormously successful speculator in his own right. In 1837 he was elected Chicago's first mayor and from then on his life and success were intimately connected with that of Chicago. He was involved in all phases of public improvements from railroads (he was a moving force behind the Galena and Chicago Union Railroad, the first to run west out of Chicago, and was eventually the first president of the Union Pacific Railroad) to sewers. He helped found many of the important institutions in the Chicago area from banks to theological seminaries. He was much more than a successful businessman and philanthropist. He was a city builder. His range of interests extended into nearly every part of community life. He supported the Chicago Lyceum, a wide variety of religious denominations including Roman Catholic, and many of the reforms previously mentioned. Thus in spite of his speculative interests and grand vision for Chicago, Ogden perhaps still owed something to the New England tradition of community building.[37]

Another booster of Chicago was John Wentworth. Wentworth was born in Sandwich, New Hampshire, into a family that extended back to Exeter in 1639. He had gone to Dartmouth College and taught school in Michigan before coming to Chicago in the 1830s. In the years that followed Wentworth represented the area in Congress, served as Chicago's mayor, and was the long-time publisher of the *Chicago Democrat*. In 1853 Wentworth wrote in his paper:

> No one need here beg the poor privilege, or vainly assert the right to toil. . . . Let the starving thousands of our eastern cities, whom poverty is driving to crime and the alms-house, swarm and scatter over the busy teeming west. . . . Here their labor will be appreciated and receive its just reward, and they will find themselves the citizens of a land abounding in gold more plentiful than California and Australia, and flowing with milk and honey.[38]

This was hardly the rhetoric of the covenanted community. It was Wentworth's version of the "myth" of the West.

In 1843 Wentworth had given a speech before Congress in which he had referred to Chicago as the "city in the garden" and had again rehearsed the advantages and promise of the West in general and Chicago specifically. In the midst of that speech, however, he had referred to Chicago as "a city not set on a hill, yet it will never be hid."[39] He thus invoked the biblical phrase John Winthrop had used more than two centuries earlier, though whether Wentworth was conscious of the connection can only be guessed. Also, while mayor, Wentworth carried out crusades against various forms of vice and is said on one occasion to have literally pulled a building down. In spite of the frontier brusqueness and egalitarian style that endeared him to many Chicagoans, Wentworth too, perhaps, owed something to his New England origins.

On occasion the values that had once been part of the covenanted community were proclaimed more openly, however. An example is a speech of Joseph Balestier, a young Chicago lawyer who eventually returned to his hometown of Brattleboro, Vermont. In a speech before the Chicago Lyceum in 1840 he first celebrated the present and future prosperity of Chicago and then went on to say:

> It is true that the elements of prosperity surround us; but let us remember that mere physical greatness is as nothing without moral and mental culture. It is essential to both, that we should be a united people. We should aim at unity of spirit and unity of action; sectional jealousies should be forgotten; selfish consideration should yield to the public good, and like a band of brothers we should march onward to that brilliant destiny which the God of nature has ordained for us. Especially should we promote the interests of religion, morality,

and education. Then indeed shall we arrive at true greatness, and our children will point with honest pride to the Annals of Chicago.[40]

The lore of Chicago may not be filled with such statements, but there were some who held such sentiments. Chicago was not a New England village, but the influence of New Englanders was felt in a variety of ways in its early history.

Much later, in 1895, a congressman from Evanston was able to say in a speech before the Vermont Society of Brooklyn that the desire of New York City to annex Brooklyn might be interpreted as the result of a Puritan cyclone having struck in New York and that New York was therefore catching up with Chicago, which had been settled by Yankees and was still led by a Puritan spirit.[41]

Whatever the congressman may have been thinking of in making such a statement, a kind of symbolic turning point had been passed much earlier, during the term of Joseph Medill as mayor from 1871 to 1873. Medill had been the editor of the *Tribune* and was to be its editor again (his daughter married Robert McCormick). In 1871, however, he ran for mayor on a "fire-proof" ticket that also pledged itself to enforce laws restricting the sale of liquor. Medill was elected, but it was to be the last victory of temperance forces in Chicago.[42] Ethnic groups were to acquire political power and a new set of names was to make its appearance, supplanting William B. Ogden, "Long John" Wentworth, and others. It was the year that Medill left office, 1873, that saw the *Tribune* mourn the passing of Chicago's village aspects. The New England influence would have to take different forms. One of the forms it took was to provide leadership for the suburbs of Evanston and Oak Park.

TWO

Origins

It has been said of Boston that it is not a place, but a state of mind. With even greater truthfulness the same could be said of Oak Park.
            William E. Barton, Oak Park

I had thought that as a village we were a pretty good illustration of unity in diversity—diversity in form, unity in spirit. So may we ever be.
            Francis D. Hemenway, Evanston

Even relatively rapid and important changes in the life of a community often proceed without any major dislocations in everyday life and without clearly identifiable benchmark events to signal a transition from one set of circumstances to another. This is perhaps especially true when what is at stake is something as intangible as a "sense of community." Yet the growth of a sense of community from somewhat obscure origins is precisely what, in some way, must be described if important dimensions of Evanston and Oak Park as they appeared toward the end of the nineteenth century are not to be overlooked. These two "ultrarespectable" suburbs, offering clear alternatives to both urban and rural ways of life through the explicit and implicit covenants that defined their communal ideal, did not just suddenly appear, even if in retrospect observers might be impressed with the speed with which things had happened.[1] From the time settlers first began to establish homesteads and small business enterprises in the areas, it was roughly thirty to forty years before expectations and aspirations of individuals and small groups had coalesced into somewhat stable communal self-understandings.

Neither Evanston nor Oak Park was established as a colonized town, much less in any sense a covenanted community. Beginning in the 1830s, after the close of the Black Hawk War had opened the Chicago region to settlement, a few people began to establish homesteads and businesses to serve travelers to the North and West. There were few signs of permanent settlement as few people owned the land on which they resided. Some were squatters, while much of the land was owned by speculators who never saw it.[2] The land was largely uninhabitable. Oak Park was the first dry land one encountered traveling west from Chicago, and the only convenient places for settlement were along the trails that connected Chicago to the hinterland and along the Des Plaines River to the west of Oak Park. In Evanston the only dry land was along the lake shore and along a ridge (now Ridge Avenue), that ran north-south roughly two miles inland. Thus as settlement slowly proceeded, clusters of cabins and a few taverns and other businesses were all that defined the regions that would eventually become Evanston and Oak Park.

Only the most rudimentary signs of community existed to modify a picture that otherwise might be described in terms derived from the myth of rugged pioneer individualism. One resident of Oak Park described the early stages of settlement in these terms:

> It is easy to see that in these very early days Oak Ridge (an early designation of the Oak Park area) was a little country village, not a city suburb. Each homestead was an independent domain. . . . True, that satisfaction was conducive to a moat and drawbridge type of mind. . . . In the primitive village the chief counter influence to this self-centered satisfaction came from the little white church at Lake and Forest.[3]

The little white church was a small frame building that served the few settlers in the area as both a nondenominational Protestant meetinghouse and a schoolhouse. It suggests what was in fact the case: whatever "community" there was in Evanston and Oak Park was built almost entirely around the few functions the settlers considered necessary.

Until 1849, when state legislation provided for the establishment of township organization within Cook County, Evanston and Oak Park were little more than outposts with no defined boundaries. What was later to become Evanston was a part of a larger region known as Grosse Point, which existed primarily as an election district. Oak Park was known as Kettlestring's Grove after the man who first settled in the area. Later, after Cicero Township had been established, there was a post office named Noyesville, a railroad station named Harlem, and a school district named Oak Ridge. The need to provide certain services and to perform certain functions—elections, postal delivery, transportation, schooling, and religious services—did provide some of the foundations for community life. But the coordination of such functions within a defined space and within the framework of shared values occurred only slowly and with difficulty.

By the latter years of the nineteenth century Oak Park and Evanston had become phenomena quite different from the primitive settlements of the 1840s. In many respects they were similar. Robert St. John, whose family moved from Chicago to Oak Park around the turn of the century, commented in his autobiographical reminiscences:

> There were two suburbs in those days which were considered ultra-respectable, Oak Park and Evanston. They had much in common. Each was seven or eight miles from the Loop and each had a population of about twenty thousand. Both were served by elevated lines and by the Chicago and Northwestern steam railroad. Both had many large homes with spacious grounds. Persistent attempts at legal adoption or absorption by Chicago were periodically defeated by autonomy-loving Oak Parkers and Evanstonians, most of whom would have been relieved if, awakening some morning, they were to have learned that during the night their raucous big neighbor had been magically moved to the open spaces of some far-Western state.[4]

Growth had transformed Evanston and Oak Park from pioneer settlements to prestigious suburbs of a metropolis.

By and large this growth had been cumulative. In Evanston Northwestern University had provided an institutional center that helped to ensure that a significant portion of those who came to Evanston shared some interests and values. In Oak Park there is circumstantial evidence that friendship or word-of-mouth communication resulted in many of the early leaders coming from the same area of western New York, Onondaga County, and sharing certain values.[5] Yet in neither case did these circumstances cause large blocs of people to move to the area within a relatively short period of time, as would typically have been the case in the colonized town.

By the end of the formative period for each community, however, both Evanston and Oak Park were firmly established as temperance communities. This temperance "covenant" was to be symbolic of a more inclusive covenant that, it will be argued, provided a foundation both for specific actions and policies pursued in the communities and for interpretive statements about the meaning of community life in Evanston and Oak Park. The development of this argument is a concern of following chapters. It is important, however, to attempt to describe the transition that occurred in each place from mere settlements to well-defined communities.

Commenting on this type of development, Page Smith generalized that:

Those towns whose origin was wholly economic and which grew by the accumulation of heterogeneous individuals eventually acquired the social and institutional forms of the typical town. Here, indeed, time developed the "psychological fabric of a good community" but the price was high. For the town meanwhile had to go through an inchoate and formless period that often left permanent scars, while towns that were colonized as towns showed, for the first, the characteristics of developed communities. Moreover most towns continued to show evidence of the manner of their origin.[6]

In the cases of Evanston and Oak Park it is a misleading simplification to see only "permanent scars" resulting from the "inchoate and formless period" of their development. Nor, in either case, was the economic motive the only important factor in drawing people to the communities. The manner of origin is, however, important, not least because it reveals some significant differences between the two communities that might not be easily seen when comparing them at certain points in time.

Both Evanston and Oak Park began as pioneer settlements of scattered groups and individuals. Both grew in somewhat cumulative fashion. Both grew relatively rapidly to a size that would seem to deny the possibility of maintaining the characteristics of the covenanted community in any form, no matter how modified. Yet both communities developed an understanding of themselves that drew heavily on the tradition of the covenanted community. With severely limited documentary evidence from the early period, it is nearly impossible to account fully for how and when the communal ideal became central to the communities' self-understandings. But it is possible to discuss how the major symbol of covenant, temperance, came into being in each community and how a basic sense of community emerged without which the communal ideal would have been impossible.

Oak Park

The man whom Oak Parkers remember as their founder was Joseph Kettlestrings, an Englishman from Yorkshire who arrived in the Chicago area in 1833. His initial residence was on the Aux Plaines (Des Plaines) River, where he was in business with Bickerdike and Noble, the former having encouraged Kettlestrings's emigration to the area. In 1835 Kettlestrings left the sawmill and established residence in what is now Oak Park. In 1837 he bought a quarter-section of land that was later sold and subdivided. By the

1840s there were a few other settlers in the area, but none apparently were permanent settlers, since by 1880 none of the oldest residents could remember any names.[7] The area was known as Kettlestrings' Grove, a name that designated no formally defined entity but "simply . . . a location."[8]

The first important development toward community in Oak Park was the opening of the Galena and Chicago Union Railroad. The symbolic first trip was made by the locomotive *Pioneer* on October 25, 1848, and by the following year passenger service was available between Oak Park and Chicago. If the immediate effects of the railroad were insignificant, the long-term effects were not. It connected Oak Park not only to Chicago but also to points west. The link to Chicago was an attraction to future residents and also ensured that Oak Park was not to remain an isolated village. In some way Oak Park would have to come to terms with the values of progress and prosperity associated with an urbanizing environment. But also of significance was the affinity it helped to establish between Oak Park and the communities to the immediate west, an affinity that remains to the present.

The same year that the railroad went into operation part of what is now Oak Park became a part of the newly created Taylor Township, later to be renamed Proviso Township at the suggestion of Augustin Porter, a resident of Oak Park.[9] For a brief time Oak Park was thus a part of a governmental unit that consisted primarily of communities to the west of Oak Park. In 1857, however, Oak Park was incorporated into Cicero Township, which had the effect of allying the area with communities to the south with which it was to have less in common. Although Oak Park residents may have played a major role in the creation of Cicero Township, this governmental reorganization may have contributed to the later tension between Oak Park and the rest of Cicero Township.

This is not to say, however, that Oak Park's relationship to the area immediately west of it was entirely sympathetic or friendly. Recalling this connection, a later historical summary commented:

In later years, the growth of Oak Park was affected chiefly by the removal of some of the best families of Chicago to this attractive suburb; but in the beginning it was not so. The village was not a growth of Chicago westward but a growth eastward of the village of Harlem, of which it was essentially a part. When Mr. Herrick and Miss Fisher came to Oak Ridge as teachers a majority of the children in the school spoke German in their homes. As the village grew eastward, there was a time when there were more beer saloons on this side of

Harlem Avenue than on the other. There was nothing to distinguish this as a place of piety and enlightenment.[10]

It was perhaps the habits and customs of the German population that caused residents of Oak Park to look toward the establishment of Cicero Township as a way of distinguishing themselves from their western neighbors, though the lack of specific evidence makes this a matter of speculation. In any case, if the creation of Cicero Township was an early effort on the part of Oak Parkers to set themselves apart as a distinct community, it largely failed. Not until the early 1870s did such aspirations begin to be fulfilled.

In the meantime, while Oak Ridge and Ridgeland (the area now constituting the eastern portion of Oak Park) were together established as school district Number One of Cicero Township, what constituted the community in any other than this respect remained vague. The railroad station serving the Oak Park area was named Harlem. Originally it had been located east of Harlem Avenue, which was to become the border between Cicero and Proviso townships, but it was moved across Harlem Avenue sometime before 1861. The community of Harlem at the time included portions of what are now Oak Park, River Forest, and Forest Park, so that at least by common usage Oak Park was assumed to be part of a community that included sections of both townships. There was a post office that served people on both sides of Harlem Avenue, and early attempts at church organization involved residents from both areas. Residents of the Oak Ridge area were thus pulled in at least two directions. They lacked the numbers, the material resources, and the natural focal points to consider themselves a separate community. But beyond this, they could not even be sure of what they were a part. For some purposes they were clearly a section of Cicero Township, while for other purposes they were a part of the "village" of Harlem.

If, however, the forms of community were lacking in the early years, the substance was beginning to emerge through a group of people who would eventually assume major leadership roles. Beginning just before the creation of Cicero Township in 1857 and continuing throughout the 1860s, the Oak Park area gradually acquired a number of strong personalities who were more or less clear in what they expected the community to become. Joseph Kettlestrings, who moved to Chicago in 1849 because of the lack of adequate school facilities for his children, returned to Oak Park in 1856. At about the same time the Scovilles—William, George, Ives, James, and their families—established their residences in Oak Park. When the first elections in

Cicero Township were held, there were fourteen votes cast. Nine were from the Oak Park area and five of those were Kettlestrings and the four Scovilles. In 1858 Milton C. Niles moved to the area from Du Page County. Then in relatively rapid succession came Henry Austin (1859), O. W. Herrick (1859), Augustin Porter (1860), Samuel Dunlop (1862), Abram and Edwin Gale (1863), and Orin Peake (1865).[11]

These men, as well as others about whom little is still known, constituted an early and coherent leadership core that began the work of community building in Oak Park. In laying out subdivisions, Kettlestrings, Niles, Scoville, and others began to define and order the space of the community as well as to provide for an increasing population. From a vast expanse of oak groves and prairie upon which a few cabins seemed to be randomly placed, Oak Park began to be transformed into an ordered settlement on the human scale with a discernable pattern of primitive streets, businesses, and residences. In establishing the first church organizations (Union Ecclesiastical Society, 1860; Oak Ridge Church of Harlem, 1863; Oak Ridge Ecclesiastical Society, 1863), they began to provide an institutional foundation for community life.[12] Because these men were capable, educated, and relatively prosperous and because such people were somewhat scarce in the area, all at one time or another held elective office and other positions of responsibility. They thus were quickly established as men of prominence and developed the skills of organization and leadership.

The importance of this group of people is not merely what they concretely initiated, for the indications are that to a large degree they thought and acted in concert. They were thus able to be a nucleus around which the community could develop. Not only did they work together in township government and church organizations. They were congenial to one another and associated informally as well as in the various tasks they undertook. Kettlestrings's son later recalled that:

> Father got good people in Oak Park, such men as Austin, Niles, Scoville, and others. He and Austin did away with saloons. And when my father sold property, he would put a clause in the deed saying if the property was used for saloon purposes it would revert back to father. . . . He kept on selling to good people who were against saloons and for good schools and churches.[13]

Allowing for some exaggeration in Kettlestrings's single-handed role in bringing all the others to Oak Park, it is clear from all descriptions that a close relationship existed among them. They visited often in one anothers' homes.

O. W. Herrick was a cousin of the Scovilles and came to Oak Park at James Scoville's suggestion. Later he married one of Kettlestrings' daughters, as did Samuel Dunlop. Herrick and Austin were the closest of friends and when Dora Kettlestrings and O. W. Herrick were married the Austins, Scovilles, and Kettlestrings all held receptions in their honor. Through a complex pattern of marriage the major family chain in Oak Park was gradually established: Kettlestrings-Dunlop-Herrick-Eastman-Scoville-Goodwillie-Tomlinson-Cotsworth.[14]

With the exception of Kettlestrings (England) and Dunlop (Ireland) all were from families of New England origin. As previously noted, Austin, Porter, Herrick, and the Scovilles were from the Pompey-Skaneateles area in Onondaga County, New York, their families having come there from New England. This was within a section of western New York that has been called the "burned-over district" because of the intense movements of religious enthusiasm that developed in the 1820s and 1830s and the utopian experiments that followed. An Owenite experiment existed near Skaneateles for about three years in the 1840s.[15] It is not surprising that these men brought with them to Oak Park a commitment to evangelical Protestantism and a zeal for certain types of reforms, chief among which was temperance.[16] That they were at least somewhat conscious of their Puritan ancestry is indicated by the custom, which developed later, of holding what were termed "Old People's Concerts" at which time all the members of a church would assume Puritan names such as Prudence, Humility, Gratitude, Patience, and the like and dress in the oldest clothing they could find before coming together for a "social."[17]

This early leadership group informally performed many of the functions that town proprietors carried out in New England communities and certain types of colonized towns in the Northwest Territory. They ordered the landscape and provided that settlement would not be too diffuse. To some degree they controlled access to the town. And they were the major figures in establishing the primary institutions of the town: schools, churches, and the town meeting.[18] To be sure, the authority and power they were able to exercise was not as well defined or as complete as would have been the case with Puritan communities or later towns that more nearly fit the classic model of the colonized town. Nevertheless, what they were able to accomplish in this regard checked any tendencies toward a merely cumulative pattern of development.

Some final insights as to who the men were who provided Oak Park with its initial energy and direction may be gained from a brief consideration of the life of James W. Scoville. If Kettlestrings is understandably remembered as Oak

Park's founder, Scoville is perhaps more representative of the group as a whole and his interests and involvements were wider in scope.

Scoville was born in Pompey, New York, in 1825, the fourth of five children. The family was said to have been conscious of its "Puritan extraction" and had made the journey to western New York from Meriden, Connecticut.[19] In 1830 Scoville's mother died, and the children were distributed among various relatives to be raised. As a child he received some schooling and worked on the family farm. At the age of twenty-one he decided to strike out on his own and entered Oneida Conference Academy, supporting himself by teaching school. He remained at the academy for only two months and then entered Manlius Academy, where he remained for two years, again teaching school to earn his way. When Scoville was a boy there had been no churches in the vicinity, but while he was at Manlius he was strongly affected by several revivals and by the wife of the principal of the academy. Under their influence he joined the Presbyterian Church of Manlius and expressed the intention of becoming a minister.

Shortly after this, however, Scoville fell ill and went to recuperate in New Hampshire. In the fall of 1848 he made his first trip to Chicago, in his own words "drawn hither by glittering reports of the golden West."[20] From Chicago he walked the distance to Beloit College, stopping overnight in Oak Park where he later remembered being impressed with the natural beauty of the site. Apparently unable to enroll at Beloit at the time, he returned to New York and was briefly engaged with his future brother-in-law in a shoe business. Later he went to work for a contractor who was engaged in widening the Erie Canal and was quickly promoted because of his mathematical and engineering skills and his success in mediating employee disputes. In 1856 he returned to Chicago and assumed the position of cashier with P. W. Gates and Co. In 1857, "consulting his own tastes" and "solicitous for the health of his family," he moved to Oak Park, where he remained until 1888. Because of health he moved to Pasadena, California, in 1888 and died there in 1893.

While in Oak Park, Scoville was involved in the founding of many of the major institutions and nearly all the public improvements that were undertaken in the 1870s and 1880s. He seems to have been concerned with everything from roads and sewers and water systems to schools and churches. In 1873 he was a major financer of the building of First Congregational Church in Oak Park and at one point when construction was held up because the workers were not being paid, Scoville met with the crew and personally guaranteed their wages if they would continue working. In 1878 he initiated the water system for Oak Park by building a limited system at his own expense. In 1888, carrying out what he claimed had been a dream for many years, he endowed the Scoville Institute as the public library for the community.

Undoubtedly Scoville made money out of his enterprises in Oak Park. For a time he operated a toll road to Chicago. Before selling out to a larger enterprise, he owned and operated the water system. Just before the outbreak of the Civil War he had gone into real estate and, on the advice of William B. Ogden, who also owned land in the Ridgeland section of what was to become Oak Park, had made significant investments in the Oak Park area. Thus all public improvements redounded to his benefit. But, like Ogden, he cannot adequately be described as either a philanthropist or a tycoon. Though his business involvements were varied and his philanthropies extended to Beloit College and Chicago Theological Seminary,[21] neither his business activities nor his charitable donations are finally separable from his vision as community builder. Judging from his concerns in Oak Park, he had an idea of Oak Park as an enlightened, modern, and progressive suburb that would, however, be able to maintain the best of the small-town tradition, and he accomplished a great deal in bringing that idea to fruition.

If we may trust descriptions from Scoville's admirers, his character was a product of a Puritan-Yankee heritage, modified but not completely altered by a nineteenth-century environment.

> His was not a commanding figure. There was a quiet, unpretentious way about him. His dress, manners, establishment were characterized by plainness and simplicity. But somehow there was a modest dignity about him. . . . Accuracy as to truth, promptness in keeping appointments, faithfulness in financial obligations, absolute honesty in form and purpose—this was the ideal after which he patterns his conduct.[22]

The institutions that mattered most to him were the school, the church, and the library. If he was concerned that Oak Park be a place of learning and piety and was himself Congregational-Presbyterian in his sympathies as a product of revivals and the fluid denominational situation of the New York frontier, he contributed to the "broad, catholic spirit of unity" that was necessary for latter-day covenanted communities to adopt. He is said not to have believed in personal charity but whenever possible sought to provide work for those in need.[23]

Even such a group of leaders as gradually emerged in Oak Park, however, might have been relatively ineffective in bringing about a well-defined and self-conscious community had it not been for a series of events that began in 1867.[24] It was in this year that one John McCaffery was elected to the Cicero Township board and began a short-lived domination of township government affairs. McCaffery lived in a community called Brighton in the southern part of the township. Beginning in 1867 he organized what Oak Parkers then and henceforth referred to as a "ring." Oak Park's grievances against the McCaffery ring were several. At the time McCaffery was elected, a section of the township was in the process of being annexed to Chicago. It was later suggested that McCaffery used his influence to prevent lawsuits against the annexation and in return received assurance that Brighton would remain a part of Cicero. This would allow him to retain his position in township affairs, a situation that was to prove quite profitable to him.

Perhaps of more significance, however, was a situation that occurred as a result of a state law passed in 1869. The revised charter of that year provided for an increase of township trustees from five to seven and allowed for public improvements to be made by borrowing on the credit of the entire township for improvements that would later be paid for by special assessment of those benefiting from the improvements. On paper this provision seemed desirable since it allowed for work to proceed on projects before the money from special assessments was actually in hand. In practice, however, the township board borrowed money for certain projects having to do with roads and drainage that only minimally affected Oak Park residents and then failed to collect the special assessments. Oak Parkers were obliged to contribute to paying off the debt in proportion to their share of general revenues rather than in proportion to the amount they benefited from the improvements. To Oak Parkers the difference was significant.

Nor was this the end of the matter. A large town hall was built in the Austin area. This offended Oak Park residents on two counts: it offended their local pride, since they felt Oak Park deserved to be the seat of government, and it was considered extravagant, only a small portion of the building being used at that time. Another grievance arose when it was discovered that McCaffery as township treasurer had been receiving many times the salary to which he was entitled through a devious interpretation of the law or an outright circumvention. Likewise several of the trustees were being overpaid according to the existing law. And finally it was noted that there was "much dissatisfaction over the handling of the saloon question in Oak Park." All these concerns, starting with the sense of having been taken advantage of in matters relating to the township, contributed to Oak Parkers' sense of their common interest and of their distinctness as a community within Cicero Township.

At about the same time steps were being taken to distinguish Oak Park more clearly from its neighbors to the west. In 1872 the post office was moved to Oak Park and the name Oak Park formally adopted because the federal officials rejected the name Oak Ridge, a post office with that name already existing in the region. Also in 1872 the Chicago and Northwestern Railroad (which had bought out the Galena and Chicago Union in 1864) moved its depot to Oak Park at the request of several Oak Park citizens. These developments, combined with certain drainage improvements and the displacement caused by the Chicago fire of 1871 caused the first relatively rapid growth in population. If by later standards this growth was still rather modest, nevertheless it was of significance at the time. It was estimated that the population in 1870 was no more than two hundred while by the end of 1872 the estimate was five hundred. Property values increased at a fantastic rate.[25]

Surveying the early history of his church, William E. Barton, minister of First Congregational Church and about whom much more will be said, wrote in 1924:

> The life of Oak Park as a town with a self-conscious existence practically dates from the organization of this Church. With that organization a social center was established east of Harlem Avenue. Movements expressive of the common will took shape in definite and concrete action, and the life of the town began and grew with the life of the church.[26]

Barton no doubt overstated First Congregational's case, but the church was certainly important, and in any case all the evidence indicates that he was entirely accurate in his dating. First Congregational was organized as a congregation in 1871 and completed a building in 1873. In 1871 a movement against the McCaffery ring was initiated and by 1873 the cleansing of town government was considered complete, with Oak Park once again feeling itself in control of township government. It was perhaps not accidental that it was also in 1873 that Oak Park achieved what had for some time been a goal of many residents: temperance. In 1873 there were three saloons left in the Oak Park area. Henry W. Austin, having received assurances that township law would henceforth prohibit the sale and distribution of intoxicants in Oak Park, bought out all three establishments. With various events and developments from 1867 to 1873, Oak Park seemed well on its way toward actualizing the intentions of its founding fathers.

Much, of course, still remained to be done. In 1870 Oak Park had no pavements, sidewalks, public utilities, police or fire protection, and other such basic community services. Even by 1880 only one-sixth of the present land area had been subdivided. Yet the events of the late 1860s and early 1870s seem to have determined what kind of a community Oak Park was to be. Needed improvements and investments could be undertaken with some confidence and a basic sense of identity. By 1883 a community newspaper, perhaps an index of the strength of a community, was begun. One important issue did remain unresolved, however. Oak Park was still not a legal entity and was not to become a self-governing village until the first years of the twentieth century.

Evanston

The early growth and development of Evanston offers contrasts to that of Oak Park in several important respects. Until the middle years of the 1850s the pattern of development and the appearance of the landscape were similar in the two communities, though even in these early years Evanston had a few more settlers than did Oak Park. Clusters of homesteads existed along the two ridges that were used as branches of the road between Chicago and Green Bay, but there was nothing approximating village life. People living on the ridges could not even communicate with one another easily because of the swampland between them. The general region was referred to as Grosse Point, but boundaries were ill-defined and the region had little importance except as a convenience for purposes of elections. In 1850 Ridgeville Township was created, to be enlarged and renamed in 1857 Evanston Township. Neither of these events was as important in defining the community, however, as was the founding of Northwestern University. Because of Northwestern's major role in establishing the village that was to become Evanston and because of the speed at which things developed after Northwestern had been chartered, Evanston takes on from the outset many more of the characteristics of a colonized town than had Oak Park.

The initial plans for Northwestern University were laid at a meeting of nine prominent Methodists of Chicago on May 31, 1850. The group consisted of the pastors of the three Methodist churches of Chicago (Richard Haney,

R. K. Blanchard, and Zadok Hall), three attorneys (Andrew J. Brown, Henry W. Clark, and Grant Goodrich), two businessmen (Jabez Botsford and Orrington Lunt), and John Evans, physician, businessman, and later territorial governor of Colorado. A number of these men were deeply involved in reform movements and were associated with those whose concern was to make Chicago into a place of piety, morality, and learning as well as of commerce and industry.[27] Their immediate concern was, of course, with education. The statement of purpose that they adopted at this meeting began:

> Whereas, The interests of sanctified learning require the immediate establishment of a university in the Northwest, under the patronage of the Methodist Episcopal Church:
> Resolved, That a committee of five be appointed to prepare a draft of a charter to incorporate a literary university, to be located at Chicago.[28]

Chicago at the time had no institutions of higher learning, high school, or college, but the proposed college and preparatory school were envisioned as meeting the needs of the entire Northwest.[29] The charter, which was approved in 1851, provided that the "institution shall remain located in or near the city of Chicago."[30] As organizational work and fund-raising proceeded, however, some difficulty was encountered in finding what the trustees considered a suitable site. Finally in 1853 Orrington Lunt, who had been holding out for a location along the lake shore, came across a plot of land he considered ideal but that had been overlooked because of the swamplands between it and the normal routes of travel to the north. The site of 380 acres was approved by the trustees and purchased for $25,000.

Once the site was selected, work proceeded quickly. The original purchase and 248 acres in addition that had been bought by Andrew Brown and Harvey Hurd was plotted by Philo Judson and named Evanston in honor of John Evans. The initial ordering of the land, a process that in Oak Park had taken a decade or more and the work of a number of different investors, was accomplished within a space of two years, 1853-54. Material improvements were begun. Quick progress was made in drainage, street grading, and building residences and business establishments. In 1854 railroad connections to Chicago were achieved through the Chicago and Milwaukee Railroad. Land values rose at a rapid rate. And even before Northwestern itself had formally opened two other institutions of learning had been established: Garrett Biblical Institute and Northwestern Female College, the latter of which was eventually to merge with the Evanston College for Ladies.

Such a village offered a number of attractions to prospective settlers in spite of its as yet rather primitive conditions. Those connected in a formal way with the institutions of course accounted for some immediate growth, though the initial staffs, officers, and agents were small in number. In connection with other real and envisioned advantages, however, they could be of influence in attracting others. The natural beauty of the area, swamps notwithstanding, was well attested. Certain business opportunities could be foreseen for a university town. And some were undoubtedly attracted by a town that seemed destined to become not only an important educational center but also a major center for midwestern Methodism. Like Oak Park, Evanston developed an image as a place of distinctive learning, piety, and morality. But unlike Oak Park this image was attained rather quickly and with the support and stability provided by major institutions.

A biblical institute, an institution of "sanctified learning," and the people these would naturally attract might have been sufficient to establish Evanston's reputation and image. But in 1855, through an amendment to the Northwestern University charter, a further evidence of the kind of community Evanston desired to become was enacted. Temperance was to become the symbol of all the qualities that the town wished to project both to itself and to the world.

> No spiritous, vinous, or fermented liquors shall be sold, under license or otherwise, within four miles of the location of said University, except for medicinal, mechanical or sacramental purposes, under a penalty of twenty-five dollars for each said offense, to be recovered before any Justice of the Peace in said County of Cook; provided, that so much of this act as relates to the sale of intoxicating drinks within four miles may be repealed by the General Assembly whenever they think proper.[31]

This charter provision was reaffirmed and strengthened through village ordinances, although throughout the 1860s and 1870s there seems to have been some trouble in actually ridding the community of alcohol.[32]

Within the space of a very few years Evanston had established itself as a village provided with the basic necessities of community life and embracing religion, education, and temperance as its fundamental values. To a large extent this was made possible by Northwestern University, and this fact had several implications. In Oak Park the development toward community had proceeded under the direction of a limited group of men, and because of their close ties with one another access to the leadership group was relatively limited. In Evanston stability and strength were provided quickly by the two major institutions, Garrett and Northwestern, but because of the nature of the institutions, personalities might come and go. Regardless of the stature of such early residents as John Evans and Bishop Matthew Simpson and the continuing later influence of such men as Orrington Lunt, a continuous, homogeneous leadership was less likely to emerge. From an early date, therefore, the potential for conflict over ideas and interests and competition for leadership existed to a greater degree in Evanston.

A further potential for conflict arose from the fact that the university and the town were not one and the same. If Northwestern in a sense acted as town proprietor, it also had its own concerns and interests to look after. Despite protestations to the contrary,[33] the interests of village and university were not always seen as identical. Those who had lived in the area previous to Northwestern's establishment did not merely vanish. And in spite of the university's influence in attracting future residents, it was neither desirous nor capable of restricting growth to those whose primary identification was with the university. A major point of tension was the tax-exempt status of university property, but on occasion other issues arose as well.[34]

The combined characteristics of village and university also produced a built-in tendency toward growth. Northwestern had intentionally been located near Chicago so that it might both serve and profit from the growth of the metropolitan area. It was unlikely that Evanston would remain a college town with a stable population. The university, in spite of its tax-exempt status, contributed directly and indirectly to the growth of the town. It made outright gifts of land and monies as well as providing a certain amount of purchasing power through the institution, its staff, and students. The nearness to Chicago and the railroad connection to the city made it an obvious locale for suburban development. The qualities that the town offered were symbolized by the temperance provision of the charter, and the university no doubt contributed to the impression that the village was going to be successful and investments there would almost certainly be well made.[35]

Under the influence of the university and, to a lesser degree, Garrett Biblical Institute, Evanston had developed in a manner that allowed it to approximate the model of a colonized and covenanted community. The temperance covenant served as a symbol of the community's intention. A single nondenominational Protestant church, begun in 1856, served the entire village.[36] Everyone knew everyone else; the people initially attracted to the village shared much in the way of religious attitudes, behavioral values, and politics.[37] A solid foundation seemed to have been laid for a village that would be able to embody and maintain the covenantal ideal of community life.

But if the university was responsible for much of this foundation, it also accounted for a set of dynamics that would not allow for the mere maintenance or stability of what had already been established. A relatively open and fluid structure of leadership, a mobile population, some uncertainty about the precise relationship between village and university, the potential for conflict and competition as a consequence of all these factors, and perhaps above all the built-in tendencies toward growth—all these made it impossible to embody fully an ideal of community that depended on a stable and limited population. By the time Oak Park was just beginning to emerge as a self-conscious community, some people in Evanston were already experiencing a sense of loss.

An occasion for the expression of some latent feelings about the growth of the village away from its original simplicity was provided by the village election of 1874. The first group of trustees elected under the revised charter of 1872 had campaigned on the promise to provide the village with a water system. With the Chicago fire a recent memory and the need for guaranteeing pure water to an increasing population becoming apparent, the proponents of the waterworks were elected in the spring of 1873 by a margin of approximately four to one. But the Panic of 1873 hit a number of the people in Evanston rather hard, and some people felt that because of this a reconsideration of the whole issue was in order. Thus in the first weeks of 1874 a public meeting was called for.[38]

As reported in the village newspaper, the major arguments presented were, in sequence, as follows: Rev. Obadiah Huse stated that the waterworks should be delayed one year because the wealthy would be able to dispute the tax collections necessary in court while the less well-to-do would not. Thus to proceed would be discriminatory and would cause hardship. Jacob Frank responded that public improvements never made anyone poor and would work to the benefit of all. John H. Kedzie made it clear that he was able to pay the taxes and would certainly do so if the majority approved of the present plan, but he nevertheless expressed alarm at the rapid rise in taxes in the village, claimed that no village of comparable size had such an ambitious project, and asserted that there were cheaper ways to meet the need. Dr. Mann felt that the basic issue was health, and the lack of waterworks had already carried people to their graves.

The meeting continued with E. S. Taylor supporting Dr. Mann and adding that too many commitments had already been made and that by the time payments were due, the panic would be over. Hugh White countered this approach by arguing that it is impossible to tell when the panic would end, and the project should be postponed a year in order to allow many of the questions to be resolved. Furthermore, the initial expense was likely to be only the beginning. Harvey Hurd also opposed the immediate construction, stating that while small landowners might be able to pay, large owners such as himself would find it more difficult. His share would be $1,200. (At this point a voice shouted that Hurd should not own so much land.) C. J. Gilbert, the president of the village board and major supporter of the waterworks, stated that the project would not be so expensive as many claimed and that many who were now unemployed might be put to work on the construction. George Watson was angered at this idea and accused Mr. Gilbert of advocating communism. E. L. Brown felt that there was a threat of "rings" and "Tweedism" in Evanston, apparently implying that whenever the amount of money spent by the government grew large, there was a danger of graft, favoritism, and the placing of friends and political supporters on the public payroll. The next two speakers, Professor Kistler and Captain Brainard, protested the use of personal invective and the lack of charity on the part of the previous speakers. Shortly thereafter the meeting was adjourned.[39]

It is evident that the concerns of those opposed to proceeding with the waterworks project were varied, and on one level they must be taken at face value. No doubt some genuinely felt that at that time the tax assessments would discriminate in favor of the wealthy members of the community while others felt equally genuinely that the discrimination would be against the wealthy. Allowance must also be made for the possibility that some of the arguments were mere subterfuge for what was basically a question of economic self-interest. Given the conditions brought about by the panic, and given that some in Evanston had not completely recovered from the losses incurred in the Chicago fire, the economic concern must be accepted as real. Yet a different level of concern, which might tie in to the material concern, can also be discerned. The unstated issue involved in the debate over this apparently commonplace public works project was: How far and how quickly was the community willing to move away from the simple, rural, village way of life it had once known and what were to be the consequences?

John Kedzie hinted at such a concern when he suggested that no other community of comparable size seemed to feel waterworks to be such an urgent concern. E. L. Brown was a bit less subtle when he raised the issue of "rings" and "Tweedism." Immediately, of course, people rushed to the defense of the incumbent board, pointing out that these were honest men and such attacks on their integrity could not be tolerated. But they missed the point. Brown's fears were doubtless unfounded in connection with the individuals on the town board, but for him the waterworks represented an increasing tendency to accept urban values and aspirations and he chose to express his vague uneasiness by referring to the image of "Tweedism." At least such is a plausible interpretation of a statement that otherwise appears to have been uncalled for, clearly unacceptable, and in general irrational.

In any case, both sides of the controversy seemed to accept its symbolic importance as the debate proceeded. The incumbent board, running for reelection on the pledge to carry through the project at the earliest possible date, was known as the "progress ticket." The other slate was referred to by proponents of the waterworks as the "anti-progress ticket"; the more neutral term, "opposition ticket," was sometimes used. The issue of taxation, as Kedzie repeatedly insisted, was not merely whether people could afford to pay the taxes, though some might not be able to. The problem was what was to be the cost of a continuing emphasis on progress. Higher taxes would place larger and larger amounts of money at the disposal of a few people. The city would indeed prosper and grow. But this might mean the gradual disintegration of the village ideal. In the March 14 issue of the *Evanston Index* Kedzie was explicit:

> Cannot my friend Judson go back in recollection with pleasure to those good old times when all worshipped in one old-fashioned church, and all attended the same sociable and companies . . . we can never have a happier community than we had then, albeit we did not have the privilege of paying one dollar for municipal taxes. The pleasures of the country which we sought in leaving the city more than compensating for the few city advantages we now possess, taxes included.[40]

In the heat of the campaign the *Index*, which strongly supported the waterworks, implicitly accepted the idea that the project symbolized a transformation in the life of the town but attempted to deromanticize the image of the past. An editorial printed just before the election stated: "The policy of opposition fully carried out would tend to drive away enterprise and make Evanston a one-horse, old fogy country town." And after the election had been won convincingly by the "party of progress" (by about the same margin as the year before), the *Index* wrote again: "The gentlemen who were beaten owe their defeat entirely to the fact that a very large majority of their fellow citizens have determined that the village shall be thoroughly progressive and be made a first-class suburban city, where we shall have all the comforts of the city and the country combined."[41]

Another aspect of the complicated debate was revealed shortly before the election when the issue of who should be allowed to vote was raised by the opposition group. The question of whether college students had enough of a stake in the community to justify their enfranchisement had already been raised. Then at a later date the more inclusive question was raised: Should not the vote be restricted to those owning property? In a letter to the *Index* of April 18 James Currey stated that nontaxpayers could burden property owners with an impossible debt. In this instance again it is difficult to separate issues and motivations. One of the levels of the argument was certainly that which was stated: the protection of the economic interests of the property holders. But a second level can reasonably be supposed to be present, namely whether the essential nature of the community was to be an association of free and relatively equal owners of property or whether the community meaningfully included renters and transients as well. The former idea more nearly approximated assumptions derived from Puritan communities while the latter tended more in the direction of urban patterns of life. That the idea of a significant renting class reminded people of urbanizing trends is illustrated by a continuing concern in the press in future years of how to provide rental accommodations in a way that would not lead to class conflict or tenements.[42]

While the issue of the waterworks assumed symbolic importance to those involved in the debate, it never resolved itself into a conflict of dichotomous ideologies: rural vs. urban, university vs. town, parochial vs. cosmopolitan, or powerful vs. powerless. As the major spokesman for the opposition, John Kedzie was not rural, parochial, or powerless. He had been born in western New York, attended Oberlin College, and admitted to the bar. He came to Chicago in 1847 and, while practicing law, invested heavily in real estate. He was a major landowner both in Chicago and in the Evanston area, especially South Evanston. He had been an abolitionist and a founder of the Republican Party in Illinois, and in later years represented the town in a number of official capacities including state legislator. Other men of the opposition were equally prominent in Chicago as well as Evanston: Harvey Hurd, James Currey, and the Rev. Obadiah Huse to mention a few. And the opposition made it clear that their intention was not to prevent the waterworks from being constructed, but merely to delay the project.

On the other side the *Index* as the vehicle for prowaterworks opinion continued to be vigilant in its campaigns against intemperance, the breaking of the Sabbath, lack of attendance at religious functions, and the like. It also concerned itself with reporting relatively insignificant actions of citizens that it considered inconsiderate and unneighborly. The press could hardly be accused of having sold out to the forces of urbanization; it still imagined Evanston as a covenanted community. After the election an *Index* editorial stated:

> We have a thousand things in Evanston to be heartily thankful for, and to prompt us to press forward with highest hopes. We have not only a natural situation unsurpassed, but our acquired advantages, taken all in all, are beyond those of any village in the Northwest. We have our University, accessibility to the great city, the temperance laws, the truly wonderful growth of the past seven or eight years giving us not only numbers, but a population that is a proverb and example in the whole nation—a people of morality, taste, and culture, containing in themselves, together with the other attractions of the place, the elements that will draw other settlers with an almost irresistible force. . . . Having definitely and thoroughly settled the matter of going on with our public enterprises, the sewerage and water works, let us see to it now that no other disturbing element arise. Let us have unity and cooperation.[43]

To the *Index* progress was in no way incompatible with the maintenance of the essential characteristics of the communal village: unity founded on religion and charitable behavior, a sense of being an example to the wider society, a preservation of natural beauties, and the absence of destructive diversity.

Those who endeavored to slow the rate of progress in Evanston had a valid intuition that to embrace and nourish an emphasis on progress without some necessary soul-searching would endanger the covenantal ideal as they had experienced and imagined it. Those who advocated that the village press forward with its planned improvements had an equally valid sense that, being located near Chicago and not wanting to be entirely out of step with the times, Evanston would not and could not spurn growth and progress. Its task would be to affirm certain characteristics of the urban-cosmopolitan outlook without sacrificing the essentials of the covenantal ideal that they still held to be valid, and indeed crucial, for the spiritual health of the human community. To adopt any other attitude would inevitably lead to defeat.

By the middle years of the 1870s both Evanston and Oak Park had achieved a basic sense of community. Both had adopted temperance as a major principle and symbol of their common life. Both conceived of themselves as Christian (read, Protestant) towns in which friendliness, pleasantness, and cooperation would characterize social relations. But interestingly, the village that had begun as a colonized venture with the temperance covenant built in seemed to have moved much more quickly toward an accommodation with certain urban forces and thought patterns. Certainly Evanston was far in advance of Oak Park in terms of population. Including South Evanston, which was not to be annexed until 1892, Evanston had a population of approximately 6,000 while Oak Park's was in the neighborhood of 500. As early as 1877 the *Evanston Index* referred to Evanston as a subcity.[44]

Yet it would be wrong to assume that Oak Park was just then entering a stage of community life that Evanston had experienced in the 1850s. What, for good or bad, had been lost in Evanston was never duplicated precisely in Oak Park. Perhaps because its growth was slower and because it had had to concern itself with the struggle to define itself apart from its geographical and political allies, Oak Park had never been a self-contained village unit. In the 1870s it was still possible for a simplicity to prevail in Oak Park that was not possible in Evanston. But in Oak Park as well as Evanston progress had become the order of the day, and many of the problems that Evanston was having to confront would affect Oak Park in much the same manner. In comparing the two communities tangible differences must be noted, but of more importance are the stories that Evanstonians and Oak Parkers told about themselves.

THREE

Ideals and Images

By the last two decades of the nineteenth century both Oak Park and Evanston had been clearly designated, or "named," suburbs. Newspapers and promotional materials from both within and without the communities referred to them as suburbs. Because the name seemed to find ready acceptance within the communities themselves, it provides a convenient point from which to begin to answer the question: What self-images and self-understandings are revealed through the labels, rhetoric, word-symbols, and stories that Oak Parkers and Evanstonians used to identify themselves?

It is not startling that Evanston and Oak Park should refer to themselves and be referred to as suburbs. Through annexation the city was moving its borders closer to the communities; a major proportion of the labor force depended on the city for their livelihood; people shopped, did volunteer work, and found recreation in the city. In countless tangible and intangible ways Evanston and Oak Park were undeniably a part of "greater Chicago." Furthermore, the existence of suburbs was nothing new to the American scene. At least as early as the beginning of the nineteenth century, towns around the periphery of cities had been called suburbs and had been described, as the *Index* described Evanston, as possessing "all the advantages of the city and country combined."[1] It required no great creativity for the label to be attached to Oak Park and Evanston.

Yet Evanstonians' and Oak Parkers' cordial acceptance and free use of the term suggests that suburb was a designation that was more than just available and appropriate in an ordinary manner of speaking; in both negative and positive ways it was of symbolic importance. It expressed, and helped to consolidate further, residents' notions both of who they were not and of who they were. And if the word was not rich enough to bear the full weight of what Evanstonians and Oak Parkers considered to be the meaning of their communal life, this was in one sense its very usefulness.

The suburb had not been an important part of the symbolic landscape in America. The pioneer in the wilderness, the yeoman farmer, the small town, the city—all these were images that might conjure associations having to do with the uniqueness of America and expressing what life was and was meant to be in the New World. The spirit of America might be embodied variously in the rugged self-sufficiency and egalitarian outlook of the frontier hero, the simple and natural virtues of an independent tiller of the soil, or the morality, cooperation, and enriching associational life of the town. The pioneer, the farmer, and the townsman all benefited from a close relationship to nature and the divine. The city was seldom viewed as embodying the essential spirit of America, but it too was a symbolic locale. Negatively it might represent vestiges of Old World influence and a danger to the innocence of the American environment. Positively it might be used as a sign that even the most potentially corrupt of phenomena could be redeemed in the American setting. With such images culturally dominant, the suburb, if it was considered at all, would likely be seen either as an adjunct to a city, as a small town that happened to be situated near a city, or more typically as a kind of haphazard assortment of characteristics borrowed from other kinds of living situations.

In the last quarter of the nineteenth century, however, the power of these images to order and to make sense of post-Civil War society began to be challenged. In 1893 Frederick Jackson Turner noted the closing of the frontier in his famous address before the American Historical Association during the Columbian Exposition in Chicago. In so doing, he articulated what was already the experience of the vast majority of Americans. Likewise the various movements of agrarian protest made it increasingly difficult to imagine the farmer's life as contented or harmonious. Such developments, of course, did not pose any immediate problems for Evanston and Oak Park. The pioneering days had clearly passed in both communities, and although a few people did farm on a small scale in the early days, neither place had ever conceived of itself as a farming community. For Oak Park and Evanston neither self-esteem nor the meaning of corporate life was at stake in the fate of the pioneer or the farmer as symbols of the American spirit.

The town and city on the other hand presented somewhat more serious conceptual problems, for without unduly stretching the imagination Oak Park and Evanston could be classed with either. Oak Parkers and Evanstonians had to decide whether they were basically the kind of place a town was or the kind of place a city was. In reality, of course, this was not a single decision nor was the issue normally confronted abstractly. But through a gradual and subtle formation of attitudes and in the debate over a wide variety of issues, the answer emerged that the communities did not precisely belong to either the city or the town; they were something new. This affirmation was articulated in various ways in those writings which confronted the question: Who are we? It was in this context that suburb became a useful designation. For if the word did not naturally and immediately bring to mind all those qualities which the communities ascribed to themselves, it at least avoided some of the misconceptions that might undermine the vision they had of themselves.

What has been called the attack on the town or the revolt from the village by literary historians is generally marked by the publication of Anderson's *Winesburg, Ohio* in 1919 and Lewis's *Main Street* in 1920. Without doubt various insights are made possible by treating literary critiques of the town in the late teens and twenties as a body. But the prominence of such men as Sinclair Lewis and H. L. Mencken should not obscure the fact that the myth of the town, if not the town itself, had begun to be seriously challenged some fifty years earlier. Edward Eggleston's *The Hoosier Schoolmaster*, Edgar Watson Howe's *The Story of a Country Town*, and Harold Frederick's *The Damnation of Theron Ware* all met with immediate popular success and had in common the fact that they viewed the plight and failings of the town from the vantage point of civilization, not nature or the wilderness. This is not in any way to imply that these authors were spokesmen for an emergent urban or cosmopolitan culture. It is merely to say that for them the town would find no salvation in adhering to an Adamic or Edenic myth. Reality was revealing those myths to be mere illusions, and if salvation lay anywhere, it lay in the acceptance of an environment divested of such products of romantic or demonic imaginations.

For those who had found meaning in the image of the New World as a place of innocence, a rediscovered paradise, it was possible for the variations on the theme to be less important than the theme itself. That is, it was the idyllic rural or natural setting that was important, not the specific kind of community or living situation. Thus it was possible for Edward Eggleston to feel that he wrote *The Hoosier Schoolmaster* as a protest against the "unreal world to which Cooper's imagination had given birth," though Cooper's hero was a man set entirely apart from society while Eggleston's concern was with the rural town of the Midwest. Eggleston and others correctly sensed that the myths that Cooper had helped to foster had been applied to the town as well as to the individual. If, for some, the town stood for civilization as against the natural man, for many others it was imagined as being the embodiment of Edenic innocence, simplicity, naturalness, and harmony.

Many of the negative images of city life needed little literary confirmation. That cities carried the potential for such evils as class conflict, the breakdown of natural rhythms and harmonies, the loss of religious and moral order, and a variety of phenomena leading to social and spiritual decline had long been recognized. What was perhaps new in the latter part of the century was the increasing recognition that cities were no passing or vestigial phenomenon in American society and that furthermore the destructive potential of cities was not to be so easily avoided in America as had once been imagined or hoped for.

This is not to say, however, that the city was imagined unambiguously. The possibility that earthly cities might be transformed into heavenly cities was, for many, symbolized by the Columbian Exposition. If the city could not be an agrarian paradise it might be a New Jerusalem. Strong himself noted the dual biblical images of the city as the outgrowth of the first murder and as the vision of "civilization perfected."[2] Washington Gladden commented that if the problems of the city could be solved in America they would be solved for the world. The city was at the very least a God-given opportunity for the evolution of a Christian civilization. And even if such notions were too extravagant for some, the glamour, the mystery, the fascination of the city could not be denied. It was this quality of the city perhaps more than any other that novelists helped to bring to public consciousness in a way that statistics and sociological commentary could not. As early as 1871 William Dean Howells noted in *Their Wedding Journey* that his protagonists felt like Adam and Eve in a New World as they walked up Broadway in New York City. And the same characters in *A Hazard of New Fortunes* are initially fascinated by the charm of even slum neighborhoods and the variety of appeals to the aesthetic sense. Theodore Dreiser begins *Sister Carrie* with the image of Chicago as a magnet, luring Carrie into unknown worlds. If this theme was not new to literature, it nevertheless reminded people of an increasingly significant fact of life in America.

The attractions of the city were never lost on Evanstonians or Oak Parkers. It had been, after all, the opportunities offered by the dynamic metropolis that had attracted many to the area in the first place. The vast majority had found at least a measure of success within this environment and were not willing to turn their backs on it. At the same time the city continually tempted young and old alike to forsake cherished values of personal and corporate life. A large part of the meaning of Oak Park and Evanston was that they offered protection against the most threatening of the city's devilish wiles.

But if Evanston and Oak Park attempted to embody a corporate ideal distinct from the city, their model was not likely to be the small town or village as it was being reconceived in the late nineteenth century. Journalistic treatments of the town showed little of the underlying sympathy expressed by novelists. For instance, in 1895 Henry Fletcher wrote in *Forum* magazine:

The decline of large cities, whenever it has occurred, has attracted universal attention, but less heed is paid to the decay of the village. One by one, family by family, their inhabitants slip away in search of other homes; a steady but hardly perceptible emigration takes away the young, the hopeful, the ambitious. There remain behind the superannuated, the feeble, the dull, the stagnant rich who will risk nothing, the ne'er-do-wells who have nothing to risk. Enough workers remain to till the soil, to manage the distribution of food and clothing, and to transact the common business of life; but the world's real work is done elsewhere.[3]

Many Evanstonians and Oak Parkers had themselves rejected the town in favor of a more cosmopolitan environment. If, in adopting Evanston or Oak Park as their home, they rejected certain aspects of the city, it was not with the intention of duplicating precisely the country village or town. To be a suburb meant at the very least that they were not to be considered in the class with either city or town. But it also meant a great deal more than that. Though many aspects of the self-image of Evanston and Oak Park are highly similar, it is instructive again, in analyzing the positive articulations of identity, to treat the communities separately.

The assertions that have been made on the basis of evidence from the wider culture were reflected in Oak Park in an article entitled "County Segregation," which appeared in *Oak Leaves*, a community newspaper, in 1903. The issue being addressed had to do with a movement for the political reorganization of Cook County. It was proposed that boundaries be changed so that the city of Chicago would become coextensive with Cook County. This would involve either the annexation to the city of those parts of Cook County outside the city limits or the separation of those areas from Cook County, in which case they would either form a separate county or be assimilated into those other counties which already existed. None of these alternatives pleased *Oak Leaves* nor, if we may trust its reporting, did they please many residents of the community. For *Oak Leaves* considerations of economic or political efficiency were not the issue. Oak Park's identity was the issue:

In all this discussion about the "segregation" of Cook County there seems to be a tendency to overlook one most important phase of the subject. The question at issue is not merely between the city on the one hand and the country town on the other. There is a third element in the problem, and that element is the suburb. The interests of such communities as Oak Park and Evanston, while not wholly in harmony with those of the city, are certainly not identical with those of the outlying country towns, and while it might be a good thing for the farming districts of the county to be cut off and made into a county by themselves, or to be annexed in sections to the surrounding counties, it certainly would be a great mistake to include these urban villages in any such plan of segregation.[4]

It was important to the editor of *Oak Leaves*, presuming in this instance to speak on behalf of as well as to his readers, that Oak Park be considered a phenomenon distinct from both city and country town. But he did not stop there, and in the development of his argument some of the positive ways Oak Park imagined itself began to emerge.

The suburbs are by rights parts of the city and their interests are so allied with those of the city that segregation would mean little less than amputation. It is true that the best interests of the suburbs cannot be served by annexation to the city under present conditions, but there can be no question but that an ideal form of city government would include the suburbs in its scope without interfering with local self government. . . . In such a city government Oak Park and Evanston and other suburbs could maintain an individuality and self-control as marked as at present, while forming organic as well as vital parts of Chicago.[5]

The clear implication is that while Oak Park must be recognized as a distinct kind of community, it cannot exist apart from the city. Indeed, a significant part of Oak Park's distinctiveness lies in the role it may assume as part of the Chicago of the future.

The editorial goes on to state, in a way that anticipates more recent criticisms of the suburbs, that there is a moral question involved. It is Chicago that has made Oak Park possible, and the problems of Chicago arise in part because Oak Parkers have chosen to isolate themselves from the city as such. "You can't have cream without skim milk, and under present social conditions, you can't have suburbs without slums."[6] Because Oak Park is the kind of community it is, it has a responsibility within the metropolitan community.

Chicago is our city and the problems it has to work out for its salvation are our problems—problems which owe their existence to the fact that we are here and are doing business there and are building up there the greatest city in the world. It does not look well for the respectable people of the suburbs to turn their backs upon their own and to seek to be absolved from the responsibility for conditions of their own making . . . the people who are looking for the civic ideal ought to frown upon this "scuttle policy" of the segregationists and turn their attention to the evolution of some plan by which the suburbs may have their full share of responsibility for the big city without sacrificing their local self-government.[7]

This extensive and somewhat impassioned editorial is quoted at such length not because it is assumed to express a consensus of Oak Parkers. *Oak Leaves* reported only that it received a large number of comments, both positive and negative, on its original editorial. It may be possible, however, to infer what the points of uncertainty and struggle were in Oak Park's image of itself. In so doing, some commonly assumed understandings may also emerge.

Three years earlier, in the first months of 1900, the *Oak Park Reporter* carried favorable notices of Oak Park's involvement in a movement of the "country towns" surrounding Chicago to band together in the formation of a separate county with the county seat in either Evanston or Oak Park.[8] This movement came at a time when the threat of annexation was apparently strongly felt by a number of communities for the stated purpose of the movement was to provide strength in avoiding annexation. For Oak Park it was a time of particular uncertainty. The community of Austin, previously a part of Cicero, had been annexed to Chicago, and a vote that had apparently separated Oak Park from the township and established "home rule" had been declared void by the state Supreme Court. The future political status of Oak Park was uncertain in the extreme. Annexation, if not an imminent likelihood, was a real possibility. Thus many of Oak Park's leaders were found attending the meetings of the secessionists.

By the time of the *Oak Leaves* editorial of 1903 the situation had changed considerably. A new state law and rulings from the state courts had made it possible for Oak Park finally to achieve a long-awaited independence. By a margin of more than five to one Oak Park had voted, in November of 1901, to separate and establish itself under a village form of government. Oak Park was now an official, legally sanctioned entity with full control over its own affairs. It was no longer merely, as William E. Barton had said, "a state of mind" for those who sensed the existence of a community and believed in it. It could, as it were, demand recognition in human affairs.

Almost immediately Oak Parkers began to use such terms as "civic ideal," "model municipality," or "model village of the west" in reference to themselves.[9] It is the image of Oak Park as a model community that can make sense of both the positive and negative reactions that *Oak Leaves* received in response to its editorial. If Oak Park was to serve as a model in the emergence of a civic ideal, it must not allow itself either to be classed as merely a country town or to be separated politically from Cook County. Political separation would remove the channels by which Oak Park could exert itself as an active force within the metropolitan arena as well as create a psychological distance between itself and the metropolis. To accept the designation of country town would be to consider itself a kind of community so different from the city as to have little relevance to it, and would, as well, open the way to self-doubt and criticism. Thus separation would mean not just a release from certain problems and responsibilities connected with the city, but a deprivation of a constitutive part of Oak Park's identity.

On the other hand, if Oak Park was to be a model, it had to avoid at all costs being assimilated into the city leviathan and becoming only one part among many that went to make up an urban conglomerate. Thus when *Oak Leaves* used such terms as "organic" and "amputation," it was likely to offend some sensibilities. To be a model, after all, is not the same thing as being an appendage, no matter how important that appendage might be. Therefore, in responding to criticisms of its initial statement, *Oak Leaves* felt it necessary to emphasize that it was against annexation and would, if forced to choose between annexation and separation, prefer the latter.[10] But it then went on to reaffirm its position that Oak Park must not accept these as the only alternatives. As a suburb Oak Park had been given a unique opportunity. It must maintain close enough connections to Chicago to be relevant while preserving sufficient distance that its integrity and purity not be violated.

The points at issue then seemed to concern the precise interpretation that the idea of Oak Park as a model community was to receive. To use somewhat incongruous terminology, was the emphasis to fall on consolidating the revolution at home or on spreading it abroad? How important in relation to each other were respective tendencies toward an isolation that might ensure the success of the model and toward an involvement that would help to ensure the relevance of the model to the larger society? The dynamics of the situation are similar to those experienced quite early in Puritan New England. The Puritans have been interpreted by Perry Miller as having undergone a crisis of identity at those points when they sensed that whatever success they might have achieved in their attempt to establish a Bible commonwealth might be met with indifference by those for whom they had hoped to serve as a model. Such a fear is unmistakable in the sentiments expressed by the editor of *Oak Leaves*.

The basic assumption that Oak Park was to be a model and that it had a mission to perform was unquestioned throughout this and other debates. Perhaps because his point of view was similar to that of the editors, *Oak Leaves* reprinted a portion of a sermon by William E. Barton of First Congregational Church that dealt directly with what it meant for Oak Park to be a suburb of Chicago. In it the sense of mission receives expression in religious terminology.

> The suburb is created by the city and is a reaction from it. It is an effect and a protest. . . . The whirr of the trolley and the whistle of the suburban train have a message of hope for the slums. To the builders of suburban lines the message comes, "Prepare ye the way of the Lord; make straight across the prairie the highway for our God; exalt the valleys and fill the swamps and drain the marshes; and the glory of the Lord shall be revealed in the rosy cheeks of children, and all flesh shall see it together, and not rich men only; for the mouth of the Lord has spoken it."

The suburb must be a refuge as well as a model; perhaps more correctly it becomes a model by establishing itself as an environment in which people crushed by the city may be rejuvenated. But Barton is not proposing the sort of rural colonization scheme that had occasionally been offered as a solution to the ills of the city. He goes on to say that while the suburb must legitimately stand as a symbol of hope, this does not mean it can turn its back on the city.

> The battle of civilization is to be fought to a finish in our cities. We must never believe that better things are impossible. The righteousness of the suburb must reinforce that of the city. "Except these abide in the ship it cannot be saved." We are out in the fresh air, thank God; we must bring fresh air to the city.[11]

For Oak Parkers their sense of mission was grounded in what they strongly felt to be the religious nature of their community. This was true in several senses. For a people who considered themselves modern and enlightened, it might be difficult to believe naively and wholeheartedly that their mission was the mission of God's chosen people. At the least, it would be difficult to articulate such a feeling in acceptable terms. Furthermore, people had come to

Oak Park as individuals with a variety of motives over an extended period of time. Since there had been no real preexisting community the analogy with the Hebrews or the Puritans could not be carried very far.

Nevertheless, the term "chosen people" does occasionally appear. In a sermon entitled "The Devil's Dead Line," Rev. H. W. Stough of Third Congregational Church adopted a sarcastic tone that perhaps enabled him to make such a reference without embarrassment while at the same time pointing to what he felt was the unspoken assumption of Oak Park residents. The devil's dead line refers to Harlem Avenue and was so named because on the west side of that street, which falls outside Oak Park's jurisdiction, there was a string of saloons that served not only residents of Harlem but backsliders from Oak Park as well. Chastising his congregation and all of Oak Park for frequenting these establishments, Rev. Stough said:

> Poor Harlem! It is a victim of the responsibility of Oak Park. We glory in our beautiful homes and in our schools and churches. We think we are not as other people. We are God's own, his chosen folk. And we keep our respectability at the expense of our neighbor over the way. Harlem bears the sins and ignominies both of her own and of ours in Godly Oak Park. I would rather see tippling houses on our streets than the present system without remedy.[12]

The sarcasm is not directed primarily at the notion that Oak Park people consider themselves "God's own, his chosen folk." The intent was rather to say: If you believe you are chosen people, see to it that no one takes advantage of being included among you whose actions betray your principles. Indications are that the numbers involved in excursions across the devil's dead line were relatively small. But as was true with Puritan communities, the actions of even a tiny minority could threaten the integrity of the whole.

Elsewhere the idea of the chosen people is applied to Oak Park's pioneers as a portion of those men who carried their Bibles and their religious convictions with them as they moved west. For instance, Elizabeth Porter Furbeck, the daughter of Augustin Porter, wrote:

> God's chosen people wandered forty years in the wilderness, seeking a land he had promised them, a land that should be flowing with milk and honey. . . . From that time until this, there has always been a land somewhere the Creator said to his children, go in and possess it. When Horace Greeley said, "go west, young man," it was but the echo of ages. . . . As I have so many years watched the settlement of so many different states, it always appears to me the way that

has been ordained to have the gospel preached to every person before the second coming of the Savior.[13]

Furbeck's point is that Oak Park was settled by just such people. By implication latter-day Oak Parkers are their spiritual heirs.

Explicit reference to Oak Parkers as a chosen people were few. It was, however, much easier to conceive that the work that Oak Park had laid out for it was God's work. A purely secular vocabulary of reform was not often used. What Oak Parkers aimed at was the salvation or redemption of themselves and the larger community. In a Fellowship Club meeting at Unity Church on the topic "Moral and Religious Conditions in Oak Park," Rev. Shayler of Grace Episcopal Church spoke to the role of the churches in the community. He began by jokingly repeating the argument that an acquaintance had made to him a few days earlier that since Oak Park had no saloons, no poor, and no Democrats, it therefore had no need of churches. Rev. Shayler then more seriously went on to point out the reasons that this was not true. The test of churches, he said, was not belief or feeling, but living. "The time is coming when the greed of the coal barons and of the labor unions will both give way to Christian living. . . . The work of the church is to bring God's heaven down here among the sons of men."[14] This was the task of Oak Park as well. For this reason the churches were central to the community.

Much more common than either of these ideas—that Oak Parkers were a chosen people or that they were involved in doing God's work—was a simpler kind of statement that merely affirmed that Oak Park lived according to religious and moral principles and that the people were God-fearing, concerned that religious principles and institutions be at the center of their common life. Everyone could certainly agree that religious institutions ought to be given full support and that religious sensitivities ought to inform every phase of the community's life. Everyone could not agree, however, on the possible implications of being a chosen people or on what God's work was with regard to Harlem or Cicero or Chicago.

An epithet that Oak Parkers half-jokingly applied to their community was "Saints' Rest." The origin of the phrase may have had to do with the number of active and retired ministers who lived in Oak Park, but as a part of the common folklore it came to mean that Oak Park was a community of saints. Another part of the folklore was a story that William E. Barton repeated in a piece entitled "The Secret Charm of Oak Park," which served as an introduction to a history of and advertisement for the community.

Two teamsters were hauling heavy loads of building material from Chicago to
the rapidly growing suburb which adjoins the city on the west. The driver who
was in the lead half turned on his load and shouted back to the teamster behind
him. "I've never been out here before. How shall I know when we get to Oak
Park?" "When the saloons stop and the church steeples begin," replied the man
on the rear load, "You'll know you're in Oak Park." This is a true story. It is also
a true description. People who go west from Chicago to find Oak Park have
little difficulty in knowing when they get there. Yet the fact that Oak Park is
more or less identified with church steeples does not mean that it is an
oppressively religious town.[15]

Barton's commentary, of course, is as interesting in what it reveals as is the
story. Oak Park has retained all the essentials of a religious foundation without
submitting to the ignorant or restrictive mentality that, in the minds of many,
had come to be associated with the small town as a descendant of the Puritan
community. Developing the idea that Oak Park is not "oppressively religious,"
Barton goes on to say:

Attractive and unostentatious homes, wide and well-kept lawns, spacious and
hospitable porches, streets of generous width overarched by spreading trees;
these are the fundamental external features of Oak Park, and out of the
conditions that make homes amid such surroundings grow churches, schools,
libraries, and places of wholesome recreation.[16]

Were one to ask what "wide and well-kept lawns, spacious and hospitable
porches, streets of generous width" have to do with not being "oppressively
religious," the answer would seem to be, though Barton does not explicitly
state it, that the spaciousness of the physical surroundings is merely an
outward manifestation of a spaciousness of the mind and spirit as well. In such
a community individuals are not likely to feel oppressed by their environment;
on the contrary, the environment is conducive to generosity, broad horizons,
and far-ranging thought.

On the other hand, expansiveness does not mean any sacrifice of
commitment or community. As the church steeples are the physical symbols,
so temperance is the moral symbol of Oak Park's commitment to an ideal of
community life.

It was determined very early that no liquor should be sold in Oak Park. This
moral stand, taken in a way when it was less frequent than it is now, may be
said to be the very cornerstone of Oak Park's intellectual and moral
supremacy.[17]

Nearly every writing or public pronouncement that attempted to interpret Oak Park's significance to residents and prospective residents included a variation on Barton's themes.[18] A speech given by A. S. Ray, the first village president of Oak Park, to a fraternal organization may be taken as representative. Asked to reflect on Oak Park's experience during its first year under home rule, Ray said in part:

> The strict principles on which it [Oak Park] was originally founded, and which are still in full force and effect, its freedom from the debasing effects of saloons and bar-rooms, so fatal to the morals and conduct of the young, and the high character of the inhabitants that a village conducted on such lines naturally draws within its circle, make Oak Park a particularly desirable residence for families who have children to rear and to whom surroundings and associations are of the very highest importance.[19]

The recognition of the "strict principles" that lie at the foundation of the community's existence, however, is made within a context that emphasizes the pride Oak Parkers may take in their accomplishments. "Beautiful residences" are said to exhibit the "taste and culture" of their inhabitants. Public improvements have been made while keeping the village practically free from debt. The school system attracts observers from throughout the country. Here is a village that is prosperous and progressive and yet adheres firmly to certain fundamental values.

The religious nature of the town was evidence that the residents were, as the Dedham town covenant had put it, "of one spirit." An important event in the early life of Oak Park as an independent village was the laying of the cornerstone for the new village hall about to be constructed. One of the speakers was Jesse Baldwin, a lawyer who had been prominent in Oak Park's efforts to achieve home rule. After reviewing some of the recent history of Oak Park, Baldwin said:

> It must be clear that this village did not come into existence by accident. It had become clear that our community was steadily losing in the town of Cicero the power to protect itself against inimical legislation, possible annexation to Chicago, or invasion by the saloon interests. We had come to realize that our people were homogeneous, having common interests and desires.[20]

Again, the temperance laws were Oak Park's assurance that the population would remain homogeneous, for only those people who accepted this symbol of the town's beliefs and aspirations would be likely to include themselves among the saints.

Behavioral standards that were presumed to flow from and manifest Oak Park's common religious commitment were, however, not the only way unity was conceived. The ideal was to remove personal pride and sectional antagonisms from any legitimate role in community life. This was, indeed, one of the most frequently repeated arguments that the advocates of separation from Cicero Township made. Oak Park, it was said, had to struggle constantly to protect its interests in the affairs of the township, and even when Oak Park was in control of the township board, as it most often was, the representatives from Oak Park had to be concerned not only with the interests of Oak Park but also with the interests of communities that had little if anything in common with Oak Park. The stretch of unoccupied prairie that lay between the northern and southern ends of Cicero Township was the physical symbol of a human and spiritual distance. This resulted, at the very least, in waste and inefficiency in government. But the advocates of separation never felt they had to go very far in demonstrating the inefficiency. The desirability of a community that might be free of the need to balance competing interests was invoked as though it were a basic article of faith.[21]

As was so often the case in both Evanston and Oak Park, a relatively minor issue might become the occasion for someone to remind people of the kind of community they were involved in creating and maintaining. One W. R. Kendall proposed a reform of the street numbering system such that numbers would begin at the eastern and northern boundaries of Oak Park and run continuously west and south.

> This system would prevent confusion for all time that we keep out of Chicago, and would bring home to everyone coming from Chicago the fact that he had entered the model village of the West. And because Chicago has a North and South side is no reason why we should have sectionalism or anything suggestive of sectionalism. . . . We should have one harmonious whole and nothing of Chicago in it. . . . A railroad track is laid down not to divide people but to unite them. Let us stand united.[22]

In Oak Park terminology, the absence of sectionalism was a way of expressing the belief that Oak Park ought to be a unified society that would be characterized by harmony and cooperation. A promotional book published in 1898 stated: "Whatever domestic battles have even been fought here have been on behalf of progress and better conditions, and no feeling of hostility animates any portion of our people."[23]

There was one apparent exception to the ideal of unity that eventually resulted in a reaffirmation of that ideal. After Oak Park had won its independence, residents were faced with the necessity of proceeding quickly to organize their government and elect the village officials. For this purpose a caucus was held that nominated a slate of candidates, adopted a platform stating their principles of government, and assumed the name Citizens' Non-Partisan League. The platform stated that village government should be free from party politics, that trustees should serve without pay, and that trustees ought to represent the whole of the village, not a portion of it, and be chosen without regard to place of residence. In this way the platform reaffirmed the ideal of unity and the vision of a town that was a homogeneous and harmonious whole, unbroken by artificial boundaries of political allegiance. The reality, however, was that a number of people felt that those who had led the flight for separation were becoming a ruling clique in the town. It was pointed out that the slate put forward by the Citizens' Non-Partisan League all lived within a very restricted area, namely that section that had originally been occupied by the founding fathers and that had retained a certain preeminence as the core of the village.

Thus an opposition slate was put forward under the name of the People's Independent ticket. Their platform was identical to that of the Citizens' Non-Partisan League with the exception that it stated the belief that as a matter of custom the candidates for president, clerk, and the six trustees ought to be chosen one from each of the eight election districts within Oak Park's boundaries. Apparently the image of Oak Park as not having sectional interests was being denied. Yet the People's Independent ticket made no proposal for a city form of government that would have given legal sanction to ward representation. And after the People's Independent ticket won a close election, the issue seems to have been closed for all practical purposes. In the several succeeding annual elections the same slate ran without opposition. John Lewis, perhaps the most influential spokesman for the Citizens' Non-Partisan League and the man who became known as the "father of Oak Park," later commented that the victory of the opposition ticket had been salutory in heading off any incipient factionalism in the young village.[24] Those who had opposed separation were given a voice in the new government; the net result had been to increase unity rather than destroy it. If sectional feeling did remain, on an official public basis the issue had been at least temporarily resolved.

65

The sense of being a model community, the belief in a missionary purpose, the consciousness that religion lay at the foundation of community life, the necessity of unity and the affirmation of homogeneity as essential to the fulfillment of the community's reason for being—all these qualities that Oak Park held as a part of its self-image had been integral to Puritan notions of community. If Oak Parkers could not quite imagine that they, and they alone, had been chosen as a group to occupy this land to reveal God's will through their community life, they could and did imagine that as a community they could choose to band together in living the kind of life that God intended for his people at this point in history. They could in effect be as a chosen people by choosing God and awaiting his blessing on their holy experiment. Much of this sentiment was summed up by O. W. Herrick speaking at the dedication of the municipal building. As a benediction on the ceremonies he said:

> What our future is to be depends on the blessing of God and what use we make of our privileges. Let us see to it that no local pride or jealousies mar our prospects. Let us see that no saloons invade our village, and that the Sabbath is not desecrated. May we be that happy people whose God is the Lord.[25]

Other evidences that Oak Park's ideals were Puritan in spirit may be mentioned briefly. Both platforms of the groups that nominated slates for Oak Park's first village election included a statement that it was the obligation of all men of the village to serve the village if asked to do so. The assumption was that such service would be without pay. Leadership would therefore be likely to fall on those who had sufficient wealth and/or leisure to allow a preoccupation with public affairs for at least a limited period of time. This had been the custom in Puritan communities. But if Oak Park took pride in its plentiful supply of such public-spirited men of means, it was less enthusiastic about the spirit of unrestrained capitalism. Success was esteemed but not apart from the communal context. One resident made his feelings explicit in a letter to *Oak Leaves*:

> The very spirit that makes it possible for some men to become vastly wealthy should be shunned. . . . Honesty of purpose, a desire to help others and more especially those who are not our equals in education and opportunity, a readiness to give rather than take, these are the principles which ought to be cultivated by our young men.[26]

Oak Park businessmen were perhaps just as legitimate heirs of the Protestant ethic as the nineteenth-century capitalists who have more often been interpreted in this manner. John Cotton had said that the Christian businessman must be diligent in business and yet dead to the world and that a "warrantable" calling must be undertaken for the public, not the private good. These were sentiments that Oak Parkers largely shared.

There is one part of Oak Park's vision of itself, however, that was not specifically Puritan in spirit or origin—the belief in the redemptive efficacy of a natural environment. As attempts were made to reproduce Puritan communities in the West, a variety of ideas and images relating to the purifying forces of nature were assimilated into the mythos of the town. For the town, however, it was not the "wilderness" but the "garden," the sublime result of nature domesticated and turned to human purposes, that was the positive metaphor. For Oak Parkers too the garden was a meaningful image, and to portray the community in this manner gave further credibility to the notion that as a suburb Oak Park was well situated to be a model community.

William E. Barton used the image explicitly:

> The motto of Chicago is "Urbs in Horto"—"A City in a Garden." Once beautiful green prairies were that garden. . . . But the prairies are now too remote to constitute the garden of Chicago's titular glory. The suburbs now are the garden of Chicago. Toward them she reaches out her system of parks and boulevards, the most comprehensive in the world, and here and there they blossom out into communities of homes. To these at night tired men return from the city, a happy homeward procession. And among all the suburban spots toward which they direct their feet none opens more invitingly before them or with more comfortable visions of rest, than Oak Park.[27]

The dominant motif here is the serenity and natural beauty of Oak Park as a place of rest, a haven from the toiling and striving of urban civilization. Had Barton restricted himself to this image, he would have been merely repeating what had been commonly understood as one of the major virtues of the small town. When Barton connected the image of the garden to the motto of Chicago, however, he introduced an interesting variation. The suburbs, he implied, do not merely surround Chicago. They are the soil out of which Chicago had grown; they nourish its industry and commerce; they restore wholeness to the urban man; and, in a sense, they are or can be living testimony to the kind of community Chicago may yet become. Had Oak Park not been so closely connected with the city, such understandings could easily be seen as reflecting the illusion and delusions that novelists were beginning to recognize as having destroyed the integrity of the small town or country village. But, as Barton explicitly and repeatedly said, Oak Park was not a small town only. It was a suburb, vitally related to Chicago, and this made all the difference.

Although interpretive statements about Oak Park dating from the period before home rule are comparatively rare, it is possible to discern a shift in emphasis away from the notion of Oak Park as a place of tranquillity and semirural contentment toward a greater acceptance of images associated with power, vitality, and progress. In 1887, the *Oak Park Reporter* published a "history" of Oak Park, the great bulk of which was little more than a compendium of information relating to the businesses and churches. In the brief introduction Oak Park is described simply as a place of residences that are "removed from the noise, stir, and confusion of daily city life." It goes on to say that while Oak Park claims many successful businessmen as residents, the desire of Oak Parkers is above all to "build up and enjoy beautiful homes and to preserve the quiet of the country in the village entire as contrasted with the daily routine elsewhere."[28]

A more extensive and revealing statement comes to us from the hands of William Halley. Halley was a newspaperman and reformer who began his association with Oak Park as the editor of a newspaper called *The Vindicator*, which started out serving both Lake and Cicero townships in 1883. Later Halley himself moved to Oak Park and the paper came to reflect more local concerns. Halley's most frequent targets are corrupt politicians and corporations. But his more fundamental concern is perhaps best reflected in the dedicatory editorial he published in the first issue of *The Vindicator*:

> That ponderous iron horse, the locomotive, whirls across the plain, the steamboat grooves the waters of the lakes. The early simple customs have been laid aside. . . . Yet with all these apparently grand improvements we are receding from the will of contentment. . . . I prefer the old systems to any other they may bring . . . everything is changed; the past simplicity is robbed of its elegance by the triflings of art.[29]

Most disquieting to Halley were the changes wrought by the new industrial order. A way must be found, he felt, to preserve the order and stability that he sensed being threatened from all sides. As a reformer and a man whose involvements and concerns had been with the urban world Halley could not adopt an attitude of escapism or nostalgia, and his statement should not be read in this manner. Nor was he concerned to be a spokesman for rural interests on any level. Contentment and simplicity had to be given a place within the life of the metropolis.

Apparently Oak Park suited Halley very well, for he not only made his home there but also published a book that extolled Oak Park's virtues and advantages. Though not published until 1898, it may be taken to represent the dominant understandings that prevailed during the entire thirty-year period between the time Oak Park achieved a basic "sense of community" and the time it became a formally self-governing village.

> Oak Park history is not strongly marked nor notably eventful. It is a story of first beginnings and quiet and assured progress. The arts of peace are the only arts that have ever been cultivated here. . . . We have not developed any marked peculiarity in the way of municipal methods, mentality, politics, or religion. . . . We have given to the world no hero, no great genius; we have cultivated no species. Our only claim is that by purpose and perseverance we have built up a beautiful town that is possessed of every home advantage. . . . Cutting down forest trees and planting ornamental ones, laying out, grading and paving streets, building sidewalks, constructing ditches, drains and sewers, has been one constant practice of our people. . . . We have reclaimed the wilderness, have set up the standard of civilization, and now freely offer of what we have to those who appreciate our labors and are desirous of joining with us in the good work of making life more enjoyable, time more precious, and results more certain. . . . Our history is free from splashes of blood and acts of violence, and open a chapter where you will there is nothing visible that is revolting or gross. We do not boast of any flush times nor lament any ruinous depressions. So we hope to have it continue until the end.[30]

Only a few years later, as a result of the successful efforts to gain independence, a new dimension had been added to Oak Park's pride that made major parts of Halley's portrait inappropriate. Achievement of Oak Park's sons and daughters in the wider culture were placed on public display. The arts, especially music, were cultivated with intense enthusiasm. The very achievement of independence made it impossible to say that Oak Park's history was not "strongly marked nor notably eventful." If Halley had been content that Oak Park remain largely unnoticed (he clearly did not want it to be completely unnoticed, or he would not have written the book) and free of aspirations to greatness, Oak Parkers of just a few years later were not likely to be so modest in their aspirations or so reluctant in proclaiming their importance.[31]

The total picture which Halley had intended to convey makes sense within its context. Halley's Oak Park was, if not exactly timeless, a place where time moved very slowly, where as Halley had put it time was precious. Because it was free of the dehumanizing consequences of events that outstripped man's ability to comprehend, Oak Park could be that place of stability and contentment which Halley felt was so important. Indeed, in the symbolic time of Oak Park the period from approximately 1871 to 1901 could be characterized in just this manner. It was a time of patience and waiting, for though Oak Park had "being" it had no power. Viewed from the later perspective provided by independence, it was not a happy time. Oak Parkers, if pressed, had had to admit that Oak Park was in fact no place at all, only a thought or feeling.[32] Time did indeed move slowly in those days; it was sadly true that there had been no notable events. But for Halley it had been precisely this fact that had endowed Oak Park with an inestimable value.

Halley had given the demands of progress and enlightenment a proper place in his portrayal of Oak Park. The proper place, however, was not as a controlling principle but as an energy controlled and adapted to the natural rhythms involved in reclaiming the wilderness. Progress was only the means whereby the wilderness could be transformed into a paradisal garden. The dream would be shattered the instant that progress came to be pursued for its own sake.

Independence did not mean that this vision was to be immediately forsaken. It was rather assimilated into a new constellation of images that included evocations of power, importance, mission, destiny. Oak Parkers were aware that what had once been the prairie still lay beneath their feet.[33] Furthermore, Oak Park was still beautiful, its air was still clean, and the notion that it could serve as a refuge from the demoralizing effects of urban life was still very much alive and important. Yet, as Joseph Fletcher had written, the "doom of the small town" was evidenced by the fact that the world's real work was being done elsewhere. It was almost as if Oak Parkers had read that statement and determined that they would not be that kind of place. The world's real work, they felt, was being done by them. As a suburb they believed themselves well situated in being able to endow the communal myths of both Puritan and midwestern heritage with renewed meaning and vitality. Independence had given Oak Parkers power over their own affairs; now there was work to be done, tasks to perform. And whether the work was to be done primarily within its own borders in building and maintaining "the model village of the West" or was to be carried out through an active exertion of influence in the affairs of the larger community, there would necessarily be some restlessness and striving attendant on that effort. A people with a mission is never really at rest. If there was an implicit conflict between this set of images and those relating to Oak Park as a place of refuge, it was a conflict that Oak Parkers found it not too difficult to live with, at least for the time being.

The composite self-portrait that Evanstonians presented to themselves and to the world was in many respects similar to Oak Park's. To dissect the image, for purposes of analysis, is to become involved in a repetition of the major themes that have been isolated with respect to Oak Park: the consciousness of having a missionary purpose, the affirmation of religion as the source of that purpose and as the foundation of communality, the belief in homogeneity and unity as essential features of community life, and the preservation of "natural advantages" in combination with a vision of the community as thoroughly modern and progressive. Careful inspection, however, reveals some significant differences between Evanston and Oak Park with regard to the way these themes were expressed. These differences arose from and were reflected in a variety of factors, the most discernible of which were Evanston's early and painless establishment as a political entity, the importance of Northwestern University, the rapid growth in population as compared to Oak Park, and Evanston's decision in 1892 to annex South Evanston and incorporate as a city. A discussion of the ways Evanston's self-image differed from Oak Park's should yield sufficient evidence of their similarities as well.

Evanston's sense of its missionary purpose may perhaps be characterized as less ambiguous but more diffuse than Oak Park's. A community that conceives of itself as a model is perhaps always faced with a potential division of its attentions and energies. On the one hand it is important to make sure that the community remains worthy of being looked to as a model, while at the same time it is necessary to find ways of ensuring that the influence of the model is being felt and appropriated. To be a model requires some degree of cooperation on the part of those for whom the model is intended. The word "model" appeared much less frequently in Evanston than it did in Oak Park. It is unlikely that this signifies any less pride in their community on the part of Evanstonians or any less desire that the municipality embody what they felt to be the ideal form of community. But it would seem to indicate that Evanstonians were less dependent for their identity on the response that Evanston as a community evoked from others.

When, on occasion, other communities copied some phase of Evanston's life, newspapers were quick to point to the fact with pride.[34] Nor was the community indifferent to whatever fame it felt it was achieving throughout the nation. It was aware that as a Christian community it had certain obligations to minister to the needs of unfortunates, such as children of the slums.[35] These were not incidental parts of Evanston's conception of its purpose. Yet the primary evidence of the community's successful execution of its mission was that those who had been nurtured within its environment could now be found carrying the "good news" throughout the nation and indeed to distant parts of the globe. Frances Willard stated this theme explicitly:

> Northwestern's vigorous sons and dauntless daughters are out yonder; I have found them as far away as my adventurous feet have wandered, and always they were preaching, teaching, toiling to lay broad and deep foundations for Christianity, for education and for the protection of the home.[36]

This conception of the way Evanston was carrying out a missionary task was made possible, perhaps was made necessary, by the nature of Northwestern University as an institution and its importance in defining the nature of the community. Evanston had to accommodate its understanding of itself as a community to the fact that many residents stayed in the community for only relatively short periods of time. For the small town, of course, mobility was not viewed positively, since the movement was inevitably away from the town and such movement was a clear sign that the town had ceased to possess those qualities which could command the loyalty of its residents. The mobility of the city, on the other hand, stood for a breakdown of communal values. People were lured to the city and left the city as individuals without having been required to make a commitment to the city as such. Evanston, however, was able to conceive of its mobility in other terms. When people came, they came not only to the university but to a community that stood for something. And when they left it was not out of disillusionment, lack of loyalty, or a desire to move on to bigger and better things. People came to Evanston to learn a way of life, and when they left it was for the purpose of spreading Evanston's ideals throughout the land.

Individuals who grew to transcend the community were thus more important to the self-image of Evanston than was the case in Oak Park. Individuals stood out from the community in a way that they did not in Oak Park.[37] Even the name of the community exemplified this fact, since Evanston bore the name of a man who himself had left Evanston in 1862. For Evanstonians John Evans was a worthy founder, but they pointed with equal pride to the fact that the man whose name they bore had carried his work and his ideals to Colorado and had been a major figure in the process of bringing the highest ideals of civilization to the far West.[38]

All this should not be taken out of context, however. The community was as important to Evanstonians as it was to Oak Parkers. The importance attached to individuals only signified a different way of conceiving of the community's mission. The people whom Evanston had sent forth were important not just because they had happened to live there, but because Evanston had nurtured them. They were not occasional residents of Evanston but, as Frances Willard had said, her sons and daughters. The kind of community Evanston was therefore had the utmost importance.

Both the difference in the way Evanston conceived of its mission and the basic similarity to Oak Park in the kind of community it imagined itself to be may be illustrated by comparing Evanston's attitude to that of Oak Park's on the "county segregation" question. The two communities shared a hostility toward any proposal that included virtual annexation to the city; they did not share the fear, which some in Oak Park held, of being separated from Cook County. In answer to the argument that Chicago needed Evanston, the *Index* stated emphatically that whatever may be the case in that regard, Evanston certainly did not need Chicago. "Evanston declines to be made a sacrifice for the city's own regeneration. . . . Let Chicago work out its own salvation along the lines which do not endanger the autonomy of Evanston."[39] Some months later an editorial in the same paper came even closer to stating the crux of the matter. It began by recognizing that there were many plans being proposed whereby the city and county might be consolidated. Some were no doubt better than others, but for Evanston there was only one issue: "Evanston will not be annexed." Then followed a simple but revealing statement: "Chicago can offer to Evanston nothing which she cannot provide herself."[40]

Chicago was not Evanston's immediate frame of reference, as it was Oak Park's. In Oak Park conditions could not support as yet a belief that Oak Park was itself the standard of civilization, but it could believe in itself as a model for the city that would become the standard of civilization. Evanston could afford to be, in a sense, more arrogant. It had many years of independence behind it and did not need to submit to any period of self-discovery such as Oak Park was experiencing in the early years of the twentieth century."[41] It was twice the size of Oak Park at the turn of the century. It was the home of a university whose very name symbolized a vision that from the start was not contained by local horizons.[42] Finally it had itself become a city in name as well as in fact. What, indeed, did Chicago have to contribute to Evanston? Oak Park might have to borrow, as it were, a part of Chicago's power and spirit and vitality. Evanston felt it did not.

At the mass meetings that were held in Evanston to discuss various plans for consolidation, not a single person could be found who would speak, even with reservations, for any of the proposed schemes.[43] The one proposal that found a favorable response was the one that would have restricted Cook County to the existing boundaries of Chicago proper. Evanstonians apparently envisioned themselves as the county seat of a new and powerful governmental unit comprised of all the north shore suburbs. When it became apparent that this idea would be heartily resisted by other communities that resented what they considered Evanston's imperialistic designs, Evanstonians accepted the inevitability of the status quo while assuring their northern neighbors that their intentions had been purely honorable.[44]

Evanston envisioned itself as a city on its own terms, a city in the root sense of the word: a center of culture and civilization. Though its differences from Oak Park in this respect were in many ways subtle, they were reflected vividly in Evanstonians' designation of their community as "the Western Athens." Interestingly this had been a phrase used not uncommonly with reference to Chicago; in taking the metaphor for themselves, Evanstonians implicitly asserted that they had become the kind of city that Chicago might have become had it not strayed in other directions. It was perhaps this image that informed Frances Willard's filiopietistic history of Evanston entitled *A Classic Town*. At the least, she considered the characterization apt. "Evanston was to be the classic suburb of Chicago, the western Athens, with its face to the future and its keynote caught by college towns along the opening ways of civilization."[45]

A New Year's editorial in the *Evanston Press* attempted to articulate some of the qualities that might surround this image:

Evanston is the most celebrated and, on many accounts, the most attractive of Chicago's suburbs, by reason of its beautiful and accessible location, its educational institutions, its churches, its high social advantages; and the cultured character of its inhabitants. A great many of the residents of the village are people distinguished in the literary world and not a few of them enjoy an international reputation. . . . The character of the people, also, is distinctive. Evanstonians are nothing if not educated. The village is the Athens of the West, the home of cultivation. One feels refinement in the very atmosphere, and the crystallization of all this is the great educational institution in the midst,

Northwestern University. The character of the residents of the village has in the past few years changed considerably—and for the better. The old Puritan days are gone, though the old element which dominated the town then is still here, only softened enough to make it what it is, preeminently a live, progressive town.[46]

One cannot help but be reminded here of William E. Barton's statement that Oak Park was fundamentally a religious town, but not "oppressively" so. The "Puritan" element in Evanston is still present but it has been "softened" enough that Evanston may now consider itself a "live, progressive town." In addition, as the western Athens, Evanston is justly "celebrated," and its inhabitants are "cultured," "educated," "refined." It contains within itself all those forces which could produce what Josiah Strong felt to be the biblical image of the heavenly city, a "fitting type of civilization perfected."

Evanston had adopted a city form of government in 1892 at the same time that South Evanston had been annexed to "Evanston proper." It had become gradually apparent in the informal discussion over a period of years about the possibility of uniting South Evanston to Evanston that such a union would require the adoption of a city charter. Residents of South Evanston were firm in their conviction that their interests could not be protected without the formal assurance of adequate representation provided by a city form of government. It was not a case, however, of Evanston feeling itself forced into a position that went against its basic instincts. Though newspaper editorials and letters commonly made reference to those who "desire a rural village with all the rest and quiet of a silent country hamlet," the voices of such people were seldom manifest. The vote was taken with a minimum of controversy; it passed by a margin of 784 to 26.[47]

The relative ease with which this transition took place can be understood when it is realized that Evanston had been in the process of becoming a city in the minds of its residents for a number of years. The formal adoption of a city charter was seen as merely confirming what most people already felt to be a fact of Evanston's life. To be sure, the precise characteristics that could be understood as distinguishing a city from a village in anything but name were likely to be elusive. Had an outsider been able to press people for an explanation, they might have found it difficult. Perhaps the most tangible of those factors which were making Evanston into a city was its growth, as in this letter from one Alexander Clark:

By splitting the territory up into three villages you will not lessen a single evil that grows out of a large population; on the contrary, they will be aggravated. . . . The desire for rural quiet and the dread of ward politics and city methods cannot postpone the evil day even without union. With its present growth Evanston is soon bound to be a city in fact, no matter what it is in form. If it is going to be a city, it had better be a first-class one.[48]

In the last analysis, however, it was the intangibles that made the difference, and these could be pointed to, but not fully accounted for, by referring to Evanston's fame, the "cultured" character of its people, and the power it exerted through its ability to send forth into the wider culture so many of its loyal sons and daughters.

Evanstonians had begun to refer to themselves as a city as early as the mid-1870s. For many the resolution of the waterworks issue had settled Evanston's future course. By the late 1880s and early 1890s the word "city" was commonly used without apology or explanation. A frequently repeated phrase was: "this thriving young city which still loves to call itself a village." Nearly everyone who felt the need to speak to the issues of the 1892 election argued that Evanston was already, or at least soon to become, a city in spirit and in fact. For instance:

Doubtless many of us experience a feeling of regret in parting with the name of the village. It is suggestive of rural simplicity and of a guilelessness that does not comport with the methods of politicians. In a village wire-pulling should be unknown. There is no motive for men to seek official positions in a village except the public good. Ambition has no place there. When that condition of rural simplicity and guilelessness has in fact departed, we are justified in concluding that the village is at heart a city and should be governed as a city.[49]

The vote of 1892 can be looked on as the culmination of Evanston's efforts to distinguish itself conceptually from the small town or the village. As the *Press* put it, "There is something in the name city which has a winsome influence; it attracts people who look upon the name village as something mean and countrified."[50] Subsequently Evanstonians' efforts to describe what kind of a community they were were directed increasingly toward distinguishing themselves from Chicago. Evanston had become a city, but it was of the utmost importance to remember that this did not mean it was the kind of city Chicago was. This could even mean, on occasion, that the idea of being a suburb was deprived of much of its meaning:

> Evanston is a home and a bedroom for respectable persons who have their
> interests in Chicago. This is true, to be sure; but . . . nowhere can there be
> found the public school system, the parks, the lawns, and the pure air that are
> in Evanston. There is only one Evanston on earth. . . . The atmosphere, the
> moral conditions that obtain here . . . cannot be duplicated on the face of the
> earth.[51]

Evanston was to be considered unique. To be a suburb implied no closer
relationship to Chicago than that which resulted from its physical proximity
and the fact that many people happened to work there. Essentially Evanston
was a different kind of city altogether.[52]

On the other hand, if referring to themselves as suburbanites could serve to
accentuate their distinctiveness from Chicago, Evanstonians would assert their
suburban status enthusiastically.

> We want to be suburbanites and we will be suburbanites. We will not be lashed
> and governed by the Chicago bosses or a government which is a blot on our
> civilization. Great cities are the curse of our country. They are the breeding place
> of criminals and paupers, and we refuse to help pay for the support of crime and
> pauperism.[53]

The rhetoric here is significant, for the issue between Evanston and Chicago
had been magnified into a national issue. Civilization itself was at stake.

In Evanston local issues could assume national importance and national
issues could be seen as being of intense interest to the community, not just
because Evanston's residents were also citizens but because national issues had
a bearing on Evanston's identity as a community. This was true to such an
extent that it is sometimes difficult to ascertain whether certain statements were
intended to apply primarily to Evanston or to the nation as a whole. The
destiny of the two was viewed as almost synonymous. It is in the nature of a
city, after all, that it should embody the civilization of which it is a part. The
United States could no longer be symbolized by the yeoman farmer or the
country town. A country as civilized and progressive as the United States
would have to find its legitimate embodiment in cities. Yet the "great cities"
could scarcely be conceived as anything other than a "blot on our civilization."
It remained for Evanston to demonstrate what an American city could be,
what it was meant to be.

A few examples illustrate the point. In an editorial upbraiding Evanston
residents for not being as faithful or diligent in attending church as they
should, the writer closed with this statement: "Romans betrayed Rome, and

Americans are betraying America. But it is not too late to save ourselves. Who will do his part?"[54] He might have added, ". . . and Evanstonians are betraying Evanston." But it was hardly necessary. The clear implication throughout was that America was being betrayed when, in the most truly American of communities, people began to fail in their religious obligations. The mantle of American civilization was on their shoulders. A more extensive, and more explicit, statement of this theme came from Edward S. Taylor, later to represent Evanston in Congress, through a Fourth of July speech he made in 1876. To commemorate the nation's centennial, a fountain was being placed in what was to be known as Centennial Square. Taylor's speech was a part of the dedication ceremonies and was entitled "The Ministry of Water."

After reviewing some of the events surrounding the Revolution and quoting some of the Founding Fathers, Taylor went on to say:

> Prompted by such teaching, the colonies declared the independence—that declaration heralded to the nations the birth of a Republic—it resurrected liberty from the tomb of oppression and breathed into it anew the breath of life. It spoke to royalty and thrones tottered; it spoke to the oppressed and inalienable rights were asserted; it was heard in the hovel and inspired hope—there is indeed a propriety in commemorating a day thus immortalized, a fitness as well in the monument selected to make this centennial, typical as it is of the virtue which more than aught else commends our suburb as a home.

In one turn of phrase Taylor connected the ideals, aspirations, and destiny of the American people to Evanston. The fountain symbolized baptism, the birth of a nation and a new birth for the hopes of humanity, though the baptism of the Revolution had been a baptism of blood. The fountain also symbolized a religious baptism; its water connoted purity, sobriety, and temperance. Water also symbolized the resolution of power with purity. Through water God's power had once purified the earth. And down to the present day water symbolized both the power of commerce and the spirit of rejuvenation. It propelled trains and also quenched the thirst of body and spirit. What more fitting memorial to the nation and to Evanston! Through this fountain Evanstonians would henceforth be reminded that their purpose was to fulfill the national destiny. Taylor closed:

> As we behold this emblem of purity, its sparkling jets tinted in the sunlight with all the colors of promise, be admonished that temperance and sobriety are essential to a nation's life. Let this ornament be a perpetual reminder of the great deed in the shadow of which we stand, a century distant, proclaiming

independence, launched upon the tide of time. . . . May the youth of today, soon to be charged with the responsibilities of government, remember that righteousness exalteth a nation. Drink, then at the fountain which cheers but does not inebriate, and link sobriety with your political faith to the end that you secure to our town prosperity and peace.[55]

Still another indication of Evanston's "political faith" is furnished by an article that sought to interpret the reasons for the Prohibition Party having received only 194 votes out of a total count of 2,200 in the presidential election of 1888, this from a town as committed to temperance as Evanston held itself to be. The author states that the fundamental reason for the weakness of the Prohibitionists is that Evanstonians are not wont to conceive of themselves as a visionary minority, but as a people who have allied themselves to those large forces that seek to advance the progress, prosperity, and morality of the country. "The Republican Party," he said, "is just as truly the party of reform, of progress, of morality and the embodiment of the best intelligence of the voters today as it was in 1860."[56]

The faith was reaffirmed still another time in the support for Republican policies in the aftermath of the Spanish-American War. It cannot be assumed that Evanstonians were unanimous in their opinion that the United States should retain those territories acquired in the course of the war. Yet anti-imperialist sentiment was not reflected in the local press. One writer waxed eloquent on the subject:

Are Americans today the degenerate sons of noble sires? Our fathers carried the flag from the Alleghenies to the Pacific, from the Golden Gate to the frozen north, and with every advance the prophets of evil predicted the fall of the Republic. . . . There is more freedom to give, more school houses to build, more truth to preach, more oceans to whiten with American commerce, more tasks to dare, and all the pessimism of Tammany Hall, the solid South, the anarchy of Chicago, and the sophistry of the Platte cannot limit our growth, paralyze our commerce, stop our development, or make us recreant to our manifest destiny.[57]

Were one to dare to read between the lines, he might be tempted to comment that it is not altogether clear whether the "ours" in the last few lines are meant to refer exclusively to Americans or might be taken to refer to Evanstonians more specifically. Two points may be made, however, without engaging in such speculation. The image of the country's expansion and destiny fit in well with Evanstonians' image of themselves as an expansive power, "holding aloft the gospel torch lighted in Evanston" in "every part of the wide earth."[58] Second, Evanstonians were not nearly as hesitant as Oak Parkers in allowing partisanship and national concerns entry into local affairs. Indeed, their image of their community in many ways required that national affairs occupy a prominent place in everyday discussions. Unity, they felt, would not be seriously threatened since Democrats were small in number, and, in any case, were likely to share most of the attitudes of the majority.

It has been necessary to dwell somewhat on the ways Evanston imagined itself differently from Oak Park in order that the communities' historical individuality not be collapsed into a historian's categories. In the last analysis, however, no truer picture is gained by emphasizing differences than would be gained by ignoring them. Though some convergences in the self-concept of the two communities have been at least implicit in the discussion up to this point, the similarities must now be summarized in more explicit fashion. Those qualities that Evanstonians felt made Evanston a unique kind of city were largely those qualities that were central to Oak Park's understanding of itself: a sense of mission, a religious foundation, unity and homogeneity, the preservation of a natural landscape tempered by art and civilization. Such words can be no more than a historian's shorthand for meanings that were deeply felt by Oak Parkers and Evanstonians alike.

Page Smith's contention that communities, as they developed, were likely to manifest continuing evidence of their manner of origin would have been widely accepted by Evanstonians. When Evanstonians reflected on their early days as a community, they did so with a double purpose. On the one hand, it was important to realize how far they had come in so short a time.[59] At the same time, they could remind themselves how the healthiest and most essential traits of the original Evanston had been preserved against all temptations to the contrary. While a dwindling number of people remembered the past with a sense of nostalgia and loss, most observed only a gain. Evanston had been given a solid foundation; its progress could not be other than creative and humane. In 1873 the *Evanston Index* had written, "Whatever fluctuations may come to other towns, Evanston, we are sure, has such superior natural and acquired advantages that its course cannot fail to be constantly onward and upward, as it has always been."[60] And in 1892 the *Evanston Press*'s "platform" stated in part:

> The *Press* believes that the "rural" days of Evanston are hopelessly lost and gone forever, and appreciating the inevitable, will try and guide the progress of the

change so that all the delightful features of Evanston as a resident suburb may be preserved.[61]

A basic continuity removed uncertainty, threat, and danger from the process of change.

One of the qualities that had been present from the beginning was, of course, religion. Frances Willard, in 1889, wrote a series of historical pieces on Evanston that appeared in the *Evanston Press* and formed the basis for her book, *A Classic Town*. In one of them she quoted from a Mrs. John Pearsons, who had been among the early residents of the town:

> From the beginning the character of the town, the whole of it, was religious. That spirit was in the very air, and it was the beginning of a new Christian life to many of us; it was to me. There were so few of us that our church privileges and its interest were the main thing. It was well for the educational interests of Evanston that this should be the foundation, and it was so, very decidedly. . . . The train conductors used to call the village "Heaven's Town." It had a reputation of being a very pious town from the beginning. They used to call it, too, "Saints Rest."[62]

What a historian chooses to emphasize from the past may be assumed to reflect contemporary values where there is no indication to the contrary. Statements such as that made by Mrs. Pearsons may, therefore, be understood as something more than "mere reminiscences" in the hands of Miss Willard. What Evanston essentially was for Frances Willard in 1889 was what it had been in the beginning. In *A Classic Town* she made a point of arguing that Evanston had originated in a "prayer meeting."[63] This was perhaps a distorted description of the meeting in 1850 that had laid the original plans for Northwestern University. But her concern was to convey a meaning, not to describe the event.

The connection of past with present was made more explicit by Harvey Hurd.

> Church Street took its name from the donated site to what was to be the Cathedral Church of the town, the center of the religious and social life of this God-fearing community chiefly of the Methodist persuasion, but broad-minded enough to welcome those of other communions in their worship, and disposed when the time came, to give them a site on which to raise their own roof-tree, as the title deeds from the University to trustees of the older churches of Evanston will testify.[64]

Frances Willard, too, stated the sentiment:

> All of us alike believed in "the faith that works by duty," in rewards for right living, and punishment for wrong, not based on favoritism or on vengeance, but as the inevitable outcome of the laws written in our members and our minds and reflected on the shining mirror of the Bible's open page; and all believed in the One who came to show us what God's heart is like, the Ideal Man, the Incarnate Deity, the World's Redeemer. But for questions of method, then, we might have stayed together.[65]

The clear implication in both of these statements is that while on the surface the age of religious unity has passed and has been broken down into the separate institutional life of churches of the various denominations, still there is an underlying unity that history reveals and that will be apparent to anyone who explores beneath the surface of Evanston's life and sees into its spirit.

Unity in the fundamentals of religion was of the utmost importance but it was yet only one aspect of a unity that was presumed to permeate all phases of the social life. An example is provided by a letter arguing for various ways Evanston might be made more beautiful. A truly beautiful Evanston, the writer argued, would be an Evanston physically united as it was spiritually united. The railroad tracks, he thought, were in danger of creating division between east and west and therefore should be either raised or placed beneath street level.

> Evanston has become known the country over as a city of high ideals. . . . The city is homogeneous to an exceptional degree. Class distinctions are as near obliterated as possible. The city should remain one.[66]

Harvey Hurd went farther. The absence of class divisions and conflict was salutary, but finally Evanston's unity should be conceived in positive terms of mutual caring:

> Recognizing, as we do, "the beautiful times we are in," and the value of the rich inheritance enjoyed by the children of the present generation, let us highly resolve, here, in our truly beautiful, lake-bordered, tree-fringed, flower-crowned Evanston, to build such a monument to these pioneer home-makers as had never yet been attempted, namely, a city in which there cannot be found a neglected or friendless child.[67]

Evanston's beauty was imagined as of a piece with its other qualities. As Evanston's spirit was pure, so was its air; as its ideals were beautiful, so were its streets and parks and residences. Though Evanston had been vitally progressive from the beginning and had not, as had Oak Park, experienced a period where growth was perceived as relatively slow, the community thus assuming something of a timeless quality, still Evanston had been given a natural setting that it was careful to preserve in its embodied vision of "civilization perfected." No one who spoke or wrote about Evanston at any length failed to give testimony to its beauty. Historical summaries began not with the human history but with the natural history of Evanston. (This was largely true of Oak Park also.) And Frances Willard makes a point of saying that Evanston was "discovered" by Orrington Lunt, not founded.[68] Evanston grew out of the soil. The human histories of the people who had come to Evanston from elsewhere were relatively unimportant. When they came to Evanston, they began life anew.

Evanstonians saw their city as vital, modern, and progressive. Yet as a foundation for all the layers of change were all those qualities that had been built into the city from the beginning: religion, temperance, harmony, uncorrupted nature. William E. Barton had said that the battle for civilization would be "fought to the death" in the cities of America. Evanstonians would have agreed, but for them this meant not Chicago but Evanston itself. They were constantly in process of demonstrating that progress could be orderly and that being a city did not necessarily involve forsaking those essentially American virtues that had formed the conceptual core of community life in the New World from the time of the Puritans forward.

Oak Park was a suburban village; Evanston was a suburban city. The difference in names reflected differences in the images that could serve both to describe what the communities essentially were and to point the way toward the future. But beyond all the specific qualities that may have illustrated similarities and differences between Oak Park and Evanston, they shared a fundamental affirmation. Each insisted that it not be conceived in borrowed metaphors. They should not be imagined as country towns were being imagined; they were emphatically not the kind of place Chicago was. They were a new kind of community, yet they were the only kind that, given their historical situation, could revive and embody the vision that had endowed American communities with sacred meaning from the beginning.

FOUR

Perils and Possibilities: Building a New Puritanism for a New Age in Oak Park

The Pilgrim movement, with all its limitations, he declared, was one of the brightest pages of history, writing in letters more clear the two words God and liberty. He held it to be the duty of the new Puritanism to preserve that liberty and show to the world that in our larger faith in universal brotherhood, the Puritan spirit has gone a step nearer to God.

> Rev. William Barton at the funeral of E. S. Tomlinson, 1910

Rev. Mr. Godolphin expressed the most progressive ideas. The words of the prayer "Thy will be done on earth" is his program, and he declared that Christian people should have faith that their religion will operate here, as well as in the hereafter. He is opposed to the old time Puritanism, but at the same time he opposed the liberalism which manifests itself in the salacious songs, dances, garments, and novels of the time.

> Oak Leaves, reporting a speech of the new rector of Grace Episcopal Church, 1913

Oak Park clergy were much less inclined than their Puritan ancestors had been to draw parallels between biblical history and their own. The exodus motif could not have illumined the experience of people in Oak Park to the same degree it had for those who had first made the journey to the promised land of the New World. Yet no less than the chosen people of Israel or the settlers of the New World, many people in Oak Park were conscious of living in a kind of wilderness situation. The material, moral, and spiritual landscape into which Oak Park emerged as a self-governing village in 1902 was in its own way a "strange new world." This modern, urban wilderness presented a vast, and often confusing, array of images and realities that needed to be interpreted. The challenges that confronted people were for the most part unfamiliar ones. To guide them through this wilderness, Oak Park leaders turned to the resources of their religious faith and to a heritage that some held to be specifically Puritan in origin and that others had come to understand as more broadly American.

Like any wilderness, this one contained both threat and promise. The threat was dual in nature. On the one hand, there was the potential of being attacked by hostile forces intent on destruction. On the other hand, any vast, unsettled terrain offers the temptation for dispersion, a loss of cohesiveness, a waning of common purpose, a running after false gods. Many people in Oak Park perceived themselves threatened in both these senses, and the threat could be seen as directed alike toward themselves, their village, and the nation as a whole. At the same time a wilderness conveys a sense of unlimited possibility. Thus, while intent on carrying forward a religious and national heritage, Oak Park leaders also understood themselves as "doing a new thing." The essentially religious character of the American experiment needed to be affirmed and preserved, but to do so would involve new ideas, new attitudes, and new forms of community life. It was a "new Puritanism" that was to be affirmed and incarnated in Oak Park. Leaders saw themselves as participants in bringing about a new America, one that would be undeniably different from, and better than, the past. While one might grow anxious over the loss of fundamental values, there was little sense of mourning over a lost way of life. However serious the threats and challenges, the opportunities seemed great indeed. In 1902 many understood Oak Park to be standing at the edge of a new age, both for itself and for the country. And this chapter in Oak Park's history may be considered to extend until the entry of the United States into World War I in 1917.

One source of optimism, of course, was home rule itself. Home rule allowed Oak Park to be conceived as much more than a state of mind. On the eve of home rule, one correspondent wrote: "The thought was very nearly on every tongue that if village organization should carry, we would make an ideal municipality of ourselves. Our situation now is most favorable for the realizing of such an ideal."[1] Firmly in control of its own affairs, Oak Park could turn a hope of being a model community into reality. This notion was never far from the surface in Oak Park during this period. Besides being implied, or contained between the lines, in a large number of statements, it was given various forms of explicit expression. A visiting speaker told his audience, "The eyes of God are upon you."[2] The newspaper wrote, "The welfare of the country cannot be largely affected by Oak Park's spirit, but we may stay out of Chicago and maintain a community which shall be an example to the world."[3] And a minister told a PTA meeting that Oak Park stood as an ideal community, avoiding the "baleful influences of the small country town and the congested city."[4] Such expressions, coming from many quarters, were not uniform in their language or explicit in describing what Oak Park was to exemplify. But the idea was repeatedly conveyed that Oak Park was a kind of testing ground, and that the results of its efforts would not go unnoticed by either God or man. There was a special importance attached to Oak Park as a community.

If, however, Oak Park was to serve a purpose larger than its own welfare, more was required than the power of self-determination. The larger society would have to be ready to receive what Oak Park had to offer. Hopefulness had to be nourished by people and events on a metropolitan and national scale as well. In this sense, the timing of home rule in Oak Park might have seemed providential.

The final decision of the courts establishing home rule came in November of 1901, just two months after Theodore Roosevelt acceded to the presidency on the assassination of McKinley. Roosevelt's initial actions in the Northern Securities trust-busting case came just at the time Oak Park was electing its first slate of village officials. Also during Oak Park's first year of independence came Roosevelt's speaking tours on behalf of his policy in the anthracite coal dispute. In one sense, of course, Roosevelt's actions were mere gestures in the history of the progressive movement. But if these actions were gestures, they were at least dramatic ones. For many people in the heavily Republican Oak Park, as for so many other Americans, Roosevelt quickly became a robust embodiment of the reforming spirit of the times.

Reforming activity was certainly not new at the turn of the century. But in the previous decade it had gradually taken more of a hold in urban areas and focused more on urban problems. At the time of the World's Fair in Chicago, for instance, an Englishman, W. T. Stead, had published a book called *If Christ Came to Chicago*, which proved to be a popular rallying cry for urban reform. As a result of his efforts and those of local businessmen, the Chicago Civic Federation had been formed after the idea of London's Civic Church. In addition to Roosevelt's national leadership, there were signs after the turn of the century that urban reform was gaining strength. Mayors Seth Low of New York, Tom Johnson of Cleveland, and Mark Fagan of Jersey City were elected in 1901. In the same year, Samuel ("Golden Rule") Jones was reelected in Toledo after an unsuccessful campaign for governor. In 1902 muckraking journalism began with the publication of Lincoln Steffens's article on the Tweed ring in St. Louis and Ida Tarbell's first article on Standard Oil, both in *McClure's*. Settlement houses were making their presence felt more and more in the urban setting, not just as service institutions but as centers of a variety of reform activity.[5]

Certainly there were many kinds of reform activity that people in Oak Park might deem impractical, if not downright dangerous. And yet there appeared to be underway a search for new principles to inform the life of the metropolis. Oak Park, therefore, did not appear to be in a position of providing an answer to unasked questions. One way of expressing the strength Oak Park might receive from contemporary reform movements was voiced by a former minister of First Congregational Church on the occasion of its fiftieth anniversary:

> Within the past few years there has been a decided advance in the thoughts of men along the lines of social, business, and political righteousness. . . . This emphasis on righteousness is seen in the progress of temperance reform, the exposure of the white slave traffic, the condition of women and children in factories, the sanitary condition in tenement houses, the relations of employers and employees and various other things discussed by pulpit, platform and press. It is true that some impractical theories are advocated, but on the whole, the purpose is to secure righteousness. Since the truly righteous man is a twice-born man, it follows that the ultimate result of a revival of righteousness must be to emphasize the need of regeneration.[6]

But if persons and events from the world beyond Oak Park could help to sustain a sense of optimism and confidence about the contribution that the village might make to American life in the new century, the impact of the world beyond Oak Park could be felt in much more ambiguous ways as well. The signs of the times were not all positive, to say the least. Realities and events over which Oak Park had no control increasingly determined the public agenda. People found themselves confronting, much more urgently than ever before, the meaning of the modern city and of modernity itself.

Certainly one way of interpreting the city, and modern life in general, was to view it as a hostile environment. One minister expressed his perception this way:

> If ever a city needed a multitude of churches well-equipped, Chicago and her suburbs do. Practical infidelity, I'm afraid, is not decreasing. The poor are discontented, and the rich are intensely worldly. The vices common to large cities flourish. Thousands of our youth are being educated in crime. The saloon influence is strong, and in politics we might say paramount.[7]

One form of threatened attack from this hostile environment came in efforts toward annexation. The defeat of annexation prior to home rule did not close the issue. The issue was to come to a vote once more during this period, and the theoretical possibility of annexation could never be entirely dismissed. But in addition the seductive appeal of the city threatened to annex Oak Park morally and psychologically. Because this threat was more subtle, it was also more dangerous. The several successful efforts to avoid political annexation can be understood as symbolic of the much broader and more difficult struggle to avoid being swallowed spiritually by a hostile environment. This other struggle was not so easily or convincingly won.

One reason for this can be found in Oak Park ideals themselves. William Barton had said: "The fact that Oak Park is *more or less* identified with church steeples does not mean that it is *oppressively* religious." And this was but one way of expressing the image that leaders intended to convey. They envisioned Oak Park as appropriately modern, but not engulfed by modernity. The "old Puritanism" was rigid, small-minded, and provincial. Oak Park on the other hand was modern and progressive: physically spacious, spiritually tolerant, socially fashionable, culturally sophisticated. At the very least, this meant that not all aspects of modern and/or urban life could be treated alike. Some no doubt should be affirmed; others should meet with vocal and effective protest. But specifics did not always yield such clear distinctions.

The automobile provides one example of a change that aroused conflicting feelings and attitudes. In 1916 *Oak Leaves* waxed eloquent in editorializing on the positive influence of the automobile. After noting the benefits to public health due to the removal of the horse from public streets, and expressing the conviction that it encouraged families to do more things together, it continued:

> Again as a means of counteracting the heretofore dominating centripetal tendency of life in our large cities, the automobile is a godsend. It makes it possible for men to live farther away from their business. It substitutes the suburb for the congested city.[8]

In the view of *Oak Leaves*, the automobile was an important ally for Oak Park. But this was not the only possible view. Even in its editorial, the newspaper noted that the automobile also gave rise to new problems of "health and morals" and required new standards of propriety. Also the automobile, if it provided a centrifugal force away from cities, might also be a centrifugal force away from Oak Park. In providing increased freedom for individuals, it might detract from more communal activities. And some saw it as playing a role in changing the nature of the Sabbath. Depending on the point of view, the automobile might be seen as a blessing or as a curse.

Another example was the growth of Oak Park. In the twenty years prior to 1900, Oak Park had grown steadily from 2,000 to almost 10,000. But in the next seventeen years, more than 25,000 were added to the total population, bringing it to almost 35,000.[9] The meaning of these figures, to say nothing of the meaning of other changes that might be attributed directly or indirectly to such growth, was not clear. In 1907, when the population was around 16,000, *Oak Leaves* viewed the situation quite positively.

> It hardly seems possible that in less than two generations Oak Park could have been transformed from the open and bleak prairie to the ideal and delightful suburb of the present day. Its growth, however, has been analogous with the growth of Chicago. . . . A large percentage of the people now living in Oak Park and who lived here 25 years ago—yea even ten years ago—have witnessed a change and a transformation almost like magic.[10]

By 1915, however, when the population was approaching 30,000, the tone changed considerably.

> These figures are appalling to those of us who love to think of Oak Park as a suburban village. We are fast taking on metropolitan aspects that must be reckoned with in our ideas for the future. The development of this territory is so rapid that we can hardly keep pace with it in our minds, to say nothing of our plans. The situation is one that deserves the careful and prayerful study of all Oak Park citizens.[11]

To some extent, of course, the difference in the two statements can be accounted for by the fact that the population had doubled in the interim. But this should not obscure the fact that growth carried a double meaning. On the one hand it signified that Oak Park had a strong appeal and was gaining in power. On the other hand it meant "metropolitan aspects" and changes that people could "hardly keep pace with in their minds."

Thus it was not just a hostile, alien environment that threatened Oak Park. That environment could be viewed as ambiguous, or even as positive. Furthermore, the realities of modern, urban life were reflected, sometimes subtly and sometimes dramatically, in Oak Park itself. It was not simply a question of how one was to look upon one's surroundings, but how one was to gain a perspective on oneself. The city, for instance, was associated not only with vice, tenement districts, and saloons, evils that Oak Park could view from a distance. Extremes of wealth and poverty, class conflict, and immigrant populations who maintained a distinct identity were seen as characteristics of urban life and were thought by many to signal a breakdown in common American values and aspirations. While Oak Park might be free from the most severe forms of such stress, it was not without its analogues in the "servant girl problem," and in sectional and religious antagonisms that were sometimes readily acknowledged, other times grudgingly acknowledged, and still other times left to imagination and inference. More subtle than these indications, however, were changing attitudes toward the Sabbath, the effect of modern theater and motion pictures, modern fads in music, dance, and dress, the image of the "new woman," and the ideas of the "new theology," to name just a few. The signs were pervasive that Oak Park was part of the modern, urban world. If in some ways this was welcome, it could not be embraced without reservation. The battle for righteousness might be lost not so much in a decisive confrontation as through a process in which ideals were undermined willy-nilly and visions lost sight of in the flux and momentum of the day-by-day course of events.

Danger lay to a large degree in the very ambiguity of the changes that took place and, one might add, in the ambiguity of Oak Park's own stated ideals. There were ample opportunities to lose one's way in this "wilderness." The situations that indeed "deserved the careful and prayerful study of all Oak Park citizens" were almost endless. What was to be the shape and substance of the "new Puritanism"? And to what extent was the religious communal ideal, articulated by spokesmen, able to sustain its hold on the imagination as a means of interpreting present reality and providing a blueprint for the future?

91

No single vantage point suffices to give an adequate picture of the varied ways efforts were made to embody the ideals or the ways values were challenged, refashioned, or renewed. Nevertheless, prominence must be given to the role of the churches and organized religion during this period on at least two grounds.

First of all, leadership in articulating hopes, shaping responses to change, guarding basic principles, and guiding attitudes fell naturally to the churches. The coherence of the various images put forward by spokesmen rested on religion. Though the ideal village was often described in terms of its physical beauty or the peaceful surroundings it offered, it was not fundamentally an aesthetic or secular example that Oak Park had been imagined to offer. It was the possibility of a Christian social order that Oak Park hoped to demonstrate. Again, although the fact that Oak Park was said to attract neither the very wealthy nor the very poor was pointed to with pride, it was not primarily a unity of class that was aimed at, but a unity of spirit. Christian unity, not middle-class unity, was what was envisioned. Thus, in addition to providing moral and spiritual leadership, churches were expected to be primary institutions of socialization, nurturing that common feeling which was held to be necessary. Were the churches to abdicate such leadership, were their leadership to be successfully challenged, or were they to take such action as to set themselves at odds with the community, portions of the ideal might remain in some form, but the original vision would be lost.

Second, because leadership fell heavily on the church, one might expect to find many of the most important concerns bearing on how successfully Oak Park could incarnate its ideals brought out in the attitudes of church leaders and in the attitudes others might hold toward the church and its leadership. The church not only provided leadership; it also reflected many dimensions of life in Oak Park. Oak Park's ideals had been articulated by people who were committed to and believed in the central importance of the church in the community. As Oak Park itself was to be viewed as an experiment in Christian living, the strength of Oak Park depended on the strength of her churches. In following the efforts of church leaders, and in paying attention to the kinds of challenges they faced and the opposition they encountered, a significant and consistent perspective may be gained by which to interpret the mass of particulars that constituted Oak Park's history in the first years of the twentieth century.

The first church organized in Oak Park was the Oak Ridge Church of Harlem, in 1863. For the next eight years, in cooperation with the Oak Ridge

Ecclesiastical Society, this was the only English-speaking church in the area. Though this church later became Congregational and its founding considered to be the founding date of First Congregational, it was at the time nondenominational in tone and was spoken of as a "union" church, the spirit of unity and cooperation, which was widely held to be a chief characteristic of church life in Oak Park, as often traced back to this eight-year period. For example, a booklet published in memory of James Scoville, one of the founders of the Oak Ridge Church, contained his comment:

> Mr. Scoville was closely identified with the religious history of Oak Park. Soon after he came he was largely influential in gathering into one society all the churchgoing people of the place without reference to previous denominational affinities. Undoubtedly, this early movement is the chief source of that broad, catholic spirit of unity which still characterizes the various churches of this village.[12]

Furthermore, in speaking of the lasting influence of the early period, religious unity was tied closely to the unity of Oak Park itself. On the occasion of First Congregational's fiftieth anniversary, Rev. William Barton wrote a series for the newspaper connecting the history of the church to the history of the village:

> The principles which have made Oak Park illustrious found their first public expression during the eight years when the Oak Ridge Church of Harlem was the one church in this community. Round that social center crystallized the principles and purposes which are synonymous with the present name of Oak Park. . . . It is good to remember that no church in Oak Park has originated through strife in the present church. . . . It is not surprising therefore that the Oak Park pastors work together in the heartiest spirit of unity and that church work here is free from sectarian bitterness.[13]

On the same occasion, the minister of First Presbyterian Church sent his greetings. After quoting one of his predecessors to the effect that First Congregational had given "tone and type to the community," he went on to say:

> Through you, upon the plastic material of the pioneer period, came the molding influence of the best stock of New England and the Western Reserve, reinforced by kindred covenanter blood from Baptist, Methodist, and Presbyterian sources, all combining in a splendid force for community righteousness.[14]

The "kindred covenanter blood," however, was not to remain under one roof with their Congregational brothers and sisters for very long. In 1871 the union church formally adopted the name First Congregational, and at the same time a Universalist congregation (Unity) was established. During the next two decades additional congregations were formed and denominationalism became an accepted part of the religious life of Oak Park. First Methodist had been organized to serve a wide area in 1870, but in 1872 separated from other areas and built a place of worship in Oak Park. First Baptist Church was organized in 1873; Grace Episcopal in 1880; First Presbyterian in 1883. Thus by the mid-1880s, there were "first churches" of six denominations that formed the core of church life in Oak Park. All were located within the original area of settlement around Lake Street in the western third of the village, which was then, and remains today, the central business and shopping district. Taken together, and standing within a few blocks of one another at the functional center of the village, these church buildings were visible signs of the place religion ought to occupy in the affairs of the village and in the lives of its residents. In addition, taken together, they described the nature of the unity that the churches aimed to achieve among themselves and to provide for the village as a whole.

As Oak Park continued to grow, and as the time for home rule approached, a further process of splintering took place. Three of the six denominations represented in the core of churches began to "church" the newly developing areas, primarily to the east. By 1902 there were four Congregational churches (First, Second, Third, and Fourth), three Methodist churches (First, Third, and Euclid Ave.), and two Baptist churches (First and Austin Avenue), in addition to the other three central churches. Additional Presbyterian and Episcopal churches were to be established shortly after 1902. In at least the case of the Congregational churches, the new churches were the product of a policy of church extension and received tangible assistance from the central church. Though never as prominent, nor numerically as strong, as the central church, many of them came to command considerable recognition. They were clearly a part of the network of religious unity in Oak Park.

Churches of other denominations would have to struggle to define their relationship to this dominant "host culture" of churches. One example was the German Evangelical Church, which had been in existence since 1867 but had stood on the fringe of the other churches physically and held services exclusively in German well into the twentieth century. Other examples were the Catholic and Lutheran churches. In anticipation of future discussion, it must also be noted that even among the six denominations included in the host culture, the Universalist and Episcopal churches were faced with some special problems in defining their relationship to the others.[15]

With the understanding that a more complicated picture will emerge, it can nevertheless be said that the foundation for religious life in Oak Park was provided by churches of these six denominations: Congregational, Universalist, Presbyterian, Methodist, Baptist, and Episcopalian.[16] Occasionally, the leaders of these churches spoke as if others did not exist. For instance, in the course of describing First Congregational's influence in the community, Rev. Barton claimed that all churches in Oak Park had directly or indirectly issued from First Congregational.[17] Quite apart from whether this was true with respect to other churches, the statement certainly ignored at least the Catholic, Lutheran, and Christian Science churches. Such churches were admittedly relative latecomers, but such omissions served only to emphasize the belief that the six central churches had defined the terms of unity in Oak Park.

These churches held something in common beyond the fact that they were Protestant and English-speaking. They were also very much churches of the "new world." The precise meaning of such a statement may be elusive, but it ought not to be ignored on that account. Regardless of the fact that the genealogy of these denominations might be extended back to European roots, their effective ancestry was thoroughly American. When a religious heritage was mentioned, it was the Puritan tradition, the religion of the founding fathers, or perhaps the religious spirit of the pioneers that was pointed to. There was an assumption, occasionally articulated directly and more often reflected indirectly, that it was the spirit of these "reformed" denominations that had laid the spiritual foundations for the republic and that must continue to provide leadership for the nation. At the same time the colonial origins of these denominations separated them from other religious groupings which, though quite American, were seen more as anomalies or fads than as integral parts of the religious life of the nation.

By most outward indications, the established churches entered this period in a position of strength. When the village newspaper, *Oak Leaves*, began publication in January 1902, its covers featuring prominent people in Oak Park emphasized nonverbally these convictions as to the importance of religion and the church to the life of Oak Park. The first picture was that of the village president, Allen Ray. The next three cover photographs were of clergy: Barton of First Congregational, Soares of First Baptist, and Strong of Second Congregational. Of the first 100 covers, nineteen were adorned with portraits

95

of the pastors of local churches (some repeating because of a change in ministers). Nineteen others were of people identified by their connection with a program of a church or the YMCA. Thus 38 of the first 100 were church-related, well more than any other category.[18]

The covers of *Oak Leaves* underscored the fact that ministers were, by virtue of their office, public figures. They were expected to provide leadership not just for their respective congregations, but for the village as a whole. Although the specific roles they played need more careful attention and admittedly depended to some extent on the style and personality of the individual, the role a minister stepped into when coming to a church in Oak Park was undeniably a public one. Church news was highly visible in the press. Changes in ministerial leadership were followed conscientiously. Ministers were invited to address secular organizations. They had ready access to the press, and their pronouncements were not only noted with interest but might become matter of public controversy. If the opinions and convictions of clergy were not immune from criticism or challenge, neither were they likely to be taken lightly. The clergy of Oak Park were easily identified as people of prominence.

In addition to the rhetorical affirmations of the importance of religion and the churches and the prominence accorded to ministers, temperance stood as further evidence of the strength of the churches. This was the most firmly established and enforceable link between church and community. Just as no one had yet risen to offer an alternative understanding of Oak Park that challenged the role of religion, just as no one had yet challenged the taken-for-granted nature of the prestige of the clergy, so temperance was an unquestioned standard of conduct that people implicitly accepted when coming to live in Oak Park. And in contrast to the rhetoric and the position of clergy, it remained unchallenged throughout the period. To be sure, nothing could guarantee that an individual would accept the "covenant" of temperance on religious grounds. Nevertheless, this was a standard that the churches had identified themselves with and was therefore easily associated with the influence of the churches. Thus, on grounds such as these—the rhetorical affirmation of the churches' importance, the prominence automatically given to clergy, and the unchallenged commitment to a policy of temperance—the position of the church during the first years of home rule in Oak Park seemed secure.

This general impression, however, needs qualification. If the symbolic leadership of the churches was formally acknowledged and seemed beyond dispute, their social and institutional role in the community was much more difficult to evaluate. By 1902 Oak Park was not only quite far removed from seventeenth-century New England in the position the church might occupy in the village; it also was increasingly far removed from the situation that had prevailed thirty years earlier in Oak Park itself. One of the most noticeable of the changes was simply the growing number of congregations. While social life had once seemed to revolve around a single church, or at worst a small group of churches, it was by 1902 becoming ever more difficult for the churches to foster unity in the village in any such tangible way. This problem had been recognized prior to 1902 and was said to have contributed to the formation of a prestigious secular organization, the Oak Park Club.

In 1907 an article describing the origins of the Oak Park Club stated that it had resulted from "a movement to find a common point of contact that might result in developing a cohesive community." And it continued:

> At the time the club was organized the only social centers in the village were the churches. They performed the function very well, but as the community grew and the churches multiplied slowly, it was observed that the circle of acquaintance of many families was almost limited to the church where they happened to attend, as there was little overlapping of the circles. The result was often a narrow view which made concerted action in town matters very difficult to secure, and hence development was slow. A change was noticeable soon after the club began to bring together some of the more progressive people from the several centers of social activity on a common level.[19]

This, of course, did not mean that the churches ceased to play any important part in the process of socialization and the fostering of common spirit. In newly developing sections of the village, a church often was initially the major social as well as religious center for that section. And even as the religious situation became more pluralistic, this social function of the church could not be dismissed. Nevertheless, the situation did seem to dictate that leadership in this important area be shared more and more with secular organizations. The implications of this trend were potentially far reaching, even if they could not be precisely defined at the time.

Another change related to the increasing complexity of social organization was more subtle. This had to do with the correspondence between church leadership and secular leadership among laymen and -women. The names of the founding families of Oak Park—Kettlestrings, Scoville, Austin, Herrick, and so forth—were equally outstanding in the history of both religious and secular affairs. By 1902 it was no longer apparent at a glance that the most prominent people in the church necessarily played an important role in the secular affairs of the village, or vice versa. As the village grew, as the number of churches increased, and as more and more secular organizations came into being, the number of people involved in some form of leadership also grew. People of prominence were still often identified with church work, but they were also likely to be involved in charity and volunteer work, in social or fraternal organizations, and in the case of men were likely to have achieved some success or responsibility in business. It was no longer necessarily a matter of public knowledge as to whether a person belonged to a church. One resident recalled that at the time it was assumed that everyone belonged to some church, but it was usually not known, or considered relevant, which one.[20] The relationship between church membership and citizenship was becoming more difficult to describe, even if it was in many ways still quite real.

To illustrate who might be likely to emerge as a leader in the community, it may be helpful to compare the position of two successful department store men: Richard Warren Sears and Lindsay Woodcock. Sears, of course, was the founder of the Sears, Roebuck Company. In 1914 a brief article appeared in the local paper that noted quite simply that Sears "had lived for many years in Oak Park" but had been too busy to take any part in local affairs, the single exception being a substantial contribution to the YMCA. Though of immense importance to the world beyond Oak Park, Sears had never been a figure of consequence within Oak Park and had received only a bare acknowledgment that he had been a resident.[21]

On the other hand, Lindsay Woodcock, a longtime manager of Marshall Field's in Chicago, was for many years clearly a leader in local affairs. When he died in 1915, he was memorialized with a full-five-column article in *Oak Leaves*. He had been born in Maine but had been with Field's since 1877. It was noted that among those attending his funeral were not only his large number of friends in Oak Park, but 500 employees from Field's, forty members of the Union League Club in Chicago, numerous business associates, and so forth. At the same time, it was pointed out that he had been an elder of long standing at First Presbyterian Church, a founder and three-time president of the Oak Park YMCA, a member of the Oak Park Club, a director of the Scoville Institute and a local bank, and numerous organizations of a more cosmopolitan nature. It was held that he had been a deeply religious man, not only active in the church but also attending prayer meeting faithfully and reading the scripture every night before retiring.[22] The marks of character generally associated with persons of leadership in Oak Park were typified in the description of Mr. Woodcock: professional success sufficient to demonstrate competence and command respect, but not so great as to draw one away from local concerns or possibly taint one's integrity; demonstrated commitment to a church and its work and spirit, volunteer service to the community through public and private agencies; participation in the social, fraternal, or patriotic organizations of the village. Normally some combination of such qualities would be present in anyone held to be a leader or representative of Oak Park. But no one of them could be considered a necessary prerequisite. The churches in Oak Park, of course, had never exercised formal control over who might be entitled to full participation and leadership in the village. But increasingly, their informal role was becoming more uncertain.

It is hardly surprising that at the beginning of this period there seemed to be very little, if any, concern over the slow shift away from a direct and observable correspondence between church and secular leadership. For one thing, the change was slow. There were still many people who were known publicly for their leadership in both religious and secular matters. Also any blatant indication that a religious "test" was required for citizenship would not have been congruent with the positive image of Oak Park as a progressive, democratic, open, and tolerant community. This was perhaps part of the style of the "new Puritanism." Oak Park was not after all to be thought of as "oppressively religious." Nevertheless, it is important to note the beginnings of change in patterns of leadership, for as the period progressed there were signs that it was no longer possible to assume that leaders would necessarily hold views consistent with those of the churches. If Oak Park was not to be "oppressively religious," neither was it congruent with the articulated images of Oak Park to have leaders who were not informed by and in sympathy with the churches who had given "tone and type" to the community.

The tensions and ambiguities contained in the broadly stated ideals of spokesmen—the tensions between preserving the fundamentals of a heritage and adapting that heritage to make it relevant to the times, the ambiguity as to whether the modern, urban wilderness was to be viewed as a friendly or hostile environment—were felt perhaps most acutely by the churches. The potential of these tensions and ambiguities for producing instability is graphically illustrated in an incident involving members of First Methodist Church. In this incident, the potential for conflict in the ideals became a real conflict between well-known people in Oak Park and drew widespread public attention within and beyond Oak Park. Although this kind of occurrence was rare, especially coming so early in the period (1903), it does provide a glimpse into the kinds of growing pains involved in trying to embody a new Puritanism.

The central figure in this incident was the colorful John Farson. The conspicuous nature of his presence in Oak Park was only hinted at in his obituary notice of 1910. It merely noted that a large banking house bore his name and that he had been involved in supporting hospitals, the horse show, the Union League Club, South Shore Country Club, and so forth. None of this was unique. At the end of the article it was suggested that "to him more than any other source is due the fact that this suburb is known far and wide throughout the country as a community of beautiful homes."[23] This was an oblique reference to Mr. Farson's mansionlike structure with extensive grounds that made the other residences of Oak Park look modest by comparison. The estate, located just south of the business district and later known as the Mills house after its next owner, was often the scene of gatherings of nationally known businessmen. A few months after his death, an article reporting on personal property tax assessments claimed that Oak Park was the home of the common man and was not under control of plutocrats, since all the village officials had been assessed at less than $2,000. At the same time it reported that the Farson estate was the largest in Oak Park, being assessed at about $500,000.[24]

It was not, however, only his wealth, his connections, and his house that made John Farson stand out. He was identified with flashy clothing and a red carriage, which had come to be his trademark. Because of his association with C. T. Yerkes, the notorious traction magnate of Chicago, his support was enlisted to allow one of the newly formed churches in Oak Park to meet temporarily in a railroad station. When a Catholic church was organized in Oak Park, he offered the grounds of his estate for a reception and fund-raising event, a symbolic action that would have been considered controversial and could hardly go unnoticed. He contributed a story of his life and success, Horatio Alger style, in several installments to the newspaper, eliciting this response from an offended fellow resident of Oak Park:

> It is strange in this seeming just age that financial success should elevate a man in the estimation of his fellows, giving him prestige and advantage. *The very spirit that makes it possible for men to become vastly wealthy should be shunned.*[25]

Whether because of his personal philosophy, his business associates, his ostentatious style, or other reasons, John Farson was a conspicuous and controversial man in Oak Park. He was also, until 1903, a member of First Methodist Church.

In October of that year, Farson withdrew his membership at First Methodist. In keeping with his character, it was done with a certain flair and attracted a good deal of attention. Even *Oak Leaves*, normally loathe to print stories it considered not in the best interests of Oak Park, reported this one, noting that the attention it had received in the metropolitan press was such that it "cannot well be ignored by local papers."

The immediate cause of Farson's withdrawal seems to have been an election at which thirteen stewards were to be chosen for the congregation. A compromise slate of candidates had been nominated by the pastor, Rev. Hall, in the hope of reconciling what were described as the liberal faction, headed by Mr. Farson, and the conservative faction, headed by Mr. N. M. Jones. As a result of secret meetings and last-minute lobbying, however, one of the men most allied with Farson had not been chosen. This, it was said, not only angered Farson and his supporters, but also undermined the efforts of Rev. Hall at peacemaking and prompted him to request that he be transferred to another church. This was, however, merely the last act in a drama that had begun more than fifteen years earlier, when Farson first came to Oak Park.

Farson accused the church leadership of repeating the kind of action they had taken with regard to a previous pastor. At that time, Farson claimed, the congregation had passed a unanimous vote to retain the pastor, Dr. Rasmus, but had then sent a delegation to meet in private with the bishop to request his transfer. In the latest incident, they had again signed a petition asking for Rev. Hall to remain, and had then taken an action that made it impossible for him to keep peace with the church.

But the real source of conflict ran deeper. The reason there were factions in the church in the first place can perhaps be inferred from the kinds of statements Farson made about his opponents. The article in the *Chicago Tribune* began by quoting Farson with reference to the conservative leadership at the church: "I believe they would burn us at the stake and dance around us—if their antiquated dogma did not forbid dancing. They fight like cats and dogs and then hypocritically join hands and sing 'Blest Be the Tie That Binds.' "[26] For Farson what appeared to be at stake was whether the church was to take a stance that could be considered modern and enlightened, or whether it would cling to what he considered "antiquated dogma" and

101

hypocritical piety. He went on to say that the conservatives were busybodies who "by their morbid display of 16th century spirit are driving away from the church many desirable members, as well as making it practically impossible for young people to feel at home in the church."[27] Farson had felt personally the sting of the attitudes of his antagonists. He had been barred from holding office in the church, and he felt condemned by other members of the church: "The narrowness and bigotry of these people passes belief. Every time I go out in a red carriage, some of them call for prayer for my soul."[28]

Several weeks later Farson continued his attack on First Methodist in *Oak Leaves*. He again gave several examples of narrow attitudes, such as the pastor being visited because his daughter had worn elbow sleeves in church. He was in no mood to be gentle with his former associates: "This church has been controlled for a great many years by a little band of irreconcilables with all of the bigotry but none of the courage of the Spanish Inquisition."[29]

For their part, the spokesmen on the other side made no attempt to apologize. They portrayed Farson as a man overcome with a sense of self-importance who liked to throw his weight around and a "disturber and breeder of dissension."

> For years . . . Mr. Farson has tried to run the church, and, failing in that, he had been endeavoring in every way to make it impossible for the church to exist as an orderly, strong, and unified body. He has brought publicity upon us and has done everything in his power to harm the church which he was not allowed to govern.[30]

They also declared that Farson had brought the trouble on himself through his open championing of such causes as the opening of the Oak Park Club on Sundays. In a somewhat curious but suggestive conclusion to the *Tribune*'s report, Farson's opposition denied that a Sunday automobile ride the pastor had taken with Mr. Farson to a camp meeting had any part in the dispute. "For that matter," one of them said, "many members of the church ride in their automobiles on Sunday."

As far as the conservative leadership was concerned, John Farson had broken faith with them long before they had done so with him. To his opponents, John Farson must have appeared as a man who did not respect the claim made upon him by Oak Park as a community, by the community of faith to which he belonged, or indeed the Christian faith itself. His standards appeared to flow much more from his having been baptized by immersion in modern life than from any genuine Christian commitment. He seemed repeatedly to demonstrate a thorough insensitivity to the heritage that others valued so highly. The challenges he made to what others held important were made not on the substantive grounds as to what the fundamentals of Christianity really were or what ought to distinguish the Christian individual or the Christian community, but rather on the grounds that his opponents' views were simply out-of-date, not sufficiently modern. By his very nature he stood for a spirit of unrestrained individualism. As a self-styled Horatio Alger, as a man of ostentatious taste and flamboyant style, perhaps given to excess in speech and action, he could scarcely avoid being viewed as one who had set himself apart from and superior to the communal enterprise.

On the other hand, Farson succeeded in portraying his opposition as stern and rigid, narrow-minded and intolerant. His references to the Spanish Inquisition, a sixteenth-century spirit, and antiquated dogma communicated the idea that such people belonged spiritually to a time and place quite foreign to twentieth-century urban America. If the implication of Farson's opponents might be taken to be that no distinctive Christian form of community life would be upheld through men like John Farson, the implication of Farson's stance was certainly that there could be no grounds for an enlightened, modern world to take such people seriously. Farson was not alone in this. Rev. Hall was quoted as saying that he believed others would follow Farson's lead in withdrawing their membership, and it was also reported that his withdrawal was followed by general dissension in the church.

The issues involved, therefore, could not be reduced entirely to the level of the personalities of those most deeply involved. In one sense, of course, Farson's personality was the issue. But the tensions that nurtured this dispute were not the sole possession of the protagonists or of the First Methodist Church. Essentially these same tensions were manifested in an almost endless variety of ways and were struggled with both by individuals and churches throughout this period. The position of the churches in the first years of home rule was indeed strong, but it was not necessarily either stable or comfortable. For those most sensitive to the tasks that lay ahead, there was little room for complacency or self-satisfaction.

"Corrupting Influences All Around"

Ironically, at the time John Farson was making his attack on the conservative leadership of First Methodist, the two most prominent "conservatives" and the pastor, Rev. Hall, were deeply involved in an effort that could easily be seen as progressive and that had enormous public support. In the early spring of 1902, just three months after the first village president had taken office, a small group of Protestant laymen signed a notice appearing in local papers calling for a meeting to establish a Young Men's Christian Association in Oak Park.[31] At first the move appeared to attract little attention, but in the ensuing months a concerted effort was made to arouse interest and raise funds. A Sunday was designated for ministers to preach on the need for a YMCA. Editorials, cover stories, and letters to the editor on the subject began to appear in *Oak Leaves* with increasing frequency. Meetings were held in the church to solicit funds and other forms of support. In November, an organization was officially created with twenty-four charter members. By early 1904 a building had been erected and fully subscribed at a cost of $75,000.

Several aspects of the YMCA campaign are worthy of note. The sources of support for the Y, the reasons given for its desirability, the timing of the campaign, and the sense of urgency that can be discerned among the leaders all suggest that more was at stake than simply providing another community facility. Available records reveal very little opposition, or controversy of any kind, about the idea. The Y was by this time a well-established, respected organization, congenial to the traditions of those denominations already described as dominant in the village. A number of past and present employees of the Y were residents of Oak Park, and many others had been previously associated with the Y. Leadership and support were readily available, and the success of the campaign would seem to have been assured from the outset. Had a general support for the Y and a feeling that it might benefit the village been sufficient to establish a YMCA in Oak Park, the chances are that it would have happened sometime before 1902.

By 1902, while many people still seemed to support the Y on general principles and without much passion, many others had come to see its creation not only as desirable but as an urgent necessity. On the surface, this might have seemed strange in Oak Park, a community quite unlike those urban areas where a Y had been understood as crucial in bringing a Protestant religious and moral environment into a setting that was otherwise chaotic, full of temptations, and physically and morally destructive. The reasons why a Y might be seen as imperative, as well as the reasons why the concern came to the surface at this time, can perhaps be found in or inferred from the several statements that appeared in *Oak Leaves*.

The first such statement came in an editorial just one week after the initial notice appeared calling for an organizational meeting. It read in part:

> But we hope that the promoters of this institution will not overlook the fact that the scope and mission of a Y.M.C.A. in this suburban village must be quite different from that in the large cities, or even in the smaller cities. The Association is usually conducted as a club house and rendezvous for young men who are avowedly and exemplary Christian, who move in good society and wear good clothes. That class of young men in Oak Park is already pretty well provided for. . . . But there are plenty of young men in Oak Park who are not in the churches or clubs. They have little liking for the one and cannot afford the other. . . . These are the young men who need the good offices of the Y.M.C.A. in Oak Park. . . . The Oak Park Y.M.C.A. should be Christian in spirit without being churchy, because it should help those whom the churches cannot help because of lack of sympathy.[32]

As it turned out, this statement was somewhat uncharacteristic of the statements others were to make in support of the Y as the campaign progressed. Nevertheless, it contains some perceptions worthy of note, and it helps to highlight by contrast some of the points that were to be made later.

The basic perception, on which the attitude of the editorial seemed to rest, was that there were a sufficient number of people in Oak Park who were not related to the churches because of "lack of sympathy" to cause concern, if not alarm. Seventeenth-century Puritans had required the unregenerate among them to attend worship. This had been an important element in the manifesting and maintaining of a spirit of unity. In twentieth-century Oak Park, this was, of course, impossible. And yet *Oak Leaves* was not beyond seeing danger in the fact that some significant number of young people appeared to be untouched by the influence of the church. The stated desire to help these young men can be taken at face value, without ignoring the implication that the welfare of the village as a whole was also at stake.

But in the process of arguing for a repair in this breach of Oak Park's unity, the editorial made statements and used language that declared a stance of accommodation on several important matters. For one thing it acknowledged that the churches and the clubs were primary agents of socialization. The beauty of the Y was that it combined functions of both. Second, it suggested that a Christian spirit would have to be communicated without being "churchy." This was, no doubt, not intended as a direct attack on the churches, but it did imply that the Christian spirit of Oak Park might no longer be identical with the spirit of the churches. It also raised the possibility that the Christian spirit of Oak Park would have to become somewhat vaguer if it was to appeal to modern youth.

The nature of the support for the Y and the way the campaign was organized, however, gave a strong indication that the perception and hopes of *Oak Leaves* were not precisely those of the promoters. The effort to create a YMCA grew out of, and was sustained by, a cooperative effort of nearly all the churches existing at the time. The actions of leaders were not those of people who intended to avoid the appearance of being churchy. Planning meetings were held in the various churches. Leadership came from those already strongly identified with the churches, well-known laymen and clergy. This gave the rather clear impression that the YMCA was not to be an independent agency; it was conceived as an extension of the program of Oak Park's Protestant churches. It was to act on behalf of the churches and reflect the churches' values, attitudes, and ideas.

Insight into the thinking that lay behind this approach can be gained from a series of testimonials that were solicited to support the campaign and appeared in *Oak Leaves* in January 1903. Over three weeks approximately fifty statements were printed, first from the clergy, then from laymen, and finally from laywomen.[33] Some statements were quite brief and expressed support without elaboration. One layman had the temerity to suggest that a Y was not needed in Oak Park since practically everyone was affiliated with some church. Among the remaining statements, two thoughts appeared frequently enough to emerge as consistent themes.

The first theme was expressed most explicitly perhaps by Rev. Hall of First Methodist Church:

> Its very proximity to a great city renders a suburb a somewhat difficult place in which to bring up a boy. The attractions of a city are numerous, and many of them are utterly demoralizing. The absence of a proper surveillance is another danger in city life. Besides, the modern conveniences have left the average boy without any chores to do.[34]

Although Rev. Hall focused on the city specifically, others echoed his sentiments in broader, less explicit language. A YMCA was needed in Oak Park, it was said, to help guard against "contaminating influences," "corrupting influences all around," and a tendency to "low living" that could be observed in modern life. The Y was portrayed, primarily by the women, as an "extension of the home" and the "right arm of the church." As such it could "keep a hold on young people," "deliver them from temptation," and provide a "healthy and moral atmosphere" for the raising of children. The positive way of stating this theme was to emphasize the need for the building of character and the development of "well-rounded Christian manhood." It was the sacred duty and happy privilege of Oak Park, Rev. Barton wrote, "to keep [young manhood] pure, to make it strong, to assist it to influence and power."

A second theme was equally strong: the various Christian forces of the community need to be united in a tangible way. The time had now come to give permanent institutional expression to the belief that harmony and cooperation were outstanding features of religious life in Oak Park. The absence of serious antagonisms was not a sufficient demonstration of the positive unity that leaders held as an ideal. In arguing for the Y, State Secretary Brown, a resident of Oak Park, began by saying that a Y was necessary for the "unification of the Christian forces" in the village. Rev. Strong of Second Congregational echoed that statement, offering as his first reason for supporting the Y that it "would bring Christian workers together and stimulate them with new methods."[35] Though expressed less directly, the concern for unity can also be discerned in the several statements that argued that the Y should be seen as an evangelistic arm of the churches. The Y would stand as visible proof that the churches understood the "effecting of conversions" and the "training for Christian service" to be a common task, not a competitive one.

The perceptions, therefore, that guided the promoters of the Y were substantially larger in scope than those that had informed the original editorial in *Oak Leaves*. Though the concerns can be considered complementary rather than contradictory, there was a noticeable difference of emphasis. It was the urge to resist the "corrupting influences all around" and to build a broad-based Christian unity, not the need to facilitate the assimilation of a particular group of young men, that lent urgency and dedication to the cause of the YMCA.

In retrospect, the YMCA can be understood as a statement made by the churches in Oak Park. It issued a warning to beware of the dangers present in the potentially hostile environment in which Oak Park existed. It also exhorted people to be aware of the effort that would be needed to maintain unity of mind and spirit in a growing suburban village.

In addition to broadly defining these two kinds of challenges that the churches faced, the YMCA campaign focused attention on the need to embody and institutionalize Oak Park ideals. The YMCA stood for the united Christian spirit of Oak Park and the role the churches were determined to play in the "new age" of the twentieth century. As a uniting force it stood for the

107

covenant with God. Just as the new village government had been needed to lend reality to the idea of Oak Park as a community, the YMCA had been needed to provide the institutional expression of the united Christian spirit that was to be at the heart of the new village.

The example of the YMCA suggests that the leadership of the churches was aware that home rule did not mean that an ideal had been realized. The real work of building a model community was only just beginning. An amorphous spirit would not be sufficient to meet the challenges that lay ahead. The ideals would have to be made incarnate in concrete action and institutional life. Home rule thus seems to have inspired a sense of the need for the churches to take a more activist posture in the village, and the mobilization of church efforts to create a YMCA within a few months after home rule is a major indication of this.

As time went on, specific manifestations of the "corrupting influences" referred to in the YMCA campaign came to be more clearly identified. It was often impossible to separate personal habits and choices from public morals. This placed the churches in a difficult position, to say the least. Their unenviable task was to guard and defend the public morals that were held to distinguish Oak Park as a Christian community without communicating attitudes that were antimodern and oppressive. That changes in mores and morals could seldom be attributed to a precise source or "enemy" only made the danger seem more severe and the task more difficult.

Contemporary enthusiasms in dancing, specifically the fox-trot and the tango, were one area of concern. In a lighthearted manner, an early settler of Oak Park reflected on the changes in social customs and attitudes she had watched occur: "The ministers' sons and deacons' daughters of those days, were, according to their parents, 'kicking up their heels to the devil's music.' What would they have thought of the present day sensational dances?"[36] Not everyone, however, was disposed to view the situation with equanimity. The strongest statements were reserved for the tango. One church newsletter condemned it as "by its nature indecent and offensive to morals."[37]

The tango was seen as a symptom of more pervasive immorality, as when another statement connected the "sex gown," modern music, and "new dances, especially the tango" with the spreading influence of prostitution.[38] Distressing as the new dances might be to some, however, there could be little doubt that they were here to stay. The uneasy situation was represented in an issue of *Oak Leaves* that carried both an editorial strongly opposed to the tango and several ads for tango lessons being given in Oak Park.[39]

Cigarettes were also seen as a sign of danger. Often this concern was expressed only as a side comment or an illustration of some larger evil, as when one person criticized a play for presenting cigarette-smoking boys and women. Occasionally, however, the issue was attacked directly. The YMCA required members of its boys' club to sign an antismoking pledge and carried out several antismoking campaigns. And in 1917, the Nineteenth Century Club, the most prestigious of the women's clubs in Oak Park, lobbied successfully for a stricter smoking ordinance, prohibiting the sale of cigarettes within 800 feet of any school and raising the penalty for selling cigarettes to minors. "The action was taken," it was said, "to do something to stop cigarette smoking among schoolboys and to handicap the growth of the cigarette business, which is increasing rapidly in Oak Park."[40] As was so often the case, the statement implied that the threat came from outside the community, in this case in the form of business interests that had no appreciation for the kind of standards Oak Park was trying to maintain. In any case, cigarettes again stood for a spirit that was foreign to the image many held of their village.

Still another important concern was gambling. *Oak Leaves* represented a consensus of articulated opinion when it wrote:

> It is surprising to us that in this enlightened age there are still so many people at that, who think there may be some honest and honorable way to get something for nothing. We need more and more to understand that there is just one honest way to acquire wealth of any kind and that is to earn it—in other words to produce it.[41]

From many sources there were complaints about the extent to which gambling was a way of life in the city and other surrounding communities, praise offered for any civic group that campaigned against gambling, criticisms of lotteries run by department stores, and voices raised against "that class of men who drink, gamble, and lead impure lives."[42] But while articulate opinion was unanimous in its opposition to gambling, it was also clear that gambling, like so many other things affecting Oak Park, needed no word spoken in its defense in order to become a reality. It was charged at one point that the Oak Park telegraph station was being used to relay gambling information, and that this was just a further sign that gambling had become a common practice among many residents.[43]

Although temperance remained a firm symbol of Oak Park's common spirit throughout this period, this did not mean that drinking was of no concern. Besides the various efforts to support the extension of anti-saloon territory

109

locally, statewide, and nationally, there were from time to time concerns expressed that modern habits and patterns of association could eat away at the "temperance covenant." In a harshly worded letter to *Oak Leaves*, one person accused of hypocrisy those people belonging to the Union League Club and other clubs serving liquor, eating at hotels that serve liquor, and so forth.[44] Among the people this kind of criticism touched, of course, were many of Oak Park's recognized leaders and most respected citizens. And if such hypocrisy did not strike others as being as serious as it was to this one person, it nevertheless served to emphasize the obvious fact that Oak Park was not an isolated, total environment. Even the best-intentioned people were implicated in the moral ambiguities of cosmopolitan life.

If metropolitan clubs might be of concern because of their tendency to permit alcoholic beverages, clubs in Oak Park presented different kinds of problems. As early as 1902, the newspaper carried notices in a single issue relating to some thirty-five organizations not related to the churches. At the very least these groups competed with the churches for time and attention. It could no longer be taken for granted that people's lives revolved around the church.

That clubs were seen as an issue was indicated when Rev. Barton was invited to address the Oak Park Club banquet on "Clubs and the Clergy." His comments on that occasion were not recorded, but a year later Rev. Soares (First Baptist) addressed the topic in a symposium on "Religious and Moral Conditions in Oak Park." He said that clubs must seek to operate for the "civic good," they must avoid evils such as serving liquor and the scheduling of events in direct competition with the churches. By doing so, he suggested, the clubs could help to maintain the spiritual unity of the village.[45] The general stance was that clubs were not necessarily detrimental so long as both the churches and the clubs carefully monitored the situation. But on occasion clubs were attacked directly. St. Edmund's, the Roman Catholic church in Oak Park, editorialized against clubs in general on the grounds that they substituted the bonds of age, interest, or society for the bonds of the family and were thus responsible for the decaying of family life.[46] One may speculate that their opposition arose in part also from their perception of being excluded from many organizations. Had this been stated it would only have added to the argument that clubs were a divisive force. Fraternities at the high school also came under attack on similar grounds. They were seen as threatening unity and harmony, building elites, and in general encouraging the kinds of factionalism that should not be condoned in a place such as Oak Park intended to be.[47]

The concern with such things as smoking, dancing, and gambling, to say nothing of liquor, was not understood as an expression of conventional, middle-class morality. The moral code in question was part of a religious ethos that many people in Oak Park had inherited and that they identified with the church and religious life.[48] Rev. Barton made the connection explicit in a sermon based on the seventh commandment, where he interpreted the modern meaning of adultery:

> Keep away from cabarets and fox-trots. Do not dance any dance or witness any plays, or engage in any conversation, the natural result of which is to make you think impure thoughts. . . . Live in the top stories of your nature, above all that is gross and sensual.[49]

Where individuals no longer "lived in the top stories of their nature," this was a sign of infidelity. It undermined a common spirit. It betrayed ties to the past. It ruptured the connection between the church and secular life.

On the other hand, a gradual, if noticeable, weakening of the moral fabric was a difficult thing to combat, and the churches chose to avoid decisive confrontations over such matters. They could and did make a quiet witness through continued prohibitions against dancing in the church and the anticigarette pledge that was required of the members of the YMCA boys' club, the Knights of the Triangle. They could and did attempt to persuade and exhort people, warning them to avoid such "corrupting influences." But these were weak tools compared to the seductive appeal of popular culture in a metropolitan setting. To regulate public morality would have required stern and repressive measures, extremes to which the churches were unwilling to go. Thus while not in any way dissociating themselves from these moral concerns, the church carefully restrained itself from proposing or supporting coercive measures with regard to such matters. The real battle, after all, was not to be carried on as an intramural affair among citizens of Oak Park. The task of the church, it would appear, was not to attack the symptoms as they appeared in Oak Park, but to defend Oak Park against the invasion of hostile, demoralizing forces from beyond.

Motion pictures, and to a lesser extent the theater, elicited a different response. These were seen as powerful vehicles by which messages could be brought in to Oak Park from the wider culture. As such they bore close scrutiny. Vachel Lindsay was soon to observe that motion pictures would penetrate every town and backwoods hamlet in America, that they would be "as difficult to prevent as the rain," and that they would exercise enormous prophetic powers, playing on the imagination in a way that was bound to affect the future.[50] This intuition of the power of the medium was perhaps shared by people in Oak Park. But for the moment their concern was less with the distant future and more with the need to control the effects of a phenomenon that had already demonstrated a spectacular appeal.

The theater held a somewhat ambiguous position in Oak Park. On the one hand, there were those who held theater of any kind to be immoral, and one minister remarked to a member of his congregation that he would like to attend some of the productions, but felt he could not for fear of offending some of his members and creating dissension.[51] On the other hand, the theater established itself quite early in the period as a popular form of entertainment. The Warrington presented live productions and musical concerts that were well publicized, favorably reviewed, and pointed to with pride. The theater was a sign of Oak Park's sophistication, and when a production was shoddily done, it was roundly criticized. A review of Ibsen's *The Doll's House* stated that the production was incompetent and the prompter could be heard in the last row. "We may be in the suburbs, but we are not in the provinces, and we resent such an action."[52]

But if the theater was not condemned out of hand as immoral and might even be pointed to with pride, its productions were nevertheless watched with an eye to the values being communicated. A general statement of this principle appeared in *Oak Leaves* editorial that opposed exempting the theater from child labor laws. After stating its opposition, it went on to make a broader statement:

> Therefore, the Warrington productions must be judged not by their suitability to an adult audience, but by their formative effect upon the artistic tastes and ethical standards of children. . . . The child is worth more to this community than the theatre. . . . The community which is not willing to sacrifice its children to the demands of business is surely not willing to sacrifice them to the plea for entertainment.[53]

An example of the specific kinds of productions that might be objected to was one called "The Law," which had received a favorable review from the architect Frank Lloyd Wright. Noting that the play depicted cigarette-smoking women, free-love advocates, and the like, one resident wrote to voice his objection to such plays being presented in Oak Park.

Even tho cosmopolitanism should be conceded to demand that knowledge of the existence of the "Bohemian" life in large cities should be given to the youth of our community, it still must be admitted that that life should not be portrayed as triumphant over law, order, and justice.[54]

Ways of life and morals, in this case connected explicitly with the city, should not in any way be glorified, presented as worthy of emulation, or conceded to be the wave of the future. Neither the churches nor any other organization were well equipped to counter the effect of such messages.

The theater in Oak Park was a representation of modern civilization. The attitudes expressed toward the theater closely paralleled attitudes expressed toward the city itself. On the one hand it threatened to undermine morals. Some seemed to feel that this was so by the very nature of the theater, just as it was possible to feel that the city was by nature demoralizing. Others were inclined to make more discriminating moral judgments. At the same time, the theater, at its best, stood for taste, culture, refinement, sophistication. And, like the city, it could even inspire a passion for reform.

It is a series of gospel meetings that they have been holding at the Warrington this week. At least that is the way the performances of "Kindling" appear to those who believe that social justice is an important part of the gospel teaching. There are those who fear the influence of the theatre upon the community and we sometimes feel that there are good grounds for such misgivings. But we do not see how anyone, old or young, can witness this play and not carry away a baptism of fire for the social regeneration of the world.[55]

Motion pictures were a different story. Even before motion pictures were shown in Oak Park, they had come under attack as being "degrading and demoralizing."[56] Yet when first shown in Oak Park in 1912 at the same Warrington Theatre, *Oak Leaves* noted the tremendous interest aroused as they played to standing room audiences.[57] During the next year two theaters were constructed especially for motion pictures. By 1914 sufficient alarm had been raised that a twenty-member censorship board was established by the village to prevent any pictures that were deemed "immoral, obscene, vicious, or tending to disturb the peace, or displaying any unlawful or riotous scenes" from being shown in the village.[58] A movement was also begun to build a village-owned theater to control entertainment.[59]

Apparently this did not prove sufficient. In 1916 the West Suburban Committee for Better Moving Pictures was formed, claiming the support of eleven churches, eleven PTAs, eleven social or civics clubs, with the director

113

of the YMCA as its president. Its stated purpose was to monitor the moral effects of movies. In May a boycott was called against Oak Park's theaters, and within a week the Oak Park Theatre ran a large ad in its own defense. It began by insisting that the theater had zealously protected the community's moral standards and by pleading for reason on the part of the boycotters. It then made a counterattack, quoting at some length an editorial of the *Chicago American*:

> All the same the notion that the only proper function of the film is to afford instruction, to address the intellect, is quite too narrow. . . . The unsmiling, severe standard of conduct, as a rule, has never been effectual in producing the highest types of health, intelligence, and moral excellence either in individuals or in nations. Some way or other, diversion and amusement answer to a rooted and entirely natural demand in the human make-up and must be duly considered.[60]

The committee was not deterred by the notion that its approach was unsmiling and severe. The movement continued to gain support, and by the next month a set of standards for films in Oak Park had been agreed on. Three categories were created: pictures to be eliminated entirely, those to be cut to a flash, and those to be encouraged. Those to be eliminated entirely were in turn categorized: "social evil" (sexually suggestive or belittling marriage or family life), unlawful acts (serious crimes, resistance to police, taking the law into your hands), amusements (promiscuous dancing or gambling), and personal habits (social drinking, hero or heroine smoking, showing the details of worship). Pictures to be cut to a flash included scenes showing death, weapons used in a deadly manner, cruelty to humans or animals, the insane or feeble-minded, or showing graphically the weakness of any class or race of people. Finally, those films to be encouraged were those showing pure home life and displays of affection, action or adventure if unexaggerated, education, clean comedy, and those with an explicit moral.[61]

Motion pictures had given the churches and secular organizations the opportunity to create a somewhat extensive moral code for Oak Park. This moral code almost constituted a social program. It sketched in outline a range of values and sensitivities that these leaders believed helped to define Oak Park's way of life. This was something that could not be communicated through any piecemeal attack on specific evils.

But even in this case, where there was a focus of concern within Oak Park's control, and where there was widespread support from both church and secular organizations, the effort proved to be short-lived. Six months later a rally in support of movie censorship drew only 100 people. It was admitted that the goal had been 1,000, which was "about the number to be found in the movie theatres on any given night."[62] Two months later another attempt at a similar rally drew only fifty people. The movement appeared to have collapsed. Perhaps motion pictures were simply too captivating for an abstract moral appeal to carry any force. Perhaps the threat to public morals and morale was not sufficiently direct or apparent. Perhaps the idea of censorship was distasteful. But whatever the combination of these or other reasons, the effect was once again to demonstrate how difficult it was for Oak Park to separate itself from the growing strength of both a metropolitan and a national culture. The concern with motion pictures seemed to be stilled until it was revived in connection with the issue of Sabbath observance.

The proper observance of the Lord's day had been a continuing concern throughout the period. Even more clearly than on many other matters, the spirit of a community rooted in Christian principles and practice could be seen as coming into conflict with the spirit of modern, urban life. Yet Sabbath observance was not unlike many of the other concerns in that there appeared to be few acceptable ways to counter the menace of growing secularity. There was no convenient battleground on which the issue could be addressed, much less resolved. The concern, therefore, surfaced only sporadically, and the effort to preserve the Sabbath might have seemed somewhat halfhearted.

The "rigid Puritan Sabbath" had come under increasing attack during the last decades of the nineteenth century.[63] Few people in Oak Park, ministers or laypersons alike, would have wanted to be identified with the harshness and provincialism often associated with the most strict sabbatarians. At the same time the Sabbath did not lack its modern defenders in the culture. The city was widely recognized as a major culprit in the trend toward a total disregard of the Lord's day. While the Sabbath might still be widely regarded as a day of worship and rest in many towns and villages throughout the country, it was patently not so regarded in major urban centers. Sunday newspapers, factories operating seven days a week, public transportation in full swing, country clubs, athletic events, and other forms of amusements, to say nothing of saloons—all these things meant that in large cities almost any form of Sabbath observance had become largely a personal and private affair. The problem was, of course, compounded by the fact that it was in the cities that ethnic groups, who did not share the view of the Sabbath identified with American evangelical Protestantism, were most visible.

As an immediate suburb of Chicago, Oak Park could scarcely avoid being affected by such realities. If the Sabbath never went completely underground, so to speak, in Oak Park, neither was its observance as universal or its meaning as obvious as many would have liked it to be. Such national enthusiasms as baseball, country clubs, and automobiling turned Sunday into a day of recreation for many people, residents of Oak Park by no means excepted. The Sunday newspaper was readily available. There was an increasing likelihood of numbers of people being involved in businesses that were open on Sunday. Distractions interfering with a completely religious observance of the Sabbath were, if not compelling, at least very much available and, one might say, difficult to resist.

The ways this might be dealt with in Oak Park were several, but the success of such efforts appears to have been checkered. The story is told that Sampson Rogers, an outstanding leader of First Methodist Church, a founder of the YMCA, and a well-known figure in the community, would on occasion take matters into his own hands. When seeing that a neighbor was working on his lawn on Sunday, for instance, Rogers would approach him and firmly inform him that this was not acceptable behavior in Oak Park.[64] It is likely that most people either did not share Rogers's stern conviction or at least were not disposed to be as forthright as he was. But nevertheless even less direct pressure could be very effective. One resident remembers that although many children were allowed to play on Sunday, they were told to do so someplace outside the residential area so as not to offend others or openly flaunt an action that might be thought to transgress the Sabbath.[65] Within such an atmosphere, Sundays in Oak Park might well have maintained an appearance of respect for the Sabbath.

On the other hand, it was certainly no secret that many people no longer observed Sunday as a holy day. At the very least, ministers had to acknowledge from time to time that they were not blind to this fact. In 1903 Rev. Barton (First Congregational) noted that there was a tendency to go into the city to catch up on work on Sunday, that golf and automobiling had become "insidious foes of the religious life," and that even the Sunday newspaper was a secular trend that could not be looked on favorably. He said that such tendencies were "fatal to the spiritual health of the village" and that "we should not allow such things on the Sabbath any more than we should allow smoke and soot from the city to take over Oak Park."[66] In 1907 Rev. Johnstone (River Forest Presbyterian) focused specifically on Sunday baseball:

[Sunday baseball] is but the natural result of a commercial and a professional spirit. . . . As a minister of the church of Jesus Christ and a watchman upon the walls of Zion, I would not be true to the living God, if I did not lift up my voice in warning.[67]

By 1911 things had not changed. Rev. George Luccock (First Presbyterian) wrote a letter to *Oak Leaves* that took up the question of Sunday golf. He wrote that this was "a conspicuous encouragement to the current disposition to dishonor the Lord's Day," that it set a bad example for youth, and that it led to a neglect of church and worship.[68]

It was one thing for individuals to fall into bad habits. It was another for public businesses and even government to encourage such negligence. Even this was apparently not impossible in Oak Park. In 1907 a brief history of First Baptist Church appeared, containing this comment:

With the growing population in 1885, when God's day seemed in jeopardy among us on account of the number of persons who forgot to remember the Sabbath day to keep it holy, this church named a committee of her members to act with the other churches of the village to take steps to enforce the closing of all places of business on the Sabbath day in Oak Park and which brought forth good fruit. It would be well to revive this work in 1907, with two prominent corners occupied by concerns running day and night.[69]

In 1913 it was noted that barbershops and certain other businesses that had been operating on Sunday had made the decision to close.[70] But in 1914 a letter from Grace Obenhaus to *Oak Leaves* criticized the village government itself for a lack of respect for the Sabbath, in that street repairs were made on Sunday.

Is it not enough that private individuals flaunt their independence of thought by using the hammer and saw about their yards, that autos and motorcycles keep the street noisy, that crowds scream and cheer around a ball game during the greater part of the afternoon without the village, through her officials joining in the desecration of the day?[71]

A rationalization for the customs that could be seen emerging in Oak Park as a result of trends in metropolitan living might be the kind of sentiment that had been expressed some years earlier by a writer who, in the middle of the national debate over the Sabbath, had sought a middle ground between the unreasonable restrictions of the Puritan Sabbath and the "uncurbed sentiments of a wild democracy."

> Some need sleep, some sunshine; some domestic cheer; some, an awakening book; some the patch of fresh grass or the forest ramble; some, the inspiration of friends; some the quiet of prayer; some, the words of the spiritual teacher; some, the great sacrifice of spiritual refreshment.[72]

This view also fit in well with those who argued for the Sabbath on the grounds that it was needed to insure the workingman a day of rest but who also argued that amusements should be available to those people who had no chance to participate in such activities otherwise.

This view was not unheard of in Oak Park.[73] But to others this view of the Sabbath no doubt seemed to preserve only the form of the Sabbath without its substance. The real importance of the Sabbath, after all, lay in the religious commitments it stood for, not in its social usefulness. And to view Sunday as only a day of rest or refreshment or recreation undermined that essential significance. Yet the Sabbath was observed in Oak Park, albeit unevenly, and for the ministers or churches to do much more than issue an occasional warning would almost certainly have been seen as a return to the repressive measures of the past and would have even more surely been self-defeating in the sense of initiating conflict and spreading disunity. Coercive measures in such matters were not only unmodern, they were antithetical to that fragile, voluntary harmony on which the communal ideal ultimately depended.[74] As the least of evils, therefore, the church accommodated itself to an ambiguous situation with regard to the Sabbath.

In 1917 conflict came, and it was initiated by those who wanted greater relaxation of Sabbath standards. In January petitions carrying 2,700 names were presented to the Oak Park village clerk asking for a referendum to allow motion picture theaters to remain open on Sundays. The initial petitions were denied on a technicality, but shortly thereafter corrected petitions were presented, this time with 4,600 signatures attached. The referendum was scheduled for April 3.

From the beginning the battle lines were drawn clearly by both sides. Those who opposed the Sunday opening formed a committee that claimed to represent the churches, PTAs, and most women's clubs. Ministers or religious leaders acted as spokesmen, but saw themselves as speaking on behalf of all who believed in Oak Park ideals. They characterized their opposition as being primarily the theater owners motivated only by a commercial desire for greater profits. *Oak Leaves* had given credence to this view in its reporting of the initial petitions. It said at that time that the petitions had quietly circulated for several weeks in the theaters themselves, with the managers the ones primarily promoting a popular vote. In the same article the paper reported a statement made by H. P. Baldwin of the YMCA saying that he did not know whether a referendum would be opposed but he was certain that if church leaders had anything to say about it, there would be no Sunday movies in Oak Park.[75]

Those who supported the opening of theaters attempted to describe the issue as being between the people of Oak Park and a small elite that was attempting to prevent freedom of choice. Four years earlier, just after the opening of the theaters in Oak Park, a longtime and well-known resident of Oak Park, Philander Barclay, had argued that pool rooms and movie theaters should be open to the public on Sunday because providing such entertainment in Oak Park itself would be better than having people going outside Oak Park for such diversions, as was already happening.[76] In 1917, however, this more moderate argument was bypassed. When an attempt was made to prevent a referendum through court injunction, this was jumped on as a clear indication that the issue was freedom and democracy. A letter was mailed to every resident of Oak Park urging the opening of theaters. It began by questioning the motives of those who sought the injunction:

> Do you believe in fair play? Do you believe in majority rule? . . . Why were these injunctions asked? What are these men afraid of? What have been their motives? Why should they try to throttle the electorate of Oak Park, thereby preventing you from expressing your opinion?

Then a connection was made between the effort to prevent a vote and the desire to keep the theaters closed. Without distinguishing between the procedural matter and the substantive issue, the letter went on:

> If you personally do not care to visit moving picture shows on Sunday, is it fair to deprive your neighbor of that pleasure and compel him to go to Chicago or Forest Park? Would it be fair of you to deprive your neighbor of the right to play golf or tennis, attend a baseball game or go automobiling on Sunday?[77]

This statement hit at a sensitive problem. The religious leadership had never condoned other Sunday amusements. For these practices now to be used as a tool against them for the further erosion of Sabbath observance must have

119

seemed a low blow. The statement seemed calculated to back the defenders of the Sabbath into a corner. Were they, or were they not, in favor of prohibiting Sunday amusements? An ambiguous situation, which many already felt uneasy about, was being made more painful in the name of consistency. And another writer pressed the issue even further:

> I wish to mention the attitude of some prominent church members who go to the Oak Park Country Club, the Westward Ho Club, or to Glen Oak and play golf on Sunday. Such men and church members who drive the automobiles on Sunday have no right to demand a closed Sunday and attempt to prevent those who do not belong to country clubs or who do not have automobiles from enjoying recreation within their means. The inconsistency of some of the opponents to the opening of moving picture theatres is strange to contemplate.[78]

Thus, in addition to the general principle of free choice, the concerns of wealth and class were raised explicitly. Was there to be freedom of choice for the relatively well-to-do and none for those less well off? This too was a sensitive issue, since it challenged the ideals that held that Oak Park was not to be divided within itself along class, or any other, lines.

In presenting their side of the story, those who opposed the Sunday opening chose not to address directly the troublesome issue of inconsistency. Nor did they base their arguments on manifestly religious grounds. Writing on behalf of the committee, Revs. Carpenter and Barton began by stating their belief that it was not zealousness for individual rights of citizens, but merely the desire for extra revenues that had prompted the theater owners to undertake the campaign.

> It is covetousness for dollars which now enrich the owners of like enterprises in the city, and no desire to secure the rights of law-abiding people, that inspires this movement. For the sake of this money and for no other apparent reason, this effort is made to introduce into our quiet Oak Park Sunday this secular and commercial element which happily we have thus far escaped.

They then went on to make a distinction between personal freedom and public policy. After admitting that many people may well attend motion pictures outside Oak Park on Sunday anyway, they wrote:

> Precisely the same argument would justify the establishment of saloons in Oak Park. There is no law which can prevent an Oak Park man from going to

Chicago to buy whiskey or to attend a Sunday theatre, and there is no good argument for making it easier for Oak Park people to attend Sunday shows than there is for making it easier for them to buy liquor at home.

For Barton and Carpenter, the overriding issue was not whether people were to be allowed freedom of choice, which could not be denied them in any case. The issue was the character of Oak Park as a community. They went on to contrast Oak Park to neighboring communities, especially Chicago.

Any thoughtful person who will walk through the moving picture districts of Chicago on Sunday afternoon or evening and will note the character and atmosphere which are induced by the presence of these audiences will not need any argument to convince him that this is precisely the kind of thing we do not want in Oak Park for ourselves or for our children. Those of us who live in Oak Park instead of in the city have come here because of the quiet and good order of this community; of its respect for the law; its freedom from temptation and its ideals of education and for those interests that make for the uplift of all the better things of life. To sacrifice these interests now . . . would be to fall far below the ideals which from the beginning have characterized this community.[79]

Throughout the statement made by the Revs. Carpenter and Barton, the concern with a religious observance of the Sabbath was present only as an undertone. The major appeal was to people's pride in Oak Park as a distinct kind of community different from, and threatened by, the communities that surrounded it. If the realities of modern life did not permit purity and consistency, this was no reason to give up entirely those characteristics which set Oak Park apart.

Rev. Carpenter was apparently not entirely satisfied with the approach of the official statement, for he submitted a separate letter that included some slightly stronger statements. He suggested that people who desire Sunday movies in their community should exercise their freedom of choice and move to Chicago, Forest Park, or elsewhere. He then went on to say:

This movement is much broader than may appear at first sight. It is an opening wedge to bring to Oak Park a wide open Sunday, to destroy the influence of the churches, and to cause family life to deteriorate. It is but one phase of the same movement that would make Oak Park a part of Chicago: Chicagoize it first; then annex it.[80]

In Rev. Carpenter's view, it was more accurately the "influence of the churches" that was at stake, not just the "quiet and good order" of the community. Relieved of the responsibility of being the aggressor, the churches, in cooperation with other organizations, had the opportunity to stand and fight. But the victory was to be a costly one.

The results of the referendum were convincing but not unanimous by any means. The theaters remained closed by a vote of 4,819 to 2,768, less than 2 to 1. Among the men, the vote was only 2,333 to 2,058 to maintain the closing, while among women it was 2,486 to 710. And in the southern third of the village a clear majority favored the Sunday openings. Although at the time there was no public analysis of the results, they could not help but leave some questions unanswered. The closeness of the vote among the men would seem to have indicated that the attitudes of men toward the Sabbath had changed significantly, encouraged perhaps by their greater involvement in the ways of the city, membership in clubs, and participation in such amusements as baseball and automobiling. This in turn raised the larger question of whether church and community ideals as a whole were not losing their appeal for the male citizen of the village. The vote in the southern portion of the village represented a geographical division that was also reflected around other issues.

When, however, *Oak Leaves* came to reflect on the results of the referendum, it ignored the signs of erosion and division within the community itself and focused instead, as the pastors had previously, on the external threats to Oak Park. The editorial began by asserting two reasons why the referendum had been doomed from the start.

> The churches are the most influential organizations in the community, and their members are the most active in social affairs, and they were opposed to Sunday shows. Those not influenced by the religious appeal were opposed to Sunday performances because of the fear it would change the character of the community and give it the aspect of hustle and bustle which characterizes some city residential sections where the theatres are open on Sunday.[81]

The editorial went on to say that the idea of Oak Park being dry and not having Sunday shows was largely a pretense as long as the saloons and Sunday theaters lay so close at hand. As a remedy, the editor proposed special legislation at Springfield creating a large village, including all the western suburbs of Chicago, which would be designed to reflect the values of Oak Park. It was admitted though that "this must now wait until the war is over."

The prospect remained, however, that what lay ahead for Oak Park when the war was over was far less likely to be the realization of such a dream than a continuing uncertainty and conflict over values in Oak Park itself. The combination of community and church ideals had won a victory, temporarily. But in the process the values of greater pluralism and variety of personal choice had been raised for public discussion, proposed as public policy, and gained a substantial vote of support. In addition it was unclear to what extent the ideals that had been maintained were based on a religious idea of the Sabbath or whether those ideals themselves were becoming more secularized. In the aftermath of the debate, with the victory safely won, Rev. Barton thanked those who helped to defeat the proposal and ended by suggesting that men now voluntarily abstain from Sunday golf. But he could not have very high hopes that his suggestion would be taken to heart. If the referendum on Sunday movies had symbolically reaffirmed the position of the churches, it did little to resolve the complexity of issues and feelings that had surfaced in the course of the brief debate.

"Oak Park's Most Dangerous Habit"

Changing mores and morals served to underline the need for constant vigilance and determination in the effort to preserve Oak Park's distinguishing characteristics. Yet instead of producing renewed dedication to the task of resisting "corrupting influences," modern life sometimes seemed to go hand in hand with an increasingly casual attitude toward communal ideals in general, and toward the church in particular. When Rev. Carpenter wrote that the movement for Sunday motion pictures was an attempt to "undermine the influence of the churches," his words probably carried this double meaning. Sunday movies could be viewed as a direct transgression of a biblical commandment and the teaching of the churches. At the same time they were not just evil in and of themselves; they also contributed to a neglect of the church on a day that had once been reserved entirely for worship and other church activities. Waning commitment and susceptibility to corrupting influences seemed to nurture and feed on each other, and it was a moot question as to which was the cause of the other.

Closely related as these two kinds of problems might be, however, they were responded to quite differently. When Rev. Johnstone described himself as a "watchman upon the walls of Zion," he perhaps aptly described the stance church leaders as a whole had evolved with regard to the specific vices that seemed to threaten Oak Park. For one thing, his phrase captured the belief

123

that such vices attacked or infiltrated Oak Park from outside. Whether the attack was portrayed as coming from an identifiable source—such as the theater owners, the cigarette business, or the liquor interest—or was seen more as a result of disembodied forces—as, for instance, in relation to modern dances and the undermining of the Sabbath—in either case the danger seemed to lie in something that was fundamentally foreign to Oak Park and was consistently described as such.

Rev. Johnstone's phrase also described accurately the role the church in fact had played. Ministers issued warnings. They held up verbal pictures to people when they saw danger approaching. They were primarily watchmen, not soldiers. It is interesting to note that the churches had not acted unilaterally on any matter of public morality. In defining, defending, and enforcing moral standards, the churches acted only when it could be clear that they were acting on behalf of, not in opposition to, the village of Oak Park and its people. Given an increasingly complex social structure, this meant acting in concert with secular organizations such as the PTA and social and civic groups. For better or worse, this was part of the "new Puritanism." On the one hand, this meant that the church still acted as representing and embodying the spirit of the community. On the other hand, it might mean that the arguments made, the rhetoric used, and the visions articulated might gradually become less firmly embedded in the specifically Christian beliefs and traditions of the churches, as illustrated in Rev. Barton's and Rev. Carpenter's statement on behalf of the coalition opposed to Sunday movies.

But a sensitivity to specific dangers present in the metropolitan environment was not all that influenced the statements and behavior of church leaders. Another fundamental perception was that the power of the church and religious beliefs to unite people in common attitudes and aspirations could not be taken for granted. Insufficient depth of common commitment was much more than a question of morals. Susceptibility to specific immoral tendencies was only one kind of symptom of indifference; there were several others. Clouded visions, confused priorities, and competing loyalties were perhaps the result of the spirit of the modern city as such, not just of its most demonic elements. If this way of defining dangers seemed to make them even more intangible, it also guided the churches toward more positive and independent action. The effort to revive and strengthen support for the churches gave leaders an opportunity to call people back to fundamental beliefs and ideals without being directly involved in the divisive and questionable practice of attempting to regulate the details of personal morality.

In 1908 a meeting of the Federated Men's Clubs of Oak Park chose as its topic "The Oak Park Problem." In retrospect, this occasion appears as an indication that the problem of generating enthusiasm was henceforth to be taken much more seriously than it had been in the first years of home rule. Eight laymen from various churches expressed opinions ranging from the need for more personal evangelism to "increasing bonds with the city and the poor." One said that Oak Park's problems were not social or political but spiritual and that greater activity of the churches was urgently needed. Another argued that Oak Park was facing spiritual degeneration, noting that attendance at church was dropping and weekly prayer meeting fading. Still another bemoaned the fact that churches were no longer the social centers they once had been, and that they were no longer effective in the sense that there were not enough returns for the money invested. It was also said that modern advances had given youth too much leisure time and that people "simply did not appreciate Oak Park enough."[82] While there were several variations on the theme, all expressed in one way or another the feeling that there was something missing in the spirit of Oak Park. Two years later prominent attention was again drawn to this concern when Rev. John Elliott addressed the summer union vesper service with a sermon entitled "Oak Park's Most Dangerous Habit." This most dangerous habit he identified as a "lack of conviction." Passive support and tacit approval, he said, were not enough, and he specifically called for a dramatic increase in church attendance, membership, and participation.[83] From that time on frequent attention was paid to the problem and attempts of various kinds were made to respond to it.

One specific sign of indifference was the difficulty the churches experienced in maintaining a Sunday evening worship service. In simpler days, when the village had been smaller, a union service had been held on Sunday evening. By 1900, however, perhaps as a result of the increasing number of churches that felt themselves able to conduct a service of their own, Sunday evening services were no longer held in common.[84] In the following years various churches tried to maintain an evening service, although it appears that for many of them it was an off-again, on-again situation. By 1910 one writer, arguing on behalf of an attempt to revive evening worship at Unity Church (Universalist), found himself led to complain that "of late the village of Oak Park has become so citified that good people in certain portions of it no longer consider it quite the proper thing to be seen at church after 6 p.m."[85] The comment illustrates how the city might be understood to threaten more than morals in a narrow sense. Being citified meant that good people were being lured away from the church physically and, by implication, spiritually as well.

By 1914 a new idea was being proposed to renew interest in Sunday evening worship. It was to establish an Oak Park Sunday Evening Club. In arguing for the idea, *Oak Leaves* reflected on the seriousness of the problem:

> We believe it is true that for many years none of our central village churches has attempted to maintain a Sunday evening service, although several of the churches more or less removed from the center section seem just at present to be having a revival of this formerly popular feature of church life.[86]

As the argument developed, however, the reasons offered in support of a Sunday Evening Club, though presented in a hopeful manner, contained somewhat cynical views. It was suggested that such a club could attract popular preachers who would be able to compete with other forms of entertainment. It was suggested that the format would be secular and "not conforming to the stereotyped ecclesiastical pattern." And it was suggested that ministers relinquishing leadership to laymen would also be a positive step. The implicit criticism of indigenous clerical leadership, of the "stereotyped ecclesiastical pattern," and the apparent acceptance of the notion that churches needed to compete on the level of entertainment was not likely to be viewed with enthusiasm by the more idealistically inclined, those who looked for a renewed commitment to the church and not an accommodation to secular realities. Whether for this or other reasons, a Sunday Evening Club was not to be in Oak Park.

A few months later First Congregational Church took matters into its own hands by reestablishing an evening service and advertising it as a community affair. While not lowering itself to speak in terms of entertainment or of a secular format, it did express the intention of having an open, undogmatic style. The analysis of what caused people to stay away from church contained in the appeal was couched in more positive terms:

> Thousands of earnest men are unsettled in their religious thinking. While believing in the church as a practical instrument of good in the community, they are in serious doubt concerning many of the doctrines which they suppose churches believe and teach.[87]

In affirming that people were still earnest and fundamentally in sympathy with the church, if not all its doctrines, First Congregational took a more hopeful view. If certain barriers existed that prevented people from wholehearted commitment, these barriers could perhaps be overcome without seriously compromising the integrity, dignity, or seriousness of the church as it at present existed. But if this analysis was correct, First Congregational's effort to revive the union service on Sunday evening did little to demonstrate the fact or answer the need. It continued for a time without fanfare and was eventually abandoned.

A concern similar to that of the Sunday evening worship was the matter of how New Year's Eve was to be celebrated. In 1911 *Oak Leaves* confidently remarked: "Elsewhere perhaps dancing and other gay festivities will mark the New Year, but here all public gatherings will be of a religious nature."[88] While the statement may have been a truthful one, reflecting the respect still accorded to the churches and to the public image of Oak Park as a religious community, there can be little doubt that in this area too attitudes were quietly changing. Union watch night services had long been a part of Oak Park's ceremonial customs. The call for the New Year's Eve service at the end of 1907 stated that it would be a time of sermons, socializing, and testimony.

> The time until midnight will be occupied by a service of testimony and covenanting in charge of Dr. Denman and Dr. Armstrong. . . . It is quite fitting for the closing hours of the year to be utilized in this manner, and the call is issued to members of all churches to join in exemplification of our common faith.[89]

There was seldom, however, any significant promotion of these services beforehand, nor was there anything but the most cursory reporting of the event after the fact. Coverage of other union services was by far more extensive, as in the case of summer vespers where at least a summary of the sermon was given along with attendance figures, neither of which was given in the case of the watch night services. In addition at least one year the Oak Park Club sponsored a dance that competed with church activity. By 1913 there was no longer a union worship. Rev. Gaylord of Second Congregational announced the plans of that church:

> With the celebration which takes place in the downtown districts many are disgusted, and it is believed that there is no better protest to be made than for the people of the churches to gather in their church homes and meet the new year with such different spirit and surroundings, with earnest prayer and purpose.[90]

Rev. Gaylord felt that this form of protest and witness was important enough that he intended to call the roll of church members. People were to stand up and be counted, both literally and figuratively. While the public face of New Year's in Oak Park had not changed dramatically, there were signs that the churches no longer commanded the attention or the loyalty they once had.

The gradual erosion of interest in and support for such programs as evening worship and watch night services could be viewed only as symptomatic, however. Various attempts to maintain or reinstitute such practices were at best holding actions; they did not directly address the problem. What was needed was more of a general spiritual "awakening." And one time-honored means of accomplishing this was the revival.

In attempting to awaken people to both the dangers and the opportunities that confronted Oak Park, and in attempting to renew a sense of unity of spirit and purpose, leaders once again found themselves involved in important ambiguities. If the need for some kind of "revival" was acknowledged by both lay leaders and clergy, the specific course was not so clear. The first two decades of the twentieth century saw a renewed interest in revivals, with a series of popular evangelists becoming nationally known and attempting to adapt their methods and their messages to the realities of the nation's largest cities. Almost universally their preaching contained attacks on precisely those things that disturbed religious leaders in Oak Park: the liquor trade, gambling, modern dance and dress, a disregard of the Sabbath. Yet neither these modern evangelists nor the memories that people may have carried with them from the revivals of the past seemed to provide an adequate model for the kind of revival that would be appropriate to Oak Park. In its own efforts at revivalism, Oak Park again had to face the task of achieving its own stance and identity amid the sometimes confusing array of images and ideologies present in the larger society. And once again religious leaders were forced to seek a delicate balance in the attitudes and fundamental beliefs that were to be conveyed through their words and actions.

The several cooperative efforts to quicken the spirits of people in Oak Park took place against a background of almost complete silence on the part of religious leaders toward the popular revivalists of the time. The Chicago revivals of Reuben Torrey, J. Wilbur Chapman, and Billy Sunday received not even the barest acknowledgment, either in the village press or the publications of local churches. The names of such men were not invoked by Oak Park people when attacking the evils of the modern city, in spite of the natural alliance that might well have existed among them against common enemies. If the work of successful evangelists was not openly attacked in Oak Park, neither was it widely supported or publicly applauded. The efforts of many others involved in Christian work and various reforms, locally and nationally, was remarked on frequently with interest, but the efforts of revivalists were virtually ignored. The personalities and campaigns of revivalists often sparked intense controversy both in church circles and in the public arena, but in Oak Park leaders declined public comment. While this silence was in some ways enigmatic, and perhaps intentionally so, it is not impossible to interpret.

In 1915 a series of revival meetings was sponsored by a local church in neighboring River Forest. The feature of interest in these meetings was the "novel method of getting workers in touch with the unconverted"; it was reported that a social hour where people "milled around" and talked informally was the means of evangelism following the service. "There was perfect good feeling all around, and nobody appeared to be annoyed or embarrassed, which is a fine attainment in evangelistic services."[91] The statement suggests that for some in Oak Park, at least, revivals were viewed as primitive. They did not reflect the refinement, dignity, culture, or propriety that many had come to associate with church life.[92] The idea that revivals often proved annoying or embarrassing may indicate one of the sources of uneasiness with regard to revivals in Oak Park.

Had the alleged embarrassment caused by revivals been all that was at stake, however, one might have expected to find voices raised to challenge such snobbery and faithlessness, just as people had been called to task for being "so citified" that they no longer considered it quite the proper thing to be seen at church after 6 P.M. A further indication of underlying attitudes was provided by a rare statement made by three of Oak Park's most prominent clergy: Barton (First Congregational), Wyckoff (First Methodist), and Luccock (First Presbyterian). The occasion was the "homecoming" of Rev. B. Fay Mills.

Mills was an unusual figure; he was the only nationally known revivalist to attempt to combine the techniques of mass evangelism with the explicit concerns of what was to become known as the social gospel. He began his career as a revivalist in 1887, but it was not until 1893 that he became influenced by George Herron, a preacher and professor who first came to prominence through a sermon entitled "The Message of Jesus to Men of Wealth." Herron called for a new spirit of revivalism that would redeem society and "enthrone Christ in our national ideals."[93] Mills took up this challenge, and from that point on his preaching emphasized the duty of

129

Christians not just to effect personal conversions but also to build a righteous society, the kingdom of God on earth. Thus the themes of dancing, alcohol, the theater, and gambling gave way in Mills's preaching to concerns about the plight of labor, the need for municipal ownership of utilities, governmental corruption, and the alliance of the church with immoral wealth. While other evangelists paid lip service to reform through campaigns against vice, Mills made quite clear his position as an advocate of social Christianity. In 1899, however, he had given up his career as an evangelist in favor of a Unitarian pastorate.[94]

When Mills returned to Chicago in 1915 it was a homecoming in a double sense. He was returning, for one thing, to seek reinstatement in the Presbyterian church. For another, he was to make two addresses in Oak Park, where he had led a revival twenty-five years earlier. The occasion brought forth a public statement of support from the three clergy, who claimed to be "speaking for others."

> The greatest revival of religion ever known in Oak Park was conducted by Rev. B. Fay Mills about 25 years ago. It is not too much to say that he was the only evangelist whose message ever gripped the town. It was a shock to many people in this community when they learned a few years later that his theological views had undergone what seemed a radical change. . . . The great events of the war have made him a sadder and wiser man.[95]

It was also stated that Mills had many friends among the clergy in Oak Park, and it was implied that several had been instrumental in helping him reach his decision. Later, in his autobiography, William Barton was to repeat the claim that Mills was the only revivalist ever to have a real impact on Oak Park. Only at that point did he add his direct criticism of other revivalists, claiming that no card ever given to him of a newly converted Christian ever panned out and that they often contained false names and addresses.[96]

Though carefully worded to express firm support for Mills without being overtly antagonistic to other revivalists, the statement of the ministers could not help but carry a message for anyone who was familiar with Mills. The message the statement carried was more to the point than the criticism Barton was to make directly at a later time. Regardless of what Mills had said in Oak Park in 1890 (three years before the major change in his emphasis), regardless of whether his message had really been the only one to grip the town, the man whom the clergy supported in 1915 was still a representative of social Christianity, even if by his own admission he could no longer be so optimistic about the coming of God's kingdom on earth. It was Mills's breadth of vision, the depth of his understanding, the nature of his social theology, that the ministers implicitly affirmed. And if in aligning themselves with B. Fay Mills they did not set themselves in direct opposition to other revivalists, they at least set themselves at a comfortable distance from them.

While these indications do not describe a general and pervasive attitude toward contemporary revivalism, they do suggest a source of discomfort that is hardly surprising. Revivalism potentially affronted both the manners and substance of religion in Oak Park. But it did more than that. It challenged the integrity of self-images and ideals. It conveyed what many no doubt felt to be an unflattering image of the movement to oppose saloons and gambling and other evils of modern city life. Precisely because the stance of the churches and the themes of revivalists overlapped at these points, it was all the more necessary for some distance to be maintained. The spirit of the churches, representing the spirit of Oak Park, was to include sophistication and enlightenment as well as moral fervor. This was not an incidental concern, and the attitudes expressed in attacks on higher criticism, liberalism, societal reform, and evolution were far too apparent to be overlooked. There were more ways than one in which people in Oak Park might be embarrassed by revivalism.

Furthermore, the characteristics of revivalism that could make it appear unsophisticated, unenlightened, unprogressive, and antimodern also produced conflict. When revivalists denounced the errors they found among their fellow Christians, within the household of faith, they threatened another important source of pride and self-understanding in Oak Park. Leaders already faced enough problems in building and maintaining a unified Christian spirit without adding more provocations by allowing themselves to become engaged in debates on the terms laid down by many of the popular revivalists of the time.

Given that mass revivalism might implicitly threaten the sophistication and unity of Oak Park Christianity, it is not surprising that evangelistic efforts were independent and indigenous. Random, isolated evangelistic crusades on the part of local churches appeared throughout the period. Most often these included special services led by the pastor of the church or an evangelist employed by the denomination. Toward the end of the period, the success of Billy Sunday did seem to inspire at least some curiosity in some churches. On several occasions speakers associated with the Pacific Garden Mission, where Sunday had been converted, were invited to address church groups, presumably to shed some light on the origin of the Sunday "phenomenon."

One church even organized a campaign that it claimed was modeled after the pattern of Sunday's Kansas City revival.

Whatever the successes or failure of these sporadic efforts, however, they could not address the increasingly recognized need to do something to restore and solidify the spiritual unity of the village as a whole. Thus in 1910 the first broadly based, cooperative effort at bringing about the needed awakening took place. If gratuitous commentary on contemporary revivalism could be avoided, the needs of Oak Park could not. Theoretical concerns and visceral reactions now became practical matters to be worked out as leaders attempted to shape their own approach to revivalism. Some things were clear. The leadership was to be drawn from Oak Park itself. Likewise, the major themes were to bypass some of the major controversies of the day and were to renew a consciousness of what Oak Park stood for. Nevertheless, the revival of 1910 reflected some of the uncertainty implied by leaders' previous silence with regard to the shape of revivals as they were now experienced in contemporary religious life.

The revival of 1910 came about when the Oak Park Pastors' Union designated the first week of January, customarily a time when the churches observed a week of prayer, as a week of revival. It was an unusual event in Oak Park not only because of the explicit terminology, which said this was to be a revival, but also because it brought together nineteen churches and the YMCA in a concerted effort far beyond anything usually associated with the week of prayer. It was a revival of, by, and for Oak Park. There were to be seven meetings at First Congregational Church, and each was to be led by the pastor of an Oak Park church.[97]

In explaining the reasons for the week of revival, the Pastors' Union stated that it was an "effort to develop the spiritual life of the community and to bring unity among the churches."[98] Even such a simple statement communicated that the intent of the revival was to renew and strengthen the village of Oak Park as a whole. It was not the spiritual life of the individual alone that was at stake but the spiritual life of the *community*. Likewise, it was not the strength of the churches individually but their unity that was stated as a goal. It was the commonness of understandings, feelings, and beliefs that needed to be restored. Implicitly the revival constituted an attempt to renew the belief that the people of Oak Park lived in a covenant relationship—in unity with one another and in corporate as well as personal allegiance to God.

But the Pastors' Union statement stopped there. It made no attempt to state a theme that would be common to all the meetings or to provide a rallying cry on which to base the renewal of the covenant. There was no indication given as to what the tone or substance of the meetings was to be. The statement offered no analysis of the present situation, nor did it suggest a program of action beyond the meetings themselves. On none of these questions did the pastors attempt to speak with a unified voice. Instead sixteen statements from individual pastors appeared in support of the revival, and taken together they reflected a certain lack of clarity about what precisely people were being called to unite around.

One approach to the revival came from several ministers who emphasized personal spirituality or introspection as the major need to be met. One of them said: "The supreme question for this hour of retrospect and anticipation is: What kind of a person am I in my inmost soul?" (Walker, Cuyler Avenue Methodist). These statements did not necessarily contradict the broader communal goals of the revival, but they did convey the attitude that the spiritual life of the community must rest ultimately on the spiritual life of individuals.

This was, of course, something that covenanted communities of the seventeenth century had insisted on as well. Initially the heart of the covenant lay in that group of redeemed individuals who were admitted into full membership in the church, and the importance of the notion is attested to by the resistance of some communities to the Half-Way Covenant, and indeed by the Half-Way Covenant itself in the sense that a distinction was still maintained between those who could testify to their religious experience and those who could not. In Oak Park the vocabulary of conversion or winning souls to Christ was nowhere used in connection with the revival. But "new birth in Jesus Christ," "purity of heart," and "definiteness of religious experience" were referred to in several statements. For some, the question of personal "saintliness" was not at all irrelevant to the communal goals of the revival. "The Kingdom of God will be realized by the salvation of men as individuals" (Montgomery, Second Presbyterian).

For the majority, however, the "supreme question" of the revival was understood differently. Most other statements emphasized, in one way or another, "practical" Christianity. The revival was to renew a determination to make saintliness visible. "Is your religion translated into the terms of the practical life? Do men know more about God and His kingdom because you are living?" (Ward, Euclid Avenue Methodist). Yet even among those who emphasized the need to make Christianity visible, there were noticeable differences of approach. Some focused on the need to let Christianity direct one's own life—"We may face the work of every day with the influence of a few thoughtful moments with your own heart and with God" (Steward, YMCA). Others appealed for a renewed commitment to Oak Park itself: "Ours is a good and beautiful community. We are resolved that it shall continue so and grow better" (Barton, First Congregational). And still others called people to follow a more distant vision of social redemption: "Today we are thinking not less of the 'other world' heaven, but more of the 'this world' heaven which we identify with the kingdom of heaven of which Jesus thought and taught" (Williams, First Methodist). "We all want the town, the city, yes the whole world redeemed to righteousness" (Johnstone, River Forest Methodist).

There was nothing inherently contradictory about the variety of statements made, including those that seemed to dwell more on the "invisible." If, on the one hand, the statements might suggest some division among the clergy, for instance, on the question of the merits of a social gospel, on the other hand such differences were effectively masked by the show of unity and cooperation in support of the revival.

In any case, such possible differences would not be the most important conclusion to be drawn. Behind the varying statements were different elements of the ideal of the covenanted community. Behind the concern with individual salvation and personal spirituality lay the conviction that unity was to be built on common Christian belief and experience, not around worldly, secular categories. Behind the more practical concerns were convictions that the common spirit must be manifested in similar personal ways of life and standards of behavior, that it must be manifested in a corporate life that could become a model of Christian community, and that the ultimate goal was to be the regeneration of society, people understanding that they were engaged in a mission that reached far beyond themselves. Thus, taken together, the statements reflected a continuing awareness of those "fundamentals" that Oak Park leaders had articulated as the basis for self-understanding.

At the same time, however, the absence of any self-conscious attempt to draw all the concerns together or to state a common theme reflected, perhaps, a certain bewilderment at the situation Oak Park found itself in and what should be done about it. Why was a revival of any kind needed so soon after home rule had seemed to open the way to the realization of so many hopes? How were the signs of indifference to be interpreted and how serious were they? Such questions yielded no conclusive answers, and the variety of statements made in support of the revival may also be taken to reflect a situation of uneasiness on the part of church leadership. Oak Park had rapidly taken on "metropolitan aspects," and the nature of the response and the specific kind of leadership called for by the new and always changing situation was not obvious.

But if the statements did more to mirror a situation of unrest than they did to clarify the issues and suggest appropriate responses, this was not without virtue. The combined appeal of the clergy in fact carried a double message. On the negative side was the fact that mixed impressions might be gained as to what the "missing element" in Oak Park's spirit was and how it was to be restored. In this sense, the pastors had not gone very far, if at all, beyond what had been expressed several years earlier at the lay symposium on the "Oak Park Problem," and their leadership could hardly help but appear somewhat tentative.

On the positive side was the rather clear indication that the concerns of the leadership were not one-dimensional. This revival stood in sharp contrast, for instance, to a comparatively minor effort of some years earlier that had aimed at combating bridge, the fox-trot, and saloons. In the revival of 1910 the focus of concern was not reduced to a list of enemies or a single area of life. If the communal vision was to continue to inform the life of Oak Park, no single problem, no single threat, could be isolated to the exclusion of others. Personal spirituality as the basis for a common Christian spirit, individual and corporate morality, belief in the need for Oak Park to be exemplary Christian in character, the hope of social regeneration based on the values being preserved in Oak Park—all these were elements of the vision that the revival implicitly hoped to reawaken, and all could be understood as being threatened, both directly and subtly, by the pressures of a modern, metropolitan way of life. If the pastors only dimly perceived or poorly expressed the interrelationships of their various concerns, they did, in a random sort of way, defend the integrity of the vision by joining their various perspectives in a united effort to "renew the spiritual life of the community."

The stance of religious leaders was given somewhat more clarity about two years later when it was decided by some to enlist the churches' support for the Men and Religion Forward Movement. This national movement was broadly conceived and had the ambitious goal of uniting many of the warring factions within American Christianity for the purpose of producing a sort of national awakening. It was to be thought of as a lay movement for the "personal acceptance of Jesus Christ by the individual manhood and boyhood of our times, and the permanent enlistment in the program of Jesus Christ as the world program of daily affairs." Its objective was "to increase the permanent contribution of the Church to the best life of the continent, socially, politically, commercially, and physically, and to emphasize the modern message of the church in social service and usefulness."[99]

Although there were six divisions of the program, the heaviest emphasis seemed to fall on practical efforts to increase the activity and influence of the church in transforming the secular life of the nation. Since everything from saloon influence and the control of the "social evil" to identifying with the interests of labor might fall under this broad framework, the movement succeeded for a time in uniting people of quite diverse theological and social stances. And yet in retrospect, both supporters and cynics agreed that it had been primarily an effort to combine evangelistic outreach with the broad outlook of a social gospel.

The Men and Religion movement was based on the conception of grass-roots organization. Local committees were to be organized simultaneously throughout the country and were provided with specific suggestions as to how to proceed. These suggestions included, for instance, a thorough survey of local conditions and needs, social service committees and forums within and among churches, increased preaching related to social service, and the observance of Labor Sunday. The climax of the activity was to be a series of mass meetings held in seventy of the nation's largest cities for the purpose of awakening the city and the entire nation to the need for reorienting its life toward the gospel of Jesus Christ.

In October, Lindsay Woodcock, previously referred to as a prominent and respected layman, active in many phases of community life, hosted a planning session at his place of business, Marshall Field's department store in downtown Chicago. Present along with Woodcock were several other laymen and Graham Stewart, executive secretary of the YMCA in Oak Park. It was decided at this time to have a dinner at the YMCA to enlist the support of all Protestant churches and to plan the Oak Park phase of the campaign. In announcing this meeting, Stewart was quoted as saying: "This movement means a great deal to the country, in my opinion, and is one of the efforts which is to transform the aspect of religious and social affairs."[100]

When the dinner meeting was held, it was presided over by Sampson Rogers, the man who had been most prominently identified as a leader of the "conservative" faction at First Methodist Church in the dispute with John Farson. The featured speaker was Harry T. Williams, one of the division leaders of the national organization, but much of the evening was devoted to a series of speeches by local clergy and laymen as to the virtues of the program. The opinion was expressed that evangelistic campaigns such as those led recently by Gypsy Smith and the team of Chapman and Alexander had been much too narrow and had had little or no real impact in Oak Park. This campaign, it was said, was one that Oak Park churches could unite behind; furthermore, the work was urgently needed.[101]

As the Oak Park activity began to take shape, it was announced that the emphasis would fall on Bible study, evangelism, boys' work, and missions. The major product of the work in Oak Park was a survey of conditions among youth, which paralleled the surveys of social conditions being taken in major cities throughout the country. Although the full study was said to be "frank and unprintable," a summary of the conclusions was made available to the public. The conclusions were: (1) the play of younger children unorganized; (2) movies had harmful effects; (3) dancing was important to youth; (4) no sex instruction; (5) no vocational guidance; (6) gambling nearly universal among youth; (7) tobacco used by 75 percent; (8) profanity discovered at an alarming rate; (9) automobiles were being used for access to metropolitan dangers; (10) intoxication reported among high school students; and (11) church failing in its appeal to young people.[102]

In one sense, of course, the results of the survey only confirmed impressions that were held, for instance, in 1903 by those who had first urged the formation of a YMCA. They served to underline with "facts" what had been suspected and observed all along; namely, that social conditions in the metropolis combined with broader trends in modern life had a direct impact on Oak Park. In 1903, however, it had perhaps been hoped that the combined efforts of the Oak Park churches would be sufficient in themselves to ward off the corrupting influences of metropolitan and modern life. The evidence presented in the Men and Religion survey did not support such an optimistic belief. While gambling was said to be "nearly universal," tobacco used by 75 percent, and profanity reported at an "alarming rate," the YMCA was said to touch only 25 percent and the church itself was found to be increasingly unappealing to youth. The picture of Oak Park presented by the study spoke for itself; conclusions hardly needed to be drawn explicitly. Present efforts were not generating enough resistance to metropolitan pressures. The efforts of the religious community would have to be redoubled, but ultimately the preservation of Oak Park's integrity would depend in part on a reordering of society. The regeneration of the social order was not only a moral obligation but a practical necessity, if Oak Park's way of life was not to fall prey to a hostile and powerful environment.

It would be difficult to assess the impact of the Men and Religion Forward Movement in Oak Park. Tangible goals by which success or failure might be measured were not stated, and there is no evidence that would establish a direct connection between the movement and subsequent church activities or programs. The importance of intangibles such as mobilizing new energies, heightening awareness of problems, and renewing cooperative efforts among laymen must be largely a matter of conjecture. Nevertheless, in providing an opportunity for Oak Park laymen to demonstrate the nature of their common concerns, the Men and Religion Movement had a symbolic significance that should not be underestimated. As a large-scale attempt to cut across theological and ideological barriers in order to Christianize the social order, the national movement positively affirmed the fundamental stance of Oak Park Christians. By allying themselves with the national movement and by conscientiously carrying out a cooperative effort on the local level, Oak Park laymen were enabled to reaffirm their basic beliefs. Furthermore, they were able to express simultaneously their desire to restore and preserve the distinctive moral and religious qualities of Oak Park and their support of broader efforts at metropolitan and national reform. Whatever the concrete accomplishments may or may not have been, the Men and Religion Forward Movement in Oak Park served as a reminder of the basic commitments that the lay leadership felt they were to hold in common.

A third cooperative effort that may be classed as a revival in the Oak Park mode had a more limited and specific objective than either of the first two. In early 1914 the Oak Park Pastors' Union announced that Oak Park would observe a "Go-to-Church Sunday." Rev. Gaylord (Second Congregational) acted as spokesman in explaining the idea. He observed that too many people had come to view the church as a "moral police force" or a "dispenser of charity" and had therefore ceased to attend or belong to a church on the grounds that they were no longer in need of such services. This, he argued, was a mistaken notion.

> The churches of Oak Park serve a larger purpose than that of a moral and ethical police force or a refuge for the spiritually weak. They are the followers of Jesus Christ, organized for worship, for fellowship, and for work. And each of these stands for a vital need in the life of the world.[103]

Gaylord went on to appeal for support not on the basis of the good the church could do for the individual, but the good it would do for the community. It was an appeal based on civic pride and responsibility. After noting that Oak Park was justifiably proud of its schools, its care for youth through the PTA and YMCA, its beautiful homes and congenial surroundings, its healthful and moral tone as a community, and its public spirit working for the good of Oak Park and Chicago, Gaylord added: "But may it not be suggested that there is a very vital connection between all these facts and the further fact that Oak Park is a village of churches?" As set forth by Rev. Gaylord, the purpose of this "revival" was not to awaken personal spirituality but to renew and strengthen the connection between Oak Park ideals and the faith and practice of the churches. Again the attempt seemed to be to accomplish by voluntary action what had been required two centuries earlier, i.e., the attendance of all citizens at worship regardless of their religious convictions or experiences. In order to promote the campaign, the Pastors' Union solicited statements from a number of prominent citizens, all men, on why they believed in going to church. These statements were then published in *Oak Leaves*.

The ideas expressed by the laymen largely paralleled Gaylord's theme. A large majority of the responders were explicit in their opinion that going to church was not only a responsibility of the individual church member or the Christian believer, but was in some way connected to the duties of citizenship. One of those who responded was Henry W. Austin, the son of one of Oak Park's founding fathers and himself the president of a local bank and a former representative to the state legislature. His words are illustrative of the tone adopted by many others.

> I believe there are very few people, even though they may not be professed Christians, who will not acknowledge that the church is the most uplifting influence in the community, and that being the case, I think all good citizens should be identified with some church, and, if for nothing more than example, should regularly attend that same church. The advantage of church attendance is not only to the person who goes, but it upholds the hands of those who minister in that church in the good they be able to do to the surrounding community.[104]

The variations and elaborations on Austin's theme were many. The school superintendent said that churchgoing makes a community a good place to raise children. The postmaster averred that the church served an important educational function since it afforded people the opportunity to see the world through the eyes of the minister, and ministers in Oak Park were uniformly

139

well read and well informed on current affairs as well as philosophy and religion. A national officer of the YMCA stated that all community feeling is based on an altruistic impulse and this impulse is rooted in the church. The local secretary of the YMCA, after reminding believers of their duty as Christians, said that all fair-minded unbelievers should go to church to prove that they are fair-minded, to live up to the profession of being a good citizen by supporting the institution that actually produces the best citizenship, and to avoid the callousness of old age trained in nothing but cynicism.

A common theme was the debt people owed to the past. Churchgoing was seen as an act of appreciation for the good the church had done for civilization, for the United States, for the community of Oak Park. It was a means of honoring the work of ancestors and ensuring that their labors were not in vain. An equally common and related theme was that those who labored and sacrificed for the common good out of their religious convictions needed the support of all people, regardless of their religious beliefs. In general terms the church was described as "the most powerful agency for good the world has ever known" and as the center for the forces of righteousness in "the terrible conflict with sin and evil." And among all the other kinds of assertions that churchgoing was a duty of citizenship, August Einfelt, the president of the village, even added that he felt sure that if everyone attended church, taxes would go down.

Perhaps more important than the content of the statements, however, was the symbolic value of the procession of people who came forward to offer their support for Go-to-Church Sunday. The display included prominent local businessmen, executives of large, Chicago-based enterprises, bank presidents, physicians, attorneys, judges, past and present presidents of the village, village trustees, state legislators, and an assortment of other public officials such as the postmaster, school officials, the president of the park board, and so forth. Many of the names already carried important historic associations in Oak Park. Others were connected to a wide variety of public-spirited, voluntary service to the community. The list could almost be considered a directory of Oak Park's leadership. The impression conveyed was that it was an honor to be included in this parade of support. Thus to participate in this movement, even if only by church attendance, should likewise be an honor and a privilege. Furthermore, the village leadership as well as the ministers had united to reaffirm their belief that Oak Park had been and must continue to be a "village of churches." This was to be a revival of Oak Park's common faith.

The results of Go-to-Church Sunday had to be somewhat encouraging. When the twenty-one participating churches reported their attendance figures, it was found that the total attendance was more than double the average, with 9,100 attending morning worship and 1,000 attending evening services. Apparently people had not been unmoved by the call for a vote of confidence in what the churches stood for in Oak Park, even if the effect was not a lasting one. The reporting of attendance figures, however, did not end the story of Go-to-Church Sunday. An interesting postscript to the campaign was written in an exchange between an anonymous writer and the Oak Park Pastors' Union.

A letter from "an inquiring church member" in the February 4 issue of *Oak Leaves* questioned whether the very need for a go-to-church Sunday was not itself a disturbing sign.

> The go-to-church movement which is taking such a strong hold on the public conscience possesses a deeper significance than many good Christian people suppose. . . . When upon careful introspection by the church, it becomes evident that the men, in increasingly large numbers, are becoming lukewarm about church attendance, it behooves those who are solicitous that the church shall fulfill its mission, to look deeply for the underlying reasons why a go-to-church Sunday should, within so brief a space of our national life, become an urgent necessity. That the surface indications which call for such treatment are merely symptomatic of deep-seated maladjustment of the church to the needs of the times, would seem to be a safe hypothesis for church workers to adopt.

The letter went on to suggest that men who did not believe in the immaculate conception, the biblical account of creation, miraculous events, and the infallible authority of scripture did not feel welcome in the church. It further suggested that self-righteousness and conventionality on the part of church members prevented many others from wanting to be a part of the church. It challenged the church for placing too much emphasis on doctrine and dogma and asserted that it was not only the laboring classes that the church was not reaching.

> What has been written is sufficient to show a real difficulty which the church must face, simply because there are so many men so constituted that they cannot accept all of the beliefs the church seems to demand. What is to be the position of the church in the future upon such questions?[105]

The letter concluded by questioning whether there could not be a union of Protestant churches around a few "fundamental principles . . . such as will affect conduct" and whether such a movement could not be originated in Oak Park.

The following week a reply appeared signed by the Oak Park Pastors' Union. It first addressed itself to what it termed a misapprehension. "First, the 'Go-to-Church' movement is the expression of a healthy and growing church life, and is not a last resort of ministers and churches in distress. Our churches were not empty before, and their support is not lacking."[106] This was, of course, a matter of some significance. The suggestion that the "Go-to-Church" movement was in any way an act of desperation could not go unchallenged. The idea that the churches of Oak Park were engaged in fighting a losing battle was not an image the ministers were in any way prepared to foster. Their image was rather one in which the efforts of Oak Park and its churches would bear fruit in the unfolding of a redeemed and Christianized social order. It was thus important to conceive that the course of current history was on their side, and the ministers invoked several authorities, including Theodore Roosevelt in *The Winning of the West*, to show that from the beginnings of the republic until the present the trend of church membership had been consistently upward.

On the other hand, the Pastors' Union did not seek to dispute the basic assertion that the times called for a practical sort of Christianity, freed from dogmatic disputations. While expressing the opinion that habits of indifference and laziness were much more likely to lead a person away from the church than were matters of conscience, the pastors did seek to address the issues that had been raised. They carefully chose neither to defend nor deny any of the various beliefs that the writer had given as illustrations of what turned people away from the church. In so doing they substantially aligned themselves with his position that such matters of belief and doctrine were in no sense essential.

> We have no hesitations in declaring to him that no one of us has authority under the rules of his church, or any disposition in his own connection or practice, to make any of these questions a test of Christian fellowship. . . . The ministers of the several churches of Oak Park hold loyally to the truth as it is held by their respective denominations. . . . We hold our respective creeds with glad willingness, but we hold them as testimonies and not as tests, as standards round which to rally in one common battle for righteousness, and not as walls of division.

142

Beyond this nondogmatic stance, elaborated at some length, there were two positive statements of belief.

> We hold that the acceptance of the Lord Jesus Christ, and of his rule of human duty expressed in love to God and love to man is the sole and sufficient test of Christian character.

> We believe that the church stands in a central relation to all those ideals which make a community like Oak Park worthwhile; and we ask for the cooperation of strong men who care for the great interests of life to join with those already at work for the glory of God and the welfare of mankind.

The statement by the Oak Park Pastors' Union was a carefully worded one, and one may infer from the fact that the statement appeared over the name of the group that it was a joint effort, not as in other instances the thoughts or the rhetoric of an appointed spokesman. As a semiofficial statement of policy, the resolution bore certain similarities to the Half-Way Covenant adopted by the Puritans in 1662. The Puritan synod at that time responded to the fact that fewer and fewer people were able to make a public confession of an experience of grace. As a result, fewer people were being admitted into full membership in the church, and their children were not eligible even to be baptized. This problem was resolved by admitting baptized adults who had not had an experience of grace to halfway membership, thus entitling their children to baptism and extending the formal connection of the church to those who professed belief without the necessity of a conversion experience. In 1915 the Protestant clergy united to make a similar statement of policy. Depth of belief and certainty of conviction, they said, was not necessary for church membership. Church membership was officially declared open to all who were "in broad sympathy" with the aims of the church. The church was to unite, not to divide. It was not to insist on rigid standards of membership, but was to serve as a rallying point for all those who understood the church to stand in "a central relation" to Oak Park ideals and who were willing to "join with those already at work for the glory of God and the welfare of mankind."

If the pastors' statement was similar to the Half-Way Covenant in attempting to extend the boundaries of the churches' constituency and in seeking to counteract any tendency to view the church as a minority voice within the culture, the comparison would not likely have been welcomed by the pastors themselves. The clergy were careful not to represent this position as a departure from any previous stance, nor was there anything halfway about it in their minds. This was in no sense to be understood as a lowering of standards, an admission of defeat, or an acquiescence to unfortunate realities. It was rather a clarification of what the churches had always stood for, a reaffirmation of the common calling of the churches in Oak Park. Religious leaders had spoken before and would speak again of the need for greater personal spirituality, devotion, and the salvation of souls. But while this might be held as an ultimate goal, it was also important to focus attention clearly on the immediate and urgent task of building a village and a society that drew its inspiration from the church and gospel of Jesus Christ.

The last village-wide revival of the period, then, proved to be the most successful, not only in measurable results but in providing the clergy with an opportunity to show that the stance of the churches was fundamentally progressive and forward-looking. As a body they skillfully maintained their own orthodoxy and refused to be drawn into the debate on volatile issues such as the higher criticism or the plenary inspiration of scripture. They neither embraced nor condemned any of the specific forms of modern religious thought, but instead declared the churches willing and able to tolerate significant differences of opinion on such matters. In so doing, they declared that the foundation for Christian unity in Oak Park was to be a common concern for the "welfare of mankind." While this was something less than a formal endorsement of the ideas or programs of the social gospel, it nevertheless conveyed the notion that the churches understood themselves to have the worldly task of reforming and redeeming the social order.

To some, no doubt, the broad-mindedness and expansiveness of spirit that the pastors had attempted to communicate in their statement of 1914 seemed inconsistent, or at least paradoxical in the light of various and repeated warnings from church leaders of the dangers of modern, metropolitan living and their efforts to exhort people to abide by uniform interpretations of Christian morals and behavior. All protestations to the contrary notwithstanding, it had been possible throughout the period for the church to be viewed variously as illiberal, undemocratic, intolerant, or reactionary, as illustrated in various incidents from the Farson affair at the beginning of the period to the conflict over Sunday motion pictures at the end of the period. The several efforts at communitywide revivals were important, if for no other reason than to remind others (and perhaps themselves as well) that the underlying attitudes that informed the churches' actions were affirmative, not merely anxious or defensive. The churches intended to inspire, not merely to condemn. They hoped for a positive unity of spirit, not just an enforced uniformity. They envisioned the Christian church, and Oak Park as a Christian community, as guiding the way toward a redeemed society, not merely as a phalanx of opposition to unwelcome changes. In support of such contentions, the religious leaders could have presented detailed evidence that their local efforts to protect Oak Park from detrimental outside influences and to preserve Oak Park's distinctive qualities were always interwoven with a temperament in tune with the needs of the times and a manifest interest in reform and renewal.

"An Ambition to Be the Most Progressive Suburb in the World"

By and large progressivism in Oak Park was written with a small *p*. The early years of home rule in Oak Park were, of course, coincident with what has come to be known as the Progressive Era in American society. Progressivism, however, was not only a story that ran parallel to the story of Oak Park. People in Oak Park were much more than detached observers of the various reform movements that loosely defined the progressive movement. The spirit of reform was quite as much in evidence as the "corrupting influences" that threatened to undermine the community's distinctive character. Outside speakers often served to legitimize Oak Parkers' perceptions of what constituted threats to social well-being while at the same time broadening their perspective to include problems that were not felt acutely in Oak Park itself. They assured people in Oak Park that they were not alone in attempting to combat "corrupting influences" and that the efforts of Oak Parkers were, and ought to be, of more than parochial significance. Oak Parkers thus received encouragement to view themselves as reformers and not merely as people devoted to self-preservation. At the same time Oak Parkers themselves took up a variety of reforms ranging from simplified spelling to the single tax. Nevertheless, while being troubled by many of the same things that motivated progressive reformers and participating directly in many of the reform efforts, people in Oak Park resisted making the progressive movement the fundamental point of departure and source of self-understanding.

One place where progressive sympathies were expressed in Oak Park was at the polls, and in this regard the election of 1912 was of special significance. Oak Park was generally conceded to be a Republican stronghold and had consistently returned large majorities for Republican candidates at all levels of the ticket. A peak of Republican strength had been reached in 1904 when Theodore Roosevelt received 2,125 votes while his opponent, Alton Parker, could manage only 273, a margin of about eight to one. A more accurate reflection of the respective strength of the parties, however, was the election of 1908 when Taft defeated Bryan by a margin of about four to one.[107] Republicans typically outnumbered Democrats by about this same ratio in primary voting and in voting for lesser offices where party affiliations were likely to be the dominant factor.

The election of 1912 was a different matter. Having been defeated in his bid to be the Republican nominee, and charging that the Republican convention had fraudulently denied him the nomination, Theodore Roosevelt gathered his supporters and mounted a third-party campaign for the presidency. The party that thus came into being was the Progressive Party. Its organizing convention, held in Chicago in August 1912, seemed to some to have more the atmosphere of a religious crusade than a political meeting. "We stand at Armageddon and we battle for the Lord," Roosevelt had said, and when he addressed the Progressive Party convention, he referred to his speech as a "confession of faith." After denouncing the two major parties as corrupt and controlled by special interests, he went on to advocate a long list of reforms, including the direct election of senators; initiative, referendums, and recall; woman suffrage; abolition of child labor; minimum wage; unemployment insurance and old age pensions; and various measures relating to increased government regulation of business. Theodore Roosevelt had become the standard bearer for a wide variety of progressive reforms.[108]

In Oak Park Woodrow Wilson's brand of progressivism was not really a factor. The contest shaped up as a battle between the insurgent Progressives with Roosevelt at their head, running on behalf of "the people" and against "special interests," and the regular Republicans represented by Taft.[109]

The results were not close. Roosevelt received over 62 percent of the vote in Oak Park. Wilson garnered about the usual quota for a Democrat (22 percent), and Taft ran a poor third with only 15 percent.[110] On the one hand, this vote could hardly be considered a precise gauge of public sentiment with regard to the specific reform proposals contained in the Progressive Party platform.[111] No doubt Roosevelt's personal appeal had much to do with the results. Yet it was difficult in 1912 to separate Roosevelt's personal appeal from the reforms he stood for. He ran as a candidate for whom principles were more important than expediency.

In the gubernatorial race the results were different, but still revealing. The Progressive Party candidate, Funk, received a plurality of about 41 percent. The Republican candidate, Deneen, had been a supporter of Roosevelt all along and had parted company with him only when forced to choose whether to break with the Republican Party. He received 37 percent of the vote. The Democratic nominee, Dunne, again received about 22 percent. Given Deneen's long-standing support of Roosevelt, and the fact that he had run only slightly behind Roosevelt in Oak Park in 1904, the strength of the Progressive candidate was significant. Though it was admittedly only a rough measurement of feeling, the impression conveyed by the Oak Park election of 1912 could not have been other than that there was considerable support for progressivism in Oak Park.

One of the reforms of the Progressive Era that one might have expected to be widely and enthusiastically supported in Oak Park was temperance. Progressives were far from united on the need or desirability of prohibition legislation, and the temperance crusade bore a somewhat tangential relationship to progressivism as a whole. Nevertheless, many temperance advocates viewed the cause as merely a part of the total program of reform. Temperance activity among other things could be seen as a way to combat vice of all sorts, as a benefit to working people, a means of undermining the city political machines and purifying the political process, strengthening the family, and so forth. The separation of temperance from other issues occurred rather late and was in large measure the result of the policy of the Anti-Saloon League, the most powerful of the organizations devoted to prohibition.

The league had been founded in 1895 and spent a number of years working for the extension of "dry" territory under local option laws before turning its attention to national prohibition. For fear of losing votes, the league deliberately spurned any association with other reforms, in contrast to the policy of other organizations such as the Women's Christian Temperance Union and the Prohibition Party. This policy may have been quite effective in securing the passage of the 18th Amendment. It may also have been effective in divorcing the cause of temperance from its roots in broader movements of reform.[112]

In Oak Park the saloon was unquestionably a symbol for much that was wrong with city life: the breakdown of the family, a lack of religion, the reign of vice, the influence of special interests in government. In this sense the generalization that prohibition was a protest against the city held true for Oak Park. Yet antiurban feeling had a more varied texture in Oak Park than it did in rural communities more removed from the urban scene, and temperance crusades alone could not do justice to the feelings of Oak Parkers. Indeed, the movement for prohibition received far less attention in Oak Park than most

147

other issues of the time, so little in fact that one might begin to wonder where Oak Park people were on this issue that was so basic a part of their own community.

To be sure, speakers from the Anti-Saloon League were heard on a number of occasions at meetings in Oak Park, and when given the opportunity, Oak Parkers voted overwhelmingly to send "dry" legislators to Springfield. As the political efforts of the Anti-Saloon League gained momentum, Rev. Barton wrote an article to *Oak Leaves* commenting on the trend. "In my judgment," he concluded, "temperance people are learning how to make legislation effective. The Anti-Saloon League is rendering great service in this way and should be supported."[113] Even such a low-key endorsement, however, was relatively rare. As time went on, there were indications that Oak Park people were somewhat unsure in which direction to move on this issue. One option was to concentrate on the local scene, and there was sentiment expressed, beginning around 1910 and coming to fruition in 1916, for Oak Park to vote itself dry under local option as a means of strengthening existing village statutes. Nor was national prohibition the only possibility for those who were interested in temperance on a broader scale. Regulation by the states, local option, and high license were all held to be viable options, at least by some.[114] One person even suggested that a system of outdoor, public toilets might be a potent weapon in the war against liquor, since free rest rooms were a chief attraction of saloons.[115]

It is unlikely that there was significant opposition to prohibition in Oak Park. The community was officially committed to temperance. The denominations that presumed to define Oak Park's united Christian spirit were precisely those that formed the backbone of support for prohibition, and in Oak Park even the Catholic priest was an outspoken temperance advocate. Furthermore, conservative and socially minded Christians found they could agree on this issue. (The Federal Council of Churches added a call for prohibition to its social creed in 1912.) *Oak Leaves* was hardly sticking its neck out when it welcomed the first day of prohibition in the United States in this manner:

> Religious leaders are sure that they will be able to reach the minds and hearts of men formerly stupefied by alcohol, and that church membership will increase everywhere. Employers count on being relieved forever of the inefficiency caused by drink. . . . Gamblers wander about as if dazed by the bright sunshine of virtue spreading over the U.S.A. to warm the people into happiness, or to dry them up body and soul, as the saloon people fear.[116]

For all this, however, there had been very little fanfare or publicity in Oak Park around the campaign for prohibition, and the *Oak Leaves* editorial was one of the few signs of celebration. One reason for this may have been that Oak Park's support for prohibition was taken as a foregone conclusion and needed little comment. Equally plausible, however, is the idea that some of Oak Park's enthusiasm for prohibition was dampened slightly by the single-mindedness of the Anti-Saloon League. Oak Parkers demonstrated repeatedly their awareness that many other reforms needed attention as well, and when prohibition took effect, both secular and religious leaders in Oak Park were expressing more alarm than celebration over the state of affairs both in Oak Park and throughout the nation. There had never been any indication that people in Oak Park mistook prohibition for the kingdom of God. Prohibition by itself did not mean victory for Oak Park ideals.

A much more visible issue, and one sometimes connected with the temperance cause, was woman suffrage. The connection between woman suffrage and temperance was simply stated in an *Oak Leaves* editorial entitled "Woman Suffrage and Oak Park."

> It is hard to conceive the possibilities of the new woman suffrage law in its effect upon public affairs, especially with regard to matters that affect moral conditions in our cities. On the saloon question alone, in the various local option contests, municipal and residential, the woman vote may be expected to bring about a new forward movement of vast import.[117]

Others no doubt shared this belief. The Neighborhood Civics Club, in the course of its campaign to place Oak Park under local option, regularly included speakers at its meetings who spoke of the need for woman suffrage as an aid to temperance activity. The strongest opposition to woman suffrage, it was pointed out, came from the liquor interests.[118]

It was not, however, clear to everyone that these two issues necessarily went hand in hand. Rev. John Code of St. Edmund's Roman Catholic Church was one, for instance, who stood firmly opposed to woman suffrage in spite of his protemperance beliefs.[119] On the other side, one of the prominent suffragist leaders, Grace Wilbur Trout, also explicitly denied any connection between the two causes. Noting that the liquor interests were indeed mounting a campaign against suffrage in Illinois, she went on to say that women were interested in suffrage for no other reason than to secure their political rights.[120]

Grace Wilbur Trout was among those suffragists who believed, whether on philosophical or pragmatic grounds, that the question of woman suffrage should be treated on its own merits apart from the effect it might have in producing other reforms. The other leading suffragist in Oak Park, Anna Blount, was among those who did not hesitate to argue for woman suffrage on the grounds that it would assure the success of other reforms.[121]

Prohibition was certainly one of the hoped-for results. Many of the movement's leaders across the nation were devoted to the cause of temperance and indeed had come to the suffrage movement by way of temperance work. But this did not mean, either on the national level or in Oak Park, that the suffrage movement was to be thought of merely as an adjunct or an afterthought to the prohibition movement. The major suffrage organization in Oak Park, the Suburban Civics and Equal Suffrage Club, involved itself with a wide variety of concerns from the fight against Sunday movies locally to such broader issues as minimum wage and direct election of senators. While prohibitionists might see woman suffrage as an aid to their cause, suffragists rather tended to hope that the influence of women would bring about an entire panorama of reforms.

While it is difficult to assess the breadth and depth of support for woman suffrage in Oak Park, on the surface there was a great deal of support and little opposition. *Oak Leaves* consistently supported woman suffrage editorially, and although its statement that Oak Park was the birthplace of the Illinois suffrage law passed in 1913 (granting women the right to vote in presidential elections) was an exaggeration, Oak Park women did play significant roles in the movement at the metropolitan, state, and national levels. Pro-suffrage speakers were invited to appear before many organizations of both a religious and secular nature, and some of them, including the prestigious Nineteenth Century Club, eventually passed resolutions officially endorsing the suffrage amendment.

If, however, support for women's right to vote seemed to come frequently and from a variety of sources, the political role of women in a broader sense was more open to debate. Most organizations concerned with civic matters remained either exclusively men or exclusively women, and a newly formed Civic Association in 1911 voted to bar women from membership. In the same year a mild furor had been aroused by the efforts of some women to secure equal representation on the school board, in violation of the established custom of having the school board consist of one-third women. And in 1916 a woman candidate for village trustee had to make a statement that she still believed women's "highest sphere" to be in the home, but that the political participation of women was necessary in order to protect the home.

Such indications that Oak Park was not ready to have women fully emancipated, however, did not necessarily indicate opposition to woman suffrage. For some it was undoubtedly the separate social role of women that promised that the influence of women would be a purifying one.

The behavior of Oak Parkers at the ballot box, the continuing support for temperance without its becoming a single consuming issue, the agitation for woman suffrage, and the linkage between woman suffrage and other issues—all these things conveyed the impression that Oak Park was a community where there was a broad-based spirit of reform.

There were other signs, too. The cause of simplified spelling was taken up by a number of Oak Park people, and *Oak Leaves* put the principles of simplified spelling into practice. A strong Kindergarten Association was developed that succeeded in making kindergartens a part of the public schools in Oak Park. An Oak Park man, Henry Neil, was a national leader on behalf of mothers' pensions laws. Meanwhile, Oak Park women established the Hephzibah Home in Oak Park to care for the children of mothers who were forced to work. Oak Park women were also instrumental in establishing the Park Ridge Home for Girls. The large number of men involved in the Union League Club and the City Club in Chicago was pointed to with pride as evidence of the commitment to municipal reform. And Oak Park women established the New Future Association as a kind of halfway house for women coming out of prison. A club of young women was started for the purpose of aiding destitute families in Chicago. It seemed that the list of such examples could be extended indefinitely, and all this was to say nothing of the reform-related topics regularly dealt with in the meetings of such organizations as the Nineteenth Century Club and the Daughters of the American Revolution.

To some extent, of course, the climate of reform in Oak Park was a reflection of the climate of reform in the larger society. Such an interpretation, however, neglects the extent to which reform activity could be understood as an intrinsic part of Oak Park's communal identity and ideals, an inevitable extension of the idea of being a model community. *Oak Leaves* hinted at this when it characterized Oak Park as "the finest suburb of Chicago, with an ambition to be the most progressive suburb in the world."[122] Oak Park was not merely to tolerate reform or passively follow the lead of others. Oak Park was described as the birthplace of the Illinois suffrage law. Henry Neil was termed the "father of the mothers' pension law." And as *Oak Leaves* prepared to list the various civic activities of Oak Park men, it noted that "Oak Park men appear to be leading in progressive Chicago affairs."[123] Implicit in such statements perhaps was the belief that Oak Park itself nurtured reform and that the ideals of Oak Park were precisely those that underlay the various reform movements of the time.

Another indication of this attitude was the participation and leadership of the churches in reform. If the ultimate purpose of reform was to produce a society on the Oak Park model, churches would have to play a central role. The need for this was stated directly, for instance, by Daniel Denman, the pastor of the First Baptist Church. "Has the church a part to play in this new social drama? It must be the star actor. The ideals which must equip men for their gigantic task can come only from the inspiration of the religion of Christ."[124]

Along with such general statements and the postures taken in connection with Oak Park "revivals," there were ample other illustrations that the churches viewed social reform as a natural part of Oak Park's Christian spirit. At one level were the speakers heard and topics discussed within the framework of the individual church. Adult Sunday school classes discussed Christian socialism from biblical and contemporary perspectives, considered the writings of Josiah Strong and Washington Gladden, held discussions on social gospel novels such as Winston Churchill's *Inside of the Cup*, considered the need for a new translation of the Bible in light of the woman suffrage movement, and debated whether the church should receive tainted wealth. Likewise women's societies, organized around missions or benevolence, might hear speakers of the stature of Jane Addams speak on child labor, hear reports on the spectrum of city missions work, and entertain special appeals on behalf of work with immigrants, prisoners, prostitutes, orphans, and so forth. On occasion churches sponsored special events such as a conference on "the church and the city" at First Presbyterian where the relations between Protestant churches and urban immigrants was the focus of discussion,[125] or a mock trial held at Second Congregational where the defendant was named "Christian America" and the charges included "oppressing and permitting the oppression of the poor within her borders" and "monopolizing religious privileges."[126]

On a slightly different level were the church men's clubs. Though sponsored by an individual church, the men's clubs took on more of the style of a public forum. Their meetings were held in the evening, members of other churches or of no church were encouraged to attend, and the tenor of discussion was more frankly secular than in the case of other church organizations. Though these clubs were capable of attracting nationally known speakers such as Jacob Riis on New York tenements or Joseph Fels on the single tax, more typically the meetings would be addressed by people from Oak Park or Chicago and the major part of the evening be devoted to discussion. Urging support for these clubs, *Oak Leaves* wrote:

> [Church clubs] are in every neighborhood and for years have offered about the only opportunity citizens have had for serious consideration of public affairs outside of their own individual concerns. Membership in the churches, belief in any certain creed, or adherence to any particular political opinions are not necessary for membership in these clubs. . . . Church clubs in communities like this are taking the same position and importance in social life held by the "little red school house" in pioneer times, when so many orators and statesmen were developed in these obscure forums of the republic.[127]

The statement did a severe injustice to other organizations that regularly sponsored meetings on public affairs: the PTA, Kindergarten Association, Suburban Civics and Equal Suffrage Club, Nineteenth Century Club, Sons of the American Revolution, Daughters of the American Revolution, to mention only a few. (The fact that many of these were predominantly or exclusively women may account for the Civic Association restricting its membership to men.) Nevertheless, these men's clubs did occupy a prominent place in the life of the community and were symbolically important in providing ongoing evidence of the church's interest in secular affairs.

Other examples of Oak Park churches generating involvement with contemporary, urban problems were found in the area of settlement work and urban missions. While Jane Addams, Graham Taylor, and other lesser-known figures made frequent appearances in Oak Park, this was perhaps less important to Oak Park's self-image than the fact that a woman from Second Congregational Church, Mrs. B. W. Firman, founded and directed a project conceived as a supplement to the work of Hull House and located just west of there. Known as Firman House, it was connected with Ewing Street Congregational Church and ran a Sunday school kindergarten, summer school, and provided charity relief. It was to have an explicitly religious motive and its workers were to follow in the steps of "the one who came to minister instead of being ministered to."[128]

This action was generally thought of as an outgrowth of years of work begun under the pastorate of Sydney Strong, who in 1903 organized a group of fifty women to work once a week in city settlements.[129] Second Congregational also provided a number of leaders for the Chicago City Missionary Society, as did other Congregational churches in Oak Park. In this instance too *Oak Leaves* seized on the fact as an illustration of what kind of place Oak Park was:

> Oak Park has both attracted and produced the New England type of businessman who lends his experience and executive ability to the great Christian and philanthropic agencies. No Chicago suburb has been quicker to recognize its moral debt to the big city which occasions our village's existence. It gives us a living: we give it a life.[130]

The role of clergy on the whole seemed to be a rather general one, expressing sympathy for movements that would result in social regeneration and reminding people that Oak Park had a larger mission than its own welfare. On occasion, however, the clergy could become more specific. When the Pastors' Union unanimously endorsed the idea of the mother's pension law, it was a rare example, if not a unique one during this period, of the clergy taking a common stand on a specific measure of reform. The clergy individually, however, did speak to specific issues, most notably the question of labor. In a union service on Labor Day in 1907, William Barton had acknowledged that with the invention of the steam engine "the history of the world began anew." A revolution, he said, had been produced in which the dignity of labor had been thrown into question.

> I may say that we ministers and churches of Oak Park do not view without sympathy this profoundly significant movement. I am the more glad to say it because we are somewhat remote from it. . . . I know that in large part the labor organizations do not trust us. They say we are rich men's clubs. They say that ministers are timid, the hired men of capitalists. They do not think we understand them. Whether we do not, we are for them.[131]

Such a statement was not unusual in Oak Park. As early as 1902, during the anthracite coal strike, several Oak Park ministers had publicly sympathized with labor and pleaded for arbitration in sermons. By 1911 Labor Sunday was almost universally observed in Oak Park, at least to the extent of having the sermon address the problems of labor. While the actions of unions came in for criticism and anarchists and socialists were condemned, Oak Park ministers seemed to find little difficulty in sympathizing with the plight of labor and denouncing in general terms the captains of industry and plutocrats who showed no regard for the welfare of their workers.

Two of the most outspoken advocates of the cause of labor and associated reforms were R. J. Wyckoff of First Methodist and Harry F. Ward of Euclid

154

Avenue Methodist. Ward came to Oak Park shortly after having been a major participant in the drafting of the Methodist "social creed" that became the basis for the social creed adopted by the Federal Council of Churches in 1908. Ward had been and continued to be the secretary of the Methodist Federation for Social Service, which had originally produced the social creed. Ward was not an especially prominent figure in Oak Park, but Wyckoff was also a strong supporter of the social creed, and together they managed to add a slightly different dimension to social Christianity in Oak Park. By 1912, when Ward and Wyckoff coauthored a book on the social creed, *Oak Leaves* said:

> Oak Park is now headquarters for one of the most significant movements for the improvement of human life. It is the Methodist Federation for Social Service. Henry F. Ward of 343 Oak Park, south, is secretary of the federation. Its program for social work has been endorsed by Protestant church organizations representing 19 million members. Many Catholic clergymen are conducting similar work, notably efforts for a minimum wage law.[132]

Even in this statement there was no reference to the social gospel. Leaders in Oak Park seldom used language that would indicate that Oak Park could be understood in terms borrowed from the larger society. The roots of Oak Park's self-understanding lay not in the ideology of temperance, progressivism, or the social gospel as such, however much Oak Park people might view these movements sympathetically and see them as allies. By generally communicating a favorable attitude toward reform, while at the same time refusing to be subsumed within any reform movement, Oak Park's leaders were perhaps conveying a message: namely, that it was important to anchor all reforms to the religious, communal vision that Oak Park embodied. While other reformers might be implicitly informed by such a vision, Oak Park was in a position to bring the vision into clear focus.

For those who held to the communal vision there was no inconsistency in adopting a posture of reform while attempting to preserve the status quo in Oak Park, for the ideals that were being protected in Oak Park were precisely the ideals that were the true goals of reform in the society at large. In both instances the integrity and success of Oak Park as a model were at stake. In addition, however, to the "corrupting influences" depicted as coming from outside the community there were issues of a slightly different sort that threw open to question somewhat the nature of Oak Park's model.

The possibility of the larger society in any sense coming to approximate Oak Park's model was challenged by the increasing visibility and power of

155

immigrant populations. Like many others, Oak Parkers might be alternately horrified by the vast numbers of immigrants and inspired to take up their cause. A typical expression of feeling came from the high school principal in a speech delivered at graduation ceremonies in 1914.

> This country was settled by people of ideas, ideals, and principles of liberty. No longer does this type come. Now the people from obscure races with no national life or history and no ideals of liberty are coming in at the rate of a million a year. They soon will be in the majority. They have no opportunity and they come for merely economic motives, and we see them herded like cattle at the railway stations and at their work. But the menace of this unassimilated mass of humanity, suffering from the centuries of wrong, is counteracted by the development of the public school system.[133]

Judging by the number of meetings held in Oak Park on the question of how to Americanize the immigrant, it was not so clear to most people that the public school system would be a sufficient answer to the problem. Nevertheless, the speech illustrated the dilemma that many felt. On the one hand, there was a kind of visceral reaction against the immigrants themselves. At the same time, the need to Americanize the immigrants could lead not only to a recognition of the need for social service and religious work among immigrants but also to a recognition of the need to provide justice and opportunity so that they would not become an enormous class of the disaffected.

While urban immigration was a frequent topic for both secular and religious groups in Oak Park, it did not appear to be an urgent problem in Oak Park itself. The 1910 census did show that approximately half of Oak Park's 19,000 people were either foreign born or the children of foreign born. The overall figures, however, were perhaps somewhat misleading. Of the slightly more than 3,000 foreign-born residents of Oak Park, about 1,000 were from English-speaking Canada, England, and Scotland. About 900 had been born in Germany and another 800 were of Scandinavian origin.[134] Thus very few of the foreign born in Oak Park were part of the "new immigration," and although periodic references were made to the servant girl problem, on the whole little attention was paid specifically to the problem of immigrants in Oak Park.

Although other groups were numerically stronger, the most definite symbol of an "alien" presence in Oak Park was the Roman Catholic Church. The first Catholic church in Oak Park, St. Edmund's, was not established until 1907.

On the surface it appeared that this event was attended by little difficulty. At the first worship service Rev. John J. Code, the pastor, seemed to be promising the cooperation of Catholics in maintaining Oak Park ideals when he said: "The people of this place are evidently very religious people as is evidenced in their churches which are the glory of the village. What others have done here Catholics can do also."[135] About a month later a benefit for the new church was held at the home of John Farson, which seemed to be an expression of welcome from Oak Park Protestants. On that occasion Code responded in kind to Farson's gesture:

> I am going to tell you a little secret. For many years the Catholic Church has courted Oak Park. . . . This scene tonight emphasizes the growing charity which Catholics and non-Catholics are bearing toward each other; the blessed fruit of a large knowledge and experience. Not many years ago it would have been almost impossible to find a non-Catholic of the Farson type. But the age of misrepresentation is passing away, the result not of polemical discussion as of right human living, which reveals the Catholic faith not merely as a teaching factor, but also a potent influence in making man virtuous and moral.[136]

Within several years from this time Father Code, through sermons, writings, and speeches delivered before local groups such as the Businessmen's Association, had made it known that he shared in many of the values held by his Protestant colleagues. He took stands against gambling, dancing, and jazz and in favor of Sabbath observance and temperance. He flattered Oak Park businessmen in language that announced his belief in Oak Park and might have been used by the most Puritan of Oak Park ministers.

> [The Oak Park businessman's] respect for God and man is not colored by any thought of gain, for first and last he is a gentleman. If he is poor he counts it riches to be a man. If he is rich, no one is any the poorer, for he owns no wicked dollar.[137]

Given such reassurances from Father Code and the absence of overt hostility, it seemed that few problems were presented by the formation of a Catholic church in Oak Park.

Even the single public controversy that somewhat marred the arrival of Catholicism in Oak Park appeared to have little to do with anti-Catholic sentiment. Late in 1907 an Oak Park man, A. J. Flitcraft, sold the Catholic church a piece of his property. This occasioned a protest from the rector of Grace Episcopal, which had been using the property as a "Church House."

Rev. Shayler of Grace Episcopal claimed that he held a lease to the property, while Flitcraft claimed that the lease was invalid and he had a perfect right to sell the property. While the debate was somewhat acrimonious, there was no indication that the issue was whom Flitcraft was selling the property to. It was merely a question of Grace Church being evicted from its quarters. And indeed it may have been the case that anti-Catholic sentiment was not involved. A different light is cast on the early years, however, by a statement that appeared many years later in the Silver Jubilee Program of St. Edmund's:

> . . . The community was in little sympathy with the movement to establish a Catholic parish in its midst. They knew little of a class which formed so small a portion of their social life. Many of them had inherited grossly erroneous views as to the religious belief and practice of Catholics; many feared lest a horde of undesirables would rush in upon them with the advent of the great democrat Church which draws no line between rich and poor, which flatters no "nice" and "select" people, and recognized no barriers save those between saint and sinner. The undercurrent of opposition came to the top when it was learned that a prospective site could be secured only with the provision that no Catholic Church should be built on it. At last the present site at the northeast corner of Oak Park Avenue and Pleasant Street encumbered with two old frame buildings was satisfactorily secured.[138]

Several explanations suggest themselves as to how this picture can be reconciled with the fact that at the time the Protestant majority appeared unruffled by the establishment of a Catholic church while the Catholics themselves expressed no resentment and made no charges of ill treatment either publicly or in their own church publication. One factor, no doubt, was the eagerness of the Catholic church to gain acceptance and the desire to do or say nothing that might jeopardize their standing in the community or arouse sentiment against them. From the viewpoint of the Protestant majority, it must also be noted that the initial impact was quite small. The erection of a church building in 1910 and then the opening of a parochial school in 1914 were much more significant in establishing Catholicism as a visible and permanent feature of Oak Park life than the fifty families who gathered in 1907. The school question furthermore was one issue where the Catholic church showed itself to be more definitely not in sympathy with the dominant value system. In the pages of St. Edmund's newsletter the public schools were often attacked as being implicitly Protestant while maintaining the official position that religion was not taught in the schools.[139] Even without such statements, however, the establishment of a parochial school in itself could easily be seen as an act of disloyalty to Oak Park, especially in view of the expectation that schools were indispensable to the process of socialization (as in the high school principal's speech quoted above).

Thus it may not be too surprising that overt concern or hostility about Catholic influences appeared toward the end of the period. Even then it was relatively rare and not directed specifically against Catholics in Oak Park. One example was a debate carried on in the press over what should be the national anthem. One person wrote:

> Our Puritan forefathers are the ones who made the country and put liberty, freedom in the Declaration of Independence and why should any sect or creed now take exception to our old and historic song America. . . . No wonder the Navy has adopted the Star Spangled Banner in preference, for on 14 of the 18 American battleships, a Catholic priest is the chaplain, and the flag of Rome floats above the Stars and Stripes at times.

This prompted the editor of *Oak Leaves* to reply:

> The editor of *Oak Leaves* was born and reared in New England, the son of a Protestant clergyman, and thoroughly imbued with the Puritan spirit. Perhaps therefore he will be excused for saying that it is just such sentiments and expressions . . . that keep a lot of petty jealousies and prejudices alive in American life. . . . To our mind one of the things most needed in American society is a better mutual confidence between races and sects, and especially between Protestants and Catholics.[140]

It is perhaps not surprising that exchanges such as this were infrequent. On the one hand, it would have been difficult, if not unthinkable, for Protestant leaders to indicate publicly their opposition or hostility to Roman Catholicism in Oak Park given that the absence of religious antagonisms was such an important part of the ideals they proclaimed. On the other hand, such positive statements as that by the editor of *Oak Leaves* were not likely to be forthcoming either, for the Catholic presence could not have been an entirely comfortable one. While Oak Park Protestants considered ways to "Americanize the immigrant," the Protestant leadership almost completely ignored the existence of the Roman Catholic Church in Oak Park.[141] At the same time, it may be said, Father Code was also warning Catholics against intermarriage and against attending any form of Protestant worship.[142] The threat of Catholics losing their identity in an overwhelmingly Protestant milieu was no doubt quite real. By and large the relationship between Catholics and Protestants appeared to be one of a comfortable, or perhaps one should say, uncomfortable, distance. While this had the virtue of avoiding confrontation, it also complicated somewhat the nature of Oak Park's communal model.

The increasing visibility and strength of the Catholic church beginning around 1910 with the opening of St. Edmund's church building was perhaps only symptomatic of an overall pattern of growth that almost inevitably meant greater diversity and a trend away from the image of Oak Park as a tightly knit, orderly, controlled environment. Between 1910 and 1920 the population of Oak Park increased from about 20,000 to almost 40,000. Much of this growth occurred in the southern and eastern sections of the village, which had been previously undeveloped. As this growth occurred, sectional antagonisms appeared that seemed to indicate that many of the newcomers did not necessarily share in or appreciate the ideals of community life leaders had articulated up to that time.

The first confrontation along sectional lines came at the beginning of 1910 when a petition was circulated on the south side to establish a city form of government in Oak Park. A South Side League had been formed that claimed those on the south side of the village were paying the same high taxes as everyone else but were not receiving the same benefits. As redress they proposed that Oak Park be made a city so that the south side would be assured of representation in the village government.[143] A month later *Oak Leaves* reported a speech of R. S. Fuertado to the Ninth Precinct Improvement Association on the south side.

> He said he had that evening talked with a friend in north Oak Park who had said, "We like you alright but we don't like your company." From this he concluded that the "Millionaires to the north of us" are exclusive, and looked down on the homemakers to the south.[144]

The ultimate result of the activity in 1910 was not a vote on the city form but a vote on annexation. This was resoundingly defeated, though the margin of defeat was significantly less in the far south side wards.

The following year the question of annexation was again before the voters, and again it appeared that the movement had been organized and found its greatest support on the south side. A "Progressive Party" was formed with a platform that called for the extension of various village services to the south side and threatened secession if this was not accomplished.[145] Meanwhile, the rhetoric was considerably more heated than in the previous year, as accusations were made that the campaign for annexation was being organized and financed by unnamed outside interests that wished to see the destruction of Oak Park, and *Oak Leaves* referred to the proannexationists as "Enemies of the Oak Park Ideal."[146] Again annexation was defeated by about a three-to-one margin, but in the still relatively unpopulated southern section annexation was defeated by only thirty-nine votes.[147]

A similar pattern appeared in 1914 when the question of a city form of government finally came to a vote. This time the southern precincts showed a narrow majority in favor of the city form, while slightly more than 60 percent of the total vote went against the proposal. No precinct outside the south side came close to a majority in favor of city government.

By 1915 it was estimated that about one-third of the village's population lived south of Madison Street (about a half mile south of Lake Street), while ten years earlier there had been few homes in this area and no paved streets. It was in 1915 also that the New Citizens Party was formed, which fielded a south side candidate for village president and adopted the slogan "Down with the Old Gang." Though several of the leaders of the New Citizens Party, including the candidate for village president, had served as village trustees, Oak Park was accused of being run by a "coterie of millionaires" from the north and central section of the village. Ignoring the feelings that may have produced such a statement, *Oak Leaves* treated the statement as though it had been intended literally and responded indignantly that "Mr. Krauth knows we have never had a village president who came within a gunshot of being a millionaire."[148] In the election, the candidate of the Primary Association, which had previously been the only organization nominating candidates for village office, won with more than 60 percent of the vote, but the New Citizens Party candidate showed surprising strength not only in southern precincts but also on those at the eastern edge of the village.

This was sufficient encouragement for the New Citizens Party to run a slate of people for village trustee the following year. The basic issue again was the charge of elitism in village affairs. "The New Citizens Party," wrote one of their leaders, "stands for the cause of the many and not of the few, that Oak Park shall not be governed by the Union League Club of Chicago and the inner circle of the Oak Park Club of Oak Park."[149] This time, however, the rebel candidates were able to muster only about 30 percent of the vote. At the same time another vote on the city form of government was taken. This also lost by about 70 percent to 30 percent, a significantly greater margin than had prevailed just two years earlier. The trend of discontent seemed to have been reversed.

By the end of the period Oak Park's leaders could take satisfaction in the several indications that the fundamental commitments of Oak Park remained intact. In 1916 Sunday movies had been defeated, Oak Park voted dry under local option with 85 percent in favor, the division of the village into wards had been defeated, and the established leadership had been given a vote of confidence in village elections. All this was in spite of the fact that Oak Park was now a community of 30,000 people and was continuing to grow at a rate that made the orderly assimilation of Oak Park's "immigrants" difficult, to say the least.

Despite these impressive victories, however, the signs of ferment, of "corrupting influences," of increasingly urban-cosmopolitan patterns of behavior, of changing manners and morals, of waning commitment to the church, of internal pluralism, division, and even animosity could not be easily ignored. At the least they need to be interpreted and placed within a framework of meaning. One possibility was to break with the past and affirm a new set of values, to begin to search for a new foundation for community life. From among the Protestant clergy there emerged one person who openly took this stand: Bernard I. Bell.

Controversy surrounded Bell's brief time in Oak Park. He had come to the community as an assistant at Grace Episcopal Church, but soon left Grace to form a new congregation, St. Christopher, of which he was the pastor. Though denied by Bell, this was commonly thought to be the result of a split within Grace Church, with those desiring a "high church" having left to form the new congregation. Bell was known also as an outspoken advocate of labor, often using strong language and expressing sympathy for socialism. In February of 1913 he publicly objected to a proposal for a Sunday "noon forum" on current affairs to be held as an ecumenical effort open to the community at large. Bell claimed that in effect these meetings would not be open. He noted that the time excluded all except those who worshiped on Lake Street and the fact that it was to be held in a Protestant church excluded Jews, Catholics, and Anglo-Catholics. On this occasion he questioned the Christian unity of Oak Park, saying that "Christians in Oak Park are not one happy family, much as we might like them to be."[150]

In a sermon a few months later, however, he challenged Oak Park ideas at an even more basic level.

We think that intellectually we are of superior stuff. In attending the meetings of women's clubs, in hearing men talk going into the city, one perceives that our people think themselves far more able to figure out the proper policies of the world than the common run of folks. . . . Spiritually we are conceited. Oak Park is a very religious town—on paper . . . the churches of this town have too much led men to believe that all religion was for was to make men respectable. There is little feeling of a call of God to men to sell their souls and all they have to aid the bleeding hearts of a common humanity. We are spiritually decadent, living in an isolated backwater and glad to have it so.

Christ is crying to Oak Park, as he did for the rich young man. And this I hear as the burden of his cry.

Oak Park you are starving in your plenty. Oak Park, tear down the fence that shields you from the rest of men before it is torn down for you. Oak Park, you are proud and conceited. You are not fit to teach other men. You ought to be learning at the feet of humanity. Oak Park go sell what you have and give it away, for it is making you different from other men, lower than other men. Oak Park, find what the world of men is thinking. Merge your petty loves in a greater passion. Pledge yourselves to Me. Love, live, sacrifice, die for the fiery love of men and the burning heart of God.[151]

In effect, Rev. Bell was pleading for Oak Park to give up the notion that it was in any sense a model community in favor of a quest for greater solidarity with people who did not fit the Oak Park mold.

But his was a lonely voice. Though Oak Park leaders may have been aware of the pharisaical dangers involved in being a model community, the belief in the communal ideal was simply too strong for them to be able to hear Christ speaking the same words that Bell heard him speak. They were not able to imagine that a "fall" for Oak Park would be a "fall upward." Thus they continued to proclaim the possibility of a redeemed society made in Oak Park's image, while in partial but significant ways Oak Park itself was at the same time taking on the image of the city.

FIVE

Winds of Change:
Ambiguities of the
New Age in Evanston

It is imperative that we study the urban life for its larger advantages to humanity.

Rev. John Boyd, 1902

Boston is called the Athens of the West, but her streets were laid out by a cow.

Rev. William McElveen, 1916

An Evanston resident surveying the urban scene and his own community in the years surrounding the turn of the century might well have felt a strong sense of kinship with the people of Oak Park. Their communities were tangibly similar in many respects. Although adjacent to Chicago, both maintained and prized an air of natural beauty and relative peace and quiet. Annexation to Chicago was inevitably a recurring threat in both places, and just as surely would be overwhelmingly defeated whenever it came to a vote. Temperance too was a feature common to the two communities. It was perhaps the most obvious, but certainly not the only, indication that both Oak Park and Evanston had been strongly influenced by religious attitudes and beliefs often referred to as Puritan. At the center of the community, churches were physically prominent and architecturally dominant, and as outlying sections developed, they too were well churched. Both Oak Park and Evanston were sometimes called "Saints' Rest."

Less tangibly, but just as certainly, the Evanston resident would have been aware that a great many people in Evanston shared with their cousins in Oak Park common perceptions and feelings as they viewed the city. The American city, so well and fully embodied in Chicago, stood in need of reform and redemption. The prospect of the United States becoming an urban nation was troubling if it meant, as it seemed to mean in Chicago, a breakdown of the family, class division and conflict, and unassimilated groups of immigrants who neither understood nor appreciated the American way. Equally offensive was the unchecked reign of vice apparent not only in the form of saloons, gambling dens, and houses of prostitution, but also in the unprincipled conduct of politics and business. Like those in Oak Park, the people of Evanston not only showed an interest in reform in the larger society, but believed themselves capable of building among themselves an exemplary form of community life.

The Evanston resident would also have been aware, however, that in some respects his community differed markedly from Oak Park. Although the issues that had to be confronted were often the same or similar, the response of both secular and religious leaders seemed to be different in tone, and often in substance, from the responses made in Oak Park. This was no doubt due in large measure to the fact that through a combination of choice and circumstance Evanston itself was becoming a city.

Again, some of the differences would have been noticeable to the casual observer. Evanston was already a city in name and by law. It was politically divided into wards that corresponded to natural and informally recognized divisions within the community. Two wards comprised what had once been South Evanston, one ward was the old North Evanston, one ward was the west side, and the three other wards covered an area sometimes referred to as Evanston proper.[1] With such divisions institutionalized, the body politic was manifestly not an unbroken fabric. Ward politics provided evidence for the more general observation that competing interests, not consensus, had become the guiding principle in Evanston's affairs.

Yet for the resident of Evanston the process of becoming a city was a continuing one, and it proceeded on many fronts. Changes in the material landscape of Evanston were accompanied by changes in the psychological and spiritual landscape. One might hear talk of the old Puritan days of Evanston that were being left behind, but one neither heard nor sensed any belief in a New Puritanism such as that which Oak Park apparently aspired to.

Evanston's aspirations appeared to be in a different direction, one at least partially dictated by changes over which the community had had very little control. Evanston seemed headed in the direction of fulfilling the idea and ideal of city life. That life was neither as mysterious nor as alien to Evanston as it appeared to be to Oak Park. Civilization had taken hold in Evanston. The community was in no sense newborn as Oak Park was in 1902. The nature of Evanston was still being determined by the realities of modern urban life. One could, and perhaps one had to, look for the hand of providence within the inexorable course of events. Yet it would not have been nearly so clear to the resident of Evanston as it was to his cousin in Oak Park that the church was destined to be the foundation for community life in the new age that was emerging in Evanston, as it was in the nation. For those who still valued the communal ideal and the religious heritage on which it was based, unresolved questions clouded the horizon of Evanston's future.

Marking the End of an Age

In 1898 the residents of Evanston responded with great feeling to two very different events: the death of Frances Willard and the Spanish American War. In each case, the response made in Evanston revealed something of the currents of thought and feeling that lay behind the daily affairs of the city and that influenced significantly the way the people of Evanston viewed themselves and their community.

On February 17, 1898 Frances Willard died in New York City. She was at that time a national, and even an international, figure. She was president of the Women's Christian Temperance Union, a crusader not only for temperance but for woman suffrage, labor, and many other causes, a woman of far-ranging interests and influence.

A few months before her death she had undertaken a pilgrimage. Her journey had taken her to the western New York town of Churchville, where she had been born, to Oberlin College, where her father had at one time studied for the ministry, to Janesville, Wisconsin, where she had spent much of her girlhood, and to Evanston, Illinois, where she had completed her education and begun her career. It was a pilgrimage that recalled not only her own past but her more distant ancestry. Both her father and mother were direct descendants of Puritans who had made their own westward journey to the New World and had settled in Massachusetts Bay in the 1630s. Churchville, where Willard's parents had grown up on adjacent farms, was a town settled by New Englanders who still held firmly to the belief that religion ought to be the foundation of community life. It was no accident that a distinctly religious atmosphere prevailed in each of the other towns the Willards chose to live in.

As Frances Willard made her pilgrimage westward shortly before her death, she might have been reminded not only of the journey made by her own family, but also of the journey made by many others whose religious beliefs and cultural values found expression in communities throughout the West. After her death, the funeral train made one more journey westward, stopping in Churchville and Chicago before arriving in Evanston a week later.

On the day of the funeral in Evanston, flags hung at half-mast and schools and businesses were closed in honor of a woman who in many ways personified the spirit of Evanston. First Methodist Church, where the services were held, became the center of activity. Hundreds of people had to be turned away from the church, and the weight of those who jammed the sanctuary caused the floor to settle and large cracks appeared in the walls. For a brief moment many of the characteristics of Evanston that Frances Willard had known when she lived there in the 1860s and 1870s were brought back to life. Once again the church occupied a central position in the life of the community. Once again people of many denominations gathered under one roof. Once again First Methodist was demonstrably the "cathedral church" of Evanston. Once again there was evidence that a common unified spirit prevailed. Many of the speakers who rose to pay tribute to Frances Willard spoke of the early days of Evanston's history. It was the village of that time that had nurtured Frances Willard. It was the village of that time that was responsible for her lasting affection for Evanston and that had informed the history of Evanston she later wrote in the midst of all her other commitments. In many ways the funeral of Frances Willard was a celebration of Evanston's past.

The close and lasting relationship Evanston and her people had had with Frances Willard, however, could not obscure the fact that she was a woman whose spirit ranged far beyond the boundaries of Evanston. She had traveled a long way physically and psychologically from the Evanston she had left in the early 1870s. As she moved into a larger arena and assumed greater responsibilities, her world had become the world of industrial strife and political conflict. Even the WCTU in later years had become a large and complex organization with its own fair share of internal conflict and dissension. As her world expanded so did her interests and involvements. She affiliated with a wide variety of groups and championed causes ranging from vegetarianism to world peace. She understood these various concerns as interrelated partly because the world she lived in was increasingly interrelated and interdependent. Problems could not be isolated from one another, and thus one reform led to another. As her social interests broadened, so did her religious views and sympathies. She experimented with such new religious movements as Christian Science, mind-cure, and theosophy. Thus while the people of Evanston mourned Frances Willard by remembering and in some ways reincarnating the past they had shared with her, they also paid homage to one whose involvement in the modern world had taken her rather far away from the times that were being celebrated. By analogy they might have been reminded of how in that short time Evanston too had come quite some distance from what it had been in the 1870s. And now with her death they were reminded of this in a different way. Precisely because she had been associated with the early days of Evanston, the death of Frances Willard was a sign that the age of the founders was passing.

The funeral of Frances Willard both celebrated the past and marked its passing in the lives of individuals and in the life of the community. While some of the speakers conjured up images of an earlier day, others lifted up visions of a hoped-for future. Commenting on the powerful effect Frances Willard seemed to have on the men and women who heard her, people who represented all parts of modern American life, one of her eulogists, Dr. Charles Little, president of Garrett Biblical Institute said:

> The New Jerusalem of the twentieth century, the transfigured homes of a new commonwealth, seemed to be so near and so real, and there . . . was always such a sublime confidence in [her listeners'] latent nobility and their ultimate righteousness, that for the time, at least, they became in their own eyes, the being that she pictured them, and they sat entranced.[2]

The New Jerusalem was, of course, a biblical image, but it was also perhaps an image well adapted to express hopes that would be consistent with the urbanizing trends of the modern age in America. The use of the image on this occasion hinted that there was much of promise in the emerging world of the twentieth century and that the vision that guided Frances Willard's life owed much to the promises contained within this new environment. At the same time the statement hinted that important elements from the past, enduring values from her heritage, had been incorporated into her hopes for the future. However eccentric she may have become in some of her secondary commitments, temperance remained the cause with which she was most identified and the cause she herself believed stood at the center of the circle of needed reforms.

169

In this regard she had not departed fundamentally from the spirit of Evanston. As the pilgrimage she made on the eve of her death indicated, she remained throughout her life both mindful and proud of her heritage, a heritage that had been clearly in evidence in Evanston's early days. Wherever she went, she had carried this with her. While in England, for instance, at a time when she was experimenting with theosophy, she had made a point of visiting the church in which her Puritan ancestors had worshiped. While believing in the promise of a new era, she had not sold her soul to the devils of modern life. The enduring values of the past might still have a redemptive effect on the present and future of American life.

In many ways Frances Willard did indeed embody what many would have considered the spirit of Evanston. She had demonstrated that it was possible to combine an openness to a broad range of modern life with a firm adherence to certain fundamental principles that not only had informed the community life of the past but must continue to inform the communities of the future. Yet what was possible for individuals might not be possible for society as a whole. As the nation, and Evanston along with it, became ever more urban and cosmopolitan in nature, it could not be so clear that what would emerge would be a New Jerusalem, or that when others spoke of the New Jerusalem they would have the same regard for the particular heritage of Frances Willard that she had had.

On the day of Frances Willard's funeral Evanston had once more taken on the appearance of a community united in covenant with one another and with God, with the church at its center. One was left to ponder whether in the new age of the twentieth century, the Evanston that appeared on that one day would be considered an anachronism or whether people had caught a glimpse of the spirit that one day might characterize the life of the American city. The funeral of Frances Willard suggested a mixture of emotions that might at any time attend the process of change in Evanston.

Also in 1898 the United States went to war. Quickly and almost painlessly, the United States liberated Cuba, Puerto Rico, and the Philippines from the burden of Spanish oppression. In the Philippines the war lasted only a week, as Dewey's squadron devastated the Spanish in Manila Bay without the loss of a life. In the Caribbean, it took a little longer, but still by the beginning of July, only ten weeks after war had been declared, the victory had been won. It was hardly a struggle of epic proportions. Nevertheless, the actual and symbolic significance of what had occurred was not to be underestimated. For four centuries Spain had tenaciously maintained a presence in the western hemisphere, and now it had been defeated decisively. Vestiges of Old World tyranny were on the run. American ideals had triumphed and were being extended to other parts of the world. The United States armed forces found themselves in control of new territories, and the government was faced with new decisions. The speed and ease with which all this transpired perhaps only served to underscore the idea that the time had come for the United States to assume greater responsibilities in world affairs.

In Evanston the press and the pulpit reflected what was, in general, the national mood. On July 16, before the terms of the peace had been proposed and well before any decision had been made as to future United States control of the new territories, Rev. John Boyd stated in a sermon at First Presbyterian Church that the United States had been the instrument of God's judgment upon Spain. He went on to say:

> In view of this, who shall say that in the providence of the God of nations it is not intended that we shall have a more significant place in the world's development. . . . With larger opportunities of human betterment opened before us, neither tradition nor constitutional limitation should bind us if the impulse of God carries us forth into the larger sphere and into ampler fields of national influence and achievement.[3]

As Boyd phrased it ("who shall say that in the providence of the God of nations it is not intended . . ."), the burden of proof now rested on those who felt that the United States should continue to adhere to its previous policies of noninvolvement in world affairs. To him it was clear that the restrictions of the past must not stand in the way of the United States heeding a sacred call toward a grander and nobler future. A few weeks later a similar sentiment was expressed editorially by the *Evanston Index*. To support its view, a Baptist minister was quoted as saying: "This nation can never again be what it was a few months ago. We cannot escape the great responsibilities which divine providence has laid upon us."[4]

There were those in Evanston, as there were throughout the nation, who were disturbed by this turn of events and felt that the United States was betraying its ideals by becoming a colonial power. The following spring President Rogers of Northwestern University and four prominent faculty members led a rally that was strongly critical of McKinley and the decision to establish American rule in the Philippines, where battles with native insurgents indicated that American presence was not entirely welcome. This was not something that others could calmly tolerate. The leaders of the rally were greeted with scorn and anger and cries of treason, and a counterrally was quickly called to demonstrate where the majority sentiment lay. Prominent in attendance at this rally, held at First Congregational Church, were the mayor, local ministers, leading businessmen, the president of Garrett Biblical Institute, and other members of Northwestern's faculty.[5]

Both opponents and supporters of the government's actions sensed that the United States was approaching a point of no return. A few foresaw disaster and felt that the nation was willfully straying from its appointed course. But by far the dominant sentiment was that new opportunities were unfolding, new responsibilities were being thrust upon the United States, and that to turn away from these new opportunities and responsibilities would constitute a denial of destiny and providence. As naturally as an individual grew to maturity, the United States was now coming of age and assuming its rightful place in world affairs. This invited a belief that a new era was dawning, as Rev. R. H. Wilkinson said in a sermon at Hemenway Methodist Church. "The logic of manifold events proclaims a new era. . . . I invite you to pass in review some things that will constitute the new era of the American Republic."[6]

The vision that Wilkinson put forth included a vanishing sectionalism and a new nationalism, the United States becoming the world leader in commerce and industry, American control of the seas, an Anglo-American alliance dominating international politics, and the United States taking on the role of a colonizing power carrying its ideals and civilization to every part of the globe. He concluded by making reference to George Washington's Farewell Address in which he stated that the controversies of other nations were essentially foreign to the concerns of the United States and that the United States should "pursue a different course," avoiding permanent alliances and involvement in the affairs of other nations. Commenting on this Wilkinson said: "Washington's advice was the law of self-preservation for a young and struggling republic. The founders of the republic were wiser than to doom it forever to go bound in swaddling bands."[7]

For America too, it seemed, the age of the founders was passing. For the nation, as well as for individuals and communities within it, new horizons were supplanting the more limited world of the past. Enthusiasm for the new identity the United States had assumed as a world power was not necessarily matched by an equivalent enthusiasm for the changes that might be needed to produce a new urban identity for Evanston. Nevertheless, when Dr. Macafee, pastor of First Methodist Church, argued at length in a Fourth of July sermon that the policy of isolation could not be pursued in the future as it had been in the past, he was using language that many people in Evanston would have recognized as just as truthful for their own community as it was with regard to the nation. Isolationism in any form was not the order of the day. Furthermore, the course of events that had led Evanston to become a city and that continued to make it increasingly citylike were just as possibly the work of providence as were the events that had led the United States to become a world power. Just as the United States had been destined from the beginning one day to become a preeminent nation in a world of nations, so perhaps Evanston had been destined from the beginning to emerge as a preeminent city in a nation of cities. In any case, there were many people in Evanston who perceived that their community, along with the nation as a whole, was crossing a boundary and that it could never again be what it once had been. Some, no doubt, viewed this new age with alarm or resignation. But others hailed it with the same kind of optimism that had been apparent in the response to the Spanish-American War.

"A Parting of the Ways"

Among those who might claim to speak for the community of Evanston and command a wide hearing, there was one voice that stood out as a rather consistent interpreter and defender of the "new age" in Evanston. That was the editorial voice of the *Evanston Index*. During the twenty-five years from 1892 to 1917 the *Index* was the major newspaper in Evanston.[8] It had established its credentials as a champion of progress in the period prior to the adoption of the city form of government. Surprisingly and without explanation, the *Index* had withdrawn its support for the city form on the eve of the election, but it quickly returned to a stance more consistent with the positions it had taken earlier. In the new phase of Evanston's history the *Index* seemed intent on interpreting the implications of that vote as broadly as possible and making sure that the people of Evanston did not retreat from those implications.[9]

Sometimes the *Index* expressed its views indirectly and subtly. But on many occasions it was quite forthright and was capable of being contentious, almost belligerent. When there were decisions confronting the community, the *Index* often presented the issue as a contest between the modern, realistic, enlightened, and progressive point of view on the one hand, and the reactionary and doctrinaire point of view on the other. When there were no such decisions to be made, the paper might take delight in drawing attention

173

to the changes that were making Evanston more citylike. In so doing, it often stated or implied the existence of an ever-widening gulf between the new Evanston and the old Evanston. Although the statements of the *Index* were not uniform in the attitudes expressed, and one could detect certain contradictions and moods of caution and conciliation, as a whole its stance was distinctly not a nonpartisan one.

One way the *Index* made its attitudes known in an indirect, though perhaps not too subtle, manner was to compare Evanston to other cities throughout the nation. On more than one occasion, tables appeared in the paper, along with appropriate commentary, that showed where Evanston ranked among the major cities of the United States on an issue such as infant mortality. When the *Index* took a stand favoring the introduction of national political parties into local politics, it noted that there was no other city in the country of Evanston's size or larger where the Democrats were in the majority that did not have the national party labels attached to the candidates for local office.[10] When it lobbied for the immediate erection of a public library, it noted that Evanston was one of the wealthiest cities in the country and that "there are few cities in the country where such a condition [i.e., no modern library building] could exist."[11] When it campaigned for the creation of a system of public parks in Evanston, the *Index* went to the effort of discovering what the situation was in a large number of other cities. For many weeks running it carried front-page articles describing how the park system developed in cities such as Buffalo, Detroit, Atlanta, Seattle, and Colorado Springs.[12] In these instances and many others the *Index* made clear, without stating it in so many words, that Evanston's point of reference and its standard of measure was properly other urban areas. It was not to be compared to other suburbs, or to other communities with a similar background or similar values.

Another indirect way that the *Index* communicated attitudes to its readers was through predictions about Evanston's future. Such was the case, for instance, in an editorial of 1894 that ostensibly addressed the issue of annexation soon to be voted on.

> Chicago is Chicago. It is our pride. It is great. It is progressive. It is destined to be the metropolis of the continent. But it is not peaceful nor quiet. Some day, years hence, Evanston will no longer be a suburb. It will have grown citified. Pretty cottages will give way to apartment buildings. Broad lawns will be covered by stores. Business will have encroached on residence. Detached houses will disappear. Not until then, if ever, may Evanston even think of becoming a part of the great city.[13]

On the surface this editorial stated the *Index*'s opposition to annexation. Both in the editorial and in the community at large, however, the result of the vote appeared to be something of a foregone conclusion. While there had been some public discussion of the matter, the response in Evanston could be characterized as much more restrained and businesslike than was the case in Oak Park on similar occasions, where the raising of the issue seemed to constitute a call to arms and called forth some of Oak Park's most impassioned rhetoric. In any case, the position the *Index* took on annexation was certainly not the most striking or interesting part of what it had to say.

It was the confidence with which the *Index* spoke of the future that was perhaps the outstanding feature of the editorial. In this light the present could not but appear insubstantial, for through a process that might be measured in years, but then again maybe only in days, Evanston was about to be transformed. That Evanston would become citified was not merely a distant possibility; it was an imminent certainty. Even annexation, though at present undesirable, was no longer unthinkable. Indeed, one might even begin to think somewhat positively of the possibility of annexation. The city that Evanston would one day be part of in spirit if not in fact was, after all, great and progressive and "destined to be the metropolis of the continent." Even as the *Index* allied itself with the views of the vast majority with regard to the immediate issue at hand, it was able to use the occasion to work on creating a climate of acceptance for what the future would bring. At the least, it indicated that annexation ought not to cause the people of Evanston to fall back into a posture of defensiveness, fear, and rigid resistance to the ways of the city and the modern age.

A year later the *Index* took a more openly controversial stand when it supported the idea of having Republican and Democratic nominees for local offices. Besides noting that other cities typically ruled by Democrats had party nominees, the *Index* and several writers who shared the paper's views went on to explain why Evanston should not be different from other cities in this regard. The initial statement said quite simply that "the city has grown too large for the town meeting idea."[14] Extending this line of thought, a correspondent later wrote that nonpartisanship had become an illusion in Evanston and that there would be parties in Evanston regardless. The question was only whether those parties would have "the prestige of national affiliations and proud historic associations."[15] Furthermore, it was said, for Evanston to cling to this outmoded and unrealistic style of nonpartisanship was accomplishing nothing but the disfranchisement of Republicans. In major cities across the country and in national affairs Republicans were barely tolerated as a necessary evil. Why should Republicans disguise themselves, abandon their principles, and allow their influence to be dissipated where they were in fact in the vast majority? As far as the *Index* was concerned, the arguments of its opponents that machine politics would take over in Evanston were not to be taken seriously. The leaders of the "independent movement" were either Democrats with only their self-interest at stake, or proannexationists.[16] This was not to be the only time an attempt was made to link the threat of annexation with the resistance to urbanizing trends in Evanston, though in this case there was no effort to make clear what the connection was.

The outcome of this affair was encouraging to the *Index*, but it was not decisive. The principle of party nominations was accepted to the extent that the Republican Party nominated a slate for village offices. The opponents to these nominees ran, however, as independents for the most part, and the election became somewhat confused. One might not have been sure whether one was casting a vote for mayor or casting a vote on a referendum to approve or disapprove partisan politics in local government. When the fog lifted, Republican nominees had carried all but one of the major offices. The margins of victory varied, but none was overwhelming, considering the fact that Evanston was said to be more than 80 percent Republican. (The new mayor, William Dyche, had won by about 3 to 2.) The *Index* admitted that the victory had been something less than complete, but felt that the majorities were "quite comfortable . . . considering that there was arrayed against the straight ticket a combination of Democrats, cranks, and soreheads, which in the aggregate looked as though it would have considerable voting strength."[17] This general situation lasted for about eight years, after which time politics in Evanston once again became nonpartisan. For the time being, though, Evanston had taken another step toward becoming a city and had showed that a town could become a city without being controlled by "Democrats, cranks, and soreheads."

There were times too when the *Index* would make its views known by letting a news item speak for itself, or at least almost speak for itself. In 1902 the Socialist Club of Evanston sponsored a meeting to discuss the "factory problem," namely, whether factories should be allowed to exist within Evanston's borders. The report of the meeting as a whole was brief. It noted that although the affair had been advertised as a debate, what materialized had instead been a discussion where the only disagreement was over the details of possible regulation. No one could be found to speak in favor of prohibiting the building of factories in Evanston. The *Index* made clear that it considered this fact significant and then went on to quote at length the speech that had been made by Frank Grover.

Grover's speech contained several themes that were also favorite themes of the *Index*. One of those was the inevitability of certain aspects of the life of cities becoming a part of Evanston and the fruitlessness of pretending that the precious tastes and preferences of some of Evanston's residents either would or should determine the nature of life in the new age.

> In the month of January, 1890, eleven years ago, this little city, then a village of 8,000 inhabitants, became very agitated on the factory question. Oratory and printer's ink both of the local and Chicago press was wasted without stint—wasted because 11 years of experience has demonstrated that speeches and newspaper interviews and editorials, to say nothing of city ordinances, will neither build nor prevent the building of a single factory. The laws of trade will attend to that and sentiment, of which we always have a surplus in this community, has little if anything to do with results.

For Grover, as for the *Index*, there was more at stake than a simple question of realism. The surplus of sentiment to which the speaker referred might produce something much more serious than wasted energy. It might place Evanston in a position that was both morally questionable and potentially self-destructive. Acknowledging that Evanston prided herself on being the "modern Athens of the West" and the "National headquarters for philanthropy and right living," Grover asked rhetorically whether this description of Evanston might not best be retained by not only supporting mission outposts in the city but also by giving working people a place to earn a living where they could at the same time benefit from the good air, fine schools, comfortable homes, and ideal surroundings of Evanston. To indulge those who had a distaste for the factory was to betray the moral ideals on which Evanston's image of itself rested. Furthermore, not only the image and reputation of the community might be destroyed; its very existence was threatened.

> On the other hand she can easily wrap her cloak of aristocracy and refinement about her, be exclusive, discourage all improvements anywhere within her borders not represented by a costly home, keep on increasing taxations, eventually annex herself to Chicago, and be the tail end of a city ward, instead of being the Evanston that is and I sincerely hope is to be.[18]

The new age, in this case represented by factories, presented Evanston with an opportunity to fulfill its destiny. To refuse would mean the complete loss of Evanston's identity.

There were, of course, many things besides partisan politics and factories that helped to define the new age in Evanston. Seldom did a change occur without the *Index* pointing to it as a sign that the community had become, was becoming, or was soon to become quite a different place from what it had been in the past. In 1899 it was the "modern office building" that caused the *Index* to comment:

> Evanston has forever lost its quiet, demure air of the time when it was a village, to which time many of our older inhabitants still look back with regret. From a coy and pretty village, Evanston has grown in a decade to a dashing and magnificent city. Paved boulevards have taken the place of dirt road, imposing residences have sprung up by the score, and even the flat and apartment building have obtruded their unwelcome presence. And now comes the modern office building to still further accentuate the lines of demarcation between the old Evanston and the new Evanston.[19]

Often it was stated or implied that Evanston's situation was somewhat paradoxical. It must accept important departures from past beliefs and practices in order to retain its identity. If it clung rigidly to characteristics that had once defined it, it would end up losing its identity. Only by accepting party politics could Evanston show its distinctiveness as a city of Republican virtues. Only by accepting the factory could Evanston preserve the image of being a home of philanthropy and the Athens of the West. Nevertheless, the *Index* did not pretend that the various changes it reported and extolled were insignificant and would leave the community essentially intact and in continuity with its past. It acknowledged the regret with which many "older residents" observed the change. A "dashing and magnificent city" had replaced the village that once was. There were distinctly two Evanstons, an old and a new, and they were separated by lines of demarcation.

Still other changes were yet to come. In 1911 Evanston's first theater was opened, and the *Index* was ready with an interpretation designed to forestall any potential opposition.

> Evanston will take its last step toward be coming a full-fledged city. A fine new theater is to open on Monday. . . . The performers are cautioned to conduct themselves carefully and avoid swearing, and they are told that no song, word,

line or situation will be permitted that could not be used with propriety in the most refined family of this city.[20]

The initial performances at the theater were vaudeville, and the paper made every effort to review them favorably. Yet the theater got off to something of a bad start. It was to come under increasing attack, not so much for its moral impropriety as for catering to the demand for crass entertainment rather than art and thus reflecting, instead of elevating, the low aesthetic standards of modern culture. For the moment, however, the *Index* was not concerned with such things. It was the theater as such that was needed to make Evanston a "full-fledged city." However, the notion that this was in any sense a last step was, of course, premature.

In 1899 it had been noted that flats and apartment buildings had already "obtruded their unwelcome presence." More than fifteen years later, however, the issue was not yet settled. In the early months of 1915 the city council passed an ordinance strictly regulating the building of flats and apartments. This was commonly interpreted as an attempt to prevent the building of such structures and it aroused a protest strong enough to require that a compromise measure be eventually substituted. After the question of public policy had been at least temporarily resolved, the *Index* went on to discuss the deeper and more lasting issue of public attitude.

> It is useless for Evanston to repine because of the spread of the apartment building in the city. That is inevitable and might as well be accepted gracefully . . . [but] if there are made no efforts to make our newcomers wish to be an integral part of the city's life, when the time comes, as it almost surely will, when there is agitation to push to the north the city's limits, there will be nothing to hold the interest and loyalty of these citizens, unfettered by property ties in Evanston. This is the real problem of the encroachment of the apartment building in Evanston.[21]

Several people wrote to the *News-Index* in support of its insight that not just the apartment building but the apartment dweller need to be welcomed and accepted in the community. One claimed that her child had been denied a seat in a crowded public school classroom because the principal had stated that property owners were to be given preference. "It requires more than pretty streets, lights, and automobiles to create municipal patriotism," she wrote. "Civic pride cannot thrive without a human atmosphere."[22]

Increasingly as the period progressed, the *Index* directed more of its attention to the less tangible aspects of the movement toward becoming a city. One of its favorite themes was the liberalization of customs with regard to the Sabbath, and in its campaign it articulated the call for a human atmosphere later to be made on behalf of apartment dwellers:

> If they go on enforcing the blue laws in Boston, many residents of that city will be seeking asylum in Evanston because this city is recognized as the Boston of the West. They can find the culture here and that air of quiet exclusiveness which dominates Boston can be found here too. In fact some of it can be seen with the naked eye. This little city was Puritanical once, quite as much so as any place in New England, but in many respects it has outgrown Puritanical customs. More liberal ideas prevail as to Sunday observance.[23]

Because this concern was by its nature connected with religious beliefs and practices, this discussion involved a different dimension of the old and new Evanston. Evanston had not only outgrown the town meeting idea and the ability to remain isolated from factories, flats, office buildings, and theaters. It had in many ways outgrown its religion. The Puritanism that admittedly had dominated an earlier day, that had been part of the old Evanston, was attacked even more directly and strongly in a later editorial.

> The Puritan in our early history could glorify God on the Sabbath Day only by making himself and his family as miserable as possible. God's gift of the sunshine and the beauties of the world must be shut out by tightly drawn blinds. Many a rebellious young heart must have found trouble keeping the sense of holiness for such a Sabbath.[24]

One of the relatively rare statements that acknowledged the existence of a positive connection between Evanston's past and present appeared, coincidentally, only a week after the first statement quoted above. Instead of picturing Evanston as having shed its Puritan past, an article on real estate prospects claimed that the community had been indelibly marked by the character of its early residents.

> Evanston was fortunate in its founders. We think of them as genuine Americans of New England descent who lived in the fear of God; and if they sat long in the Amen corner, they loved truth and believed in the axiom "in knowledge there is power." . . . Their influence to this community is henceforth ineffaceable. To them the community is largely indebted to present educational advantages not only in the college proper, but in influences which have given us our public

schools, libraries, clubs, our broad-minded pulpits, and those intellectual aspirations and social amenities which define a cultured society.[25]

One might almost be led to wonder whether the people who had once made Evanston as Puritan as anyplace in New England were in fact the same as "the genuine Americans of New England descent who lived in the fear of God."

Here, in contrast to the statement made only a week earlier, the religion of the founders was being touched on gently, almost lovingly; the reference to the "Amen corner" seemed to be a description of a harmless eccentricity rather than a sign of rigidity. Still, the *Index* did not depart too much from its general position. The lasting contributions of the founders were only those that were consistent with the modern age: schools, libraries, clubs, high culture, and, in the specifically religious realm, broad-minded pulpits. By implication, whatever else they believed and stood for had fallen prey to the principle of natural selection. Almost by definition, whatever was lasting was well adapted to the new Evanston.

The changes in Evanston's physical appearance and in such things as Sabbath observance only hinted at what was perhaps a more fundamental concern: the changing nature of Evanston's population. Even the *Index* had a bit of trouble with this issue. It consistently supported and celebrated without apparent reservation the growth of the community, and it even complained that the U.S. census had insulted Evanston by underestimating the city's numbers.[26] But the paper was evidently less sure that this growth should occur in a completely random fashion. Indeed, it made a strong statement to the contrary as its major reason for opposing a 5-cent train fare to the city.

> While Evanston is not in the least degree snobbish, it naturally flocks by itself because it there finds the best society, and there is great, decided, and emphatic objection to opening the doors with a 5-cent fare to a class of people who have nothing in common with the present residents.[27]

Perhaps the *Index* would have been unable to say, and in any case it did not choose to say, precisely what it was that the present residents held in common or what constituted the class of people that were considered unwelcome. Nevertheless, at this point it seemed to be clear to the *Index* that whatever other changes might be welcomed as part of the new Evanston, the abandonment of a certain like-mindedness or a certain social homogeneity was not one of them.

181

Perhaps its defense of apartment dwellers was an indication that the attitude of the *Index* was changing on this matter, but a more sweeping statement was yet to come. It was made in connection with an advertising campaign being organized by businessmen in order to attract residents to the community.

> The reluctance of a portion of the people to advertise the advantages the city has to offer to those who may be seeking new homes is not, in most cases, based upon modesty. It is far more likely . . . a disinclination to share with a promiscuously gathered populace, the possessions which we hold in common with every citizen. There is here a conservative element who refuse to see or fail to see that the Evanston of today is not the Evanston of twenty years ago, or even of ten years ago. We have left behind us the village of congenial groups, drawn by the university and the quiet of a place remote from the city and have grown into a city ourselves, with all the problems and possibilities of any other municipality. . . . Civic pride has nothing in common with the discouragement of acquisitions to our citizenship.[28]

Though much of the language now being used had become familiar, to say the least, there was also an important addition to the rhetoric. Among the things that had been left behind was a "village of congenial groups," and among the things that lay ahead for Evanston as a city was a vision of a "promiscuously gathered populace." In this instance, as in most others, the comments of the *Index* were more suggestive than specific, but they were not on that account insignificant. One might well ask whether a promiscuously gathered populace and uncongenial groups would have any semblance of a unified and harmonious spirit. If not, what was to make Evanston any different from other cities where the breakdown of common moral and spiritual values was endangering the civilization? In what sense could Evanston still consider itself an ideal city and not just another city? The statement that Evanston now had all the problems and possibilities of any other municipality only heightened the impression that little remained of Evanston's distinctiveness.

This statement, which the *Index* had finally been led to at the end of the period perhaps by the momentum of its own arguments, cannot be read back into the other positions it had taken in the course of twenty-five years of acting as spokesman for the new age in Evanston. What had been expressed over that period of time was not a consistent ideology but rather a general attitude and posture toward urbanizing innovations quite unlike the views articulated by Oak Park's leadership during the same period. The *Index* itself stated what was perhaps the one idea it had tried to impress on its readers again and again. In the eyes of the *Index* the two candidates for mayor in 1913 presented the voters with a choice between two fundamentally different ideas of the kind of community Evanston should become. Much of the paper's endorsement for one of the candidates ranged rather far from the specific issues of the campaign or the candidate's qualifications:

> We have frequently of late expressed the opinion that Evanston at the present time stood at a "parting of the ways." There is an era of greater and more broad horizon dawning upon its immediate future. Of all cities in this land of ours, there seems no other place which has so many advantages for becoming an ideal city.[29]

Whereas in Oak Park the leadership, wherever possible, had attempted to avoid the necessity for hard and fast choices, in Evanston at least this one important voice consistently portrayed the community as being at a turning point, a parting of the ways, where choice was unavoidable. Even where no questions of public policy were involved, the *Index* confronted people with change and asked them to choose what their attitude would be. Each of the decisions which the *Index* asked people to make was in essence a reaffirmation of the decision that had been made in 1892: Evanston was to be a city. For the *Index*, it seemed, Evanston was to be a city wholeheartedly or not at all.

"A Growing Metropolitan Character"

The authority and credibility of the *Index*'s statements seemed to rest primarily on two grounds. On the one hand, it did not take the losing side on issues where a vote was to be taken. Whenever there was a clear expression of public sentiment, the *Index* could claim that its views were those of the majority.[30] Perhaps more important, though, was the belief that its view would be vindicated by the course of events. History would confirm the stands taken by the *Index* even if temporarily the feelings of the majority would not. On at least these two grounds the *Index* laid its claim to be taken seriously, but it did not claim that its views expressed the unified spirit of the community. On the contrary, it often indicated that it stood opposed to a significant segment of the population, and the net effect of its statements was in part to communicate the impression that there no longer was a single, unified spirit among the people of Evanston.

In any case, the leadership of the community was something less than united. The press was one source of leadership; the churches were another.

And the relationship between the two had become ambiguous, to say the least. To be sure, the stance of the *Index* was not overtly hostile to the churches. Religion played only a small part in the *Index*'s discussions relating to Evanston's transformation. Indeed, this was perhaps part of the problem. The portraits of the present and future Evanston that the *Index* held up before the public did not present Evanston as a city of churches. Commerce and culture were the essential ingredients. Religion was at best just a portion of Evanston's cultural attributes, a subheading, as it were. Furthermore, it was commonly understood that churches had been an intimate and integral part of the village days of Evanston that were constantly being left behind in the *Index* editorials. The fact that the Puritan days were gone was no more disturbing to many church members than it was to the *Index*, but the continuing influence of the church on the community was a different matter. It was at least an open question whether the statements of the *Index* implied that the church was to play a much less important role in the city of Evanston than it had in the village of Evanston. In a sense this was already the case, for it was quite clear, even early in the period, that the agenda of the *Index* was different from that of the churches. It could no longer be taken for granted that the churches' order of business and priorities would be the same as the community's as the *Index* articulated them.

If the church and the press did not provide a unified front of leadership, neither was there a unified front among the churches themselves. By the beginning of the twentieth century there were thirty churches in Evanston and a population of about 20,000—one church for every 700 people. In sheer numbers the churches were strong. Evanston was a well-churched community. Churches were visible everywhere. But this was not an unmixed blessing. In general church life prospered, but it had also become fragmented. Divisions in the life of the community as a whole had come to be reflected in the life of the churches, and it was difficult to see in what sense the church was now a unifying force within the city.

There was in Evanston, as there was in Oak Park, a core of evangelical Protestant churches that had been in existence since the early days of the community. First Methodist, the "cathedral church," had been organized in 1856. First Baptist was founded in 1858 and St. Mark's Episcopal in 1864. In 1866 the Lake Avenue Church was started by the combined efforts of Congregationalists and Presbyterians, who then split to form First Presbyterian in 1868 and First Congregational in 1870. These five churches all came to occupy land that had been donated to them by Northwestern University. They stood at the center of the village and provided visible symbols of the kind of religious unity and cooperation that stood at the heart of Evanston's life and spirit.

One church organized in the early period did not receive land from Northwestern and could not be considered part of the core of churches defining the spirit of the community. That was St. Mary's Roman Catholic Church. Catholic families had been among the earliest settlers of the area, dating back to the 1830s before Evanston was "discovered." In 1864 land was purchased in central Evanston for a Catholic church and in 1866 the first mass was said and a church building was begun. Although the early membership was quite small, by the 1890s St. Mary's had a membership larger than most of the Protestant "first churches." Although the relationship of St. Mary's to the other churches was cordial and several prominent Methodists were said to have helped in the initial effort to raise money for St. Mary's,[31] the existence of St. Mary's could not help but complicate the religious picture in Evanston. By the beginning of the twentieth century, the Catholic church could scarcely be denied a status equivalent to that of any other church. It had numbered among its members some of the original settlers of the community. It was older than several of the central Protestant churches. And St. Mary's was now among the largest congregations in the city. Although the combined strength of the first churches still outweighed St. Mary's, it could not be assumed that they represented the religious spirit of the entire community.

St. Mary's seemed to have been organized primarily as an Irish Catholic church. As time went on there were to be two other Catholic churches with an ethnic identity in Evanston. St. Nicholas parish was organized in 1887 to serve German Catholics and Ascension was organized as a Polish parish. Ethnic divisions were also apparent among the Protestant churches, however. Among the thirty churches in Evanston in 1902, six were clearly Scandinavian: Swedish Baptist, Norwegian and Danish Methodist, Swedish Methodist, Swedish Evangelical Lutheran, Norwegian and Danish Lutheran, and Svenska Kristna. These churches cooperated among themselves but were not a part of cooperative efforts among the other Protestant churches of the community.[32]

According to census figures, Scandinavians were by far the largest ethnic group in Evanston. Next largest were the Germans. There were two German churches—German Evangelical Lutheran and St. John's German Evangelical—but they were not highly visible in the church life of the city. Commanding far more attention were two major black churches: Ebenezer African Methodist Episcopal and Second Baptist. While these two churches were not generally a part of cooperative efforts there was some evidence of fraternal relations. The minister of Second Baptist was part of a reorganized ministers' association for a time. White and black churches cooperated with the YMCA to promote a program designed to better serve the "colored" population of Evanston. Appeals were made to the central churches for financial aid. The ministers of First Methodist and First Presbyterian were in attendance at the cornerstone ceremony for Ebenezer A.M.E. in 1907. And when the A.M.E. church held its convention in Evanston, its offer to supply Evanston pulpits with ministers attending the meeting was accepted by all five of the white Methodist churches in Evanston. On the closing day of the convention, the bishop of the A.M.E. church in Illinois preached in Bailey's Opera House to a standing room congregation that was about half white and half black.[33]

Geography was perhaps just as important as ethnicity in dividing the churches of Evanston. When South Evanston was annexed to Evanston in 1892, it already had churches of its own. These churches were not emanations from the central churches as was so often the case in Oak Park. They had been formed as separate churches in a separate community. Thus the historical ties and associations that might help to foster a sense of unity were not present. Furthermore, the merger of Evanston and South Evanston did not put an end to the sense that South Evanston was a distinct community. The feeling was fostered from both sides and occasionally tempers flared.

In 1894, for instance, a former mayor of South Evanston, James Hibben, decided to take up the cause of annexation to Chicago, a position that was not likely to endear him to residents in other sections of the city. He gave as his reason that South Evanston had been treated unfairly and that there was a general feeling of dissatisfaction with the government of the city. This caused the *Index* to respond that if South Evanston wanted to be annexed, the rest of Evanston should consent. "The annexation of South Evanston [to Evanston] has never been productive of any great advantage to Evanston proper other than the introduction of new political factions into city politics."[34] Another time when underlying feelings came to the surface was in 1899, when a meeting was held to organize resistance to city-county consolidation. At the end of the meeting the mayor appointed a committee to pursue the matter but neglected to place anyone from South Evanston on the committee. On the vigorous protest of a resident of South Evanston, the mayor apologized for the oversight and appointed two additional members. Another speaker, however, said that this would not make up for the mistake, at which point a resident of "Evanston proper" decided to go on the attack. "I have been in politics in Evanston for some time and have always found that South Evanston wants the earth. I—" Before he could go farther, the mayor interrupted to rule the discussion out of order and adjourned the meeting. Shortly thereafter a meeting was called in South Evanston to discuss seceding from Evanston.[35]

Such outbreaks of anger cannot be assumed to have been characteristic of the relationship between the two portions of the village. More often the existence of a certain sectional feeling and rivalry was acknowledged and the hope expressed that this was being overcome. Yet South Evanston continued to have a separate identity and carried on a community life of its own. In 1916 a program of "civic cooperation" was organized in the third and fourth wards, the old South Evanston. This was applauded in the newspaper and the city council as perhaps setting an example that might eventually be extended to include all of Evanston. Commenting on this, the *Index* wrote: "Evanston has been, largely owing to the mechanical features of the city, divided rather more than the ordinary community."[36] Given such a situation it is not surprising that the churches of South Evanston seemed to find more in common with one another than they did with their sister churches in other parts of the community. To a lesser extent this was also true on the west and north sides of the community, where sectional feeling was less pronounced but still existed.

Further complicating the religious picture in Evanston were several churches that did not represent ethnic or geographical divisions, but were in a class by themselves. These included a Free Methodist Church, First Unitarian, and the First Church of Christ, Scientist. The Evanston Christian Church was founded relatively late (1896) and only gradually achieved some recognition as its pastor, O. F. Jordan, an editor of *Christian Century*, became one of the more prominent clergy in the community.

All this did not mean, of course, that there was no sense of unity among the churches in Evanston. It did mean that manifestations of any presumed unity of spirit were partial, varied, and shifting. There could be little doubt about the continuing spirit of cooperation and harmony among the four first churches of the central area. Emmanuel Methodist, established in 1890 by west siders who wanted a church closer to home and by some east siders who were "dissatisfied with the state of affairs at First Methodist,"[37] most often was a part of this group too. The relationship of St. Mark's Episcopal, to say nothing of St. Mary's, was much less clear.

There was ample direct and indirect testimony to the sense of friendship and common purpose enjoyed among these churches and their ministers. In 1896, for instance, Rev. H. A. Delano died of typhoid fever. He had been the pastor at First Baptist Church for seven years and had only recently accepted a call to an institutional church in Chicago's inner city. Six clergy participated in the memorial service held for him at First Baptist: Albion Small of the University of Chicago, who had been a close friend; Newell Dwight Hillis, then at the Central Church of Chicago, who had developed a close friendship with Delano while at First Presbyterian in Evanston; F. M. Bristol, pastor of First Methodist; J. F. Loba, First Congregational; John Boyd, First Presbyterian; and N. M. Waters, Emmanuel Methodist. The last two were recent arrivals in the community and were clearly present more to represent their churches than because of their personal association with Delano. On this occasion, as on many others like it, the speakers referred to a universal affection and esteem for the person being honored as well as to their personal and professional ties with the man.[38] The arrival or departure of a minister from any of the churches was typically accompanied by a ceremony that involved the ministers of the same churches making testimonies similar to those made on the occasion of H. A. Delano's memorial service.

First Methodist, First Baptist, First Presbyterian, First Congregational, and Emmanuel Methodist did seem to constitute a prominent and identifiable religious community at the heart of Evanston. Yet, to continue the biological metaphor, it was not clear how far or in what direction the arteries extended into the rest of the community. For example, in 1899 these five churches called off their Sunday evening services in order to have a united meeting of support of the Four Mile League, an organization devoted to facilitating the enforcement of the prohibition clause in Northwestern's charter. Various city officials were invited, and it was clearly an attempt to develop a united, cooperative effort with regard to an issue on which it was assumed Evanston was united, and yet required constant attention.[39] Yet there is no evidence that other churches were invited to be a part of the meeting; in any case only the five participated.[40]

In 1904 there was an effort made to form a new ministers' group. Prior to that time the group had been "limited to the four or five central churches." At the time the new group was announced it included the ministers of five Methodist churches (First, Emmanuel, Wheadon, Hemenway, and Central Street), First Congregational, First and Second Baptist, and First and Second Presbyterian. In addition to the five "core" churches, therefore, there were several churches from South Evanston represented, along with one from North Evanston and one black congregation.[41] Perhaps this was an indication that the five central churches were themselves becoming aware of the need to extend the boundaries of their community in some concrete way.

A trend toward wider participation can be seen also in the nature of union Thanksgiving services. In 1904, for instance, one of the union services included two of the churches whose ministers were in the expanded ministers' group: Hemenway Methodist and Second Presbyterian. These along with the five central churches were involved in one service. At the same time a second union service was held among the Free Methodist, United Presbyterian, and Christian churches. This, it was said, was a service for the west side of the city, but it was also apparent that these churches did not fit precisely the denominational mold of the churches involved in the other service.[42] By 1910 the central union service had been expanded. This time nine churches agreed to participate. There were the five core churches along with Second Presbyterian and United Presbyterian. It is unclear what the other two churches were, for although all nine pastors were scheduled to have a part in leading the worship, two of them failed to show up. This was not, however, the most disturbing part of the event. Although nine substantial congregations were invited to attend, the sanctuary of First Presbyterian Church was less than half full, significantly less than a normal Sunday attendance for First Presbyterial alone. The preacher on the occasion, James Madison Stifler of First Baptist, noted that there must have been more in attendance in 1621 than there were in First Presbyterian on that day.[43] This was hardly an encouraging sign for future attempts at wider cooperation.

The annual week of Christian prayer was another good opportunity to demonstrate a sense of unity. This was scheduled regularly for the first week in January and was organized according to guidelines put out by the Evangelical Alliance. The number of churches that observed the week of prayer together varied somewhat from year to year, but it never was many more than the five central churches. By 1909 it had become only those five. The following year the promotional notice for the week of prayer stated: "Church union is not a dream but a fact in Evanston. Nowhere in the world do the Christian churches work more in harmony than here. One expression of that harmony is the union week of prayer services the churches unite in each year."[44] It was not made clear precisely which churches participated that year, but the reports did indicate that the evening union services drew only about 100 people, and there was some discussion as to whether the week of prayer might not be more successfully conducted during Holy Week in the future.[45]

Perhaps if anything promised to bring churches together on a wide scale it was the Men and Religion Forward Movement. A meeting held at the YMCA to enlist support for the movement was attended by twelve churches, including the two Episcopal churches and the Unitarian church. This represented almost all of the churches in Evanston that were white, nonethnic, and Protestant. (First Congregational and Central Street Methodist were not listed as present and apparently did not participate in the campaign.) Even with such an unusually broad gathering, however, it might have been apparent to those in attendance that they represented a minority of the churches in Evanston. The "minority" churches—Roman Catholic, black, and those with a specific ethnic identity—together totaled as many churches as those of the "majority."[46] Partly because of this, no doubt, and partly because these churches were not accustomed to working together, and perhaps for other reasons, the Men and Religion Forward Movement did not seem to have the same impact or importance in Evanston that it did in Oak Park. The campaign consisted of eight days of workshops led by experts and held in various churches. As such it required a minimum of planning and coordination and added little to what the churches were capable of doing, and often did do, on their own. The workshops were not reported in the press and there appears to have been no follow-up activity.

In Oak Park the Men and Religion Movement had been organized in such a way as to engage members of the various churches in common tasks over an extended period of time. This allowed the churches to renew actual working relationships as well as to reaffirm a sense of their common faith and spirit. In Evanston the Men and Religion Movement seems not to have appreciably furthered the cause of church unity; instead, it may have provided an illustration of how difficult it had become for the churches to work together in Evanston. A similar comparison may be made with regard to Go-to-Church Sunday in the two communities. This was, of course, an opportunity not only to nourish a sense of unity among the churches but also to provide an occasion for a show of popular support for the churches. In Oak Park there was no indication that Go-to-Church Sunday was a national movement. It was actively and vigorously promoted by the local leadership as a demonstration of what kind of community Oak Park was. By contrast it was merely noted in Evanston that many of the churches would be participating, as would churches throughout the nation. No public appeals were made by either pastors or laymen, perhaps because no group existed that was in a position to plan a coordinated campaign. As a result, Go-to-Church Sunday at least had the appearance of being the work of only individual churches.[47] Afterward it was reported that many of the churches were filled to overflowing since specific invitations had been extended to members and friends of the church, but there was no listing of the churches involved nor of specific figures.

Apart from the Men and Religion Movement and Go-to-Church Sunday even feeble attempts at communitywide revivals or religious activities seem to have been lacking. Efforts to awaken faith and renew support for the church were not unknown, but they were either the work of a single church or, on occasion, of several churches with some natural connection. In 1898 the Swedish Methodist and Norwegian-Danish Methodist churches combined for a revival. The call concluded, "All Scandinavians are heartily invited."[48] In 1904 Harry F. Ward, then of Chicago, later of Oak Park, ran a two-week revival campaign for the men of Northwestern University.[49] In 1908 the five Methodist churches combined for two weeks of revival meetings. Perhaps because a campaign of even this magnitude was unusual, it temporarily spawned a sense of extravagant optimism. "The universal feeling is that Evanston is on the eve of a great spiritual awakening through which the whole community will be uplifted."[50] And in 1916 B. Fay Mills was engaged by the Christian, Methodist, and Presbyterian churches of South Evanston to conduct a series of revival meetings. It was described as "a community campaign for the better life, and its object will be the promotion of the higher interest of all residents of the vicinity."[51]

In addition to Mills, two other nationally known evangelists were heard in Evanston during this period, but it was not entirely clear whether their appearances were to be considered in any sense revivalistic. Dwight Moody's first appearance in Evanston was in 1893, when he spoke at a special union prayer meeting at First Methodist. On that occasion the four "first churches" called off their regular Wednesday evening worship and joined to hear Moody speak on the activities he had planned to coincide with the World's Fair in Chicago.[52] Moody made two other appearances in Evanston before he died. One was a single address delivered at First Presbyterian on his prison work. The other was a series of meetings held again at First Methodist. These meetings were advertised as "evangelistic meetings," but in the reports of the sessions it was admitted that Moody himself preferred to call them revivals, saying that Evanston was too conservative and needed a revival.[53]

Gypsy Smith was the other major revivalist to speak in Evanston. In 1909 he came to Chicago to lead a crusade against the vice district in Chicago and was invited to speak for three successive nights at First Presbyterian in Evanston. These were, apparently, not intended as merely informational talks about the work in Chicago. The accounts commented favorably on Smith's style of evangelism. He was "mild of manner and voice," and instead of attempting to build a frenzy of enthusiasm, Smith took a calm and reflective approach as he prepared to ask people to come forward at the end of the evening: "Brethren, be quiet. All is peaceful and still here. Think. Think. Think." When the call was made, however, few people in the audience responded, perhaps indicating that many had come to hear about revival more than they had come prepared to be revived themselves.[54] It may also be noted that although B. Fay Mills was attempting to return to the field of evangelism when he was called to South Evanston in 1915, his days as a major revivalist were over. He had come to Evanston before, in 1911, to lecture for a week at First Congregational. At that time he was described as "an evangelist of modern religious thought, along the lines of recent discoveries of science."[55] By 1915 he had returned to the Presbyterian church but he had also renounced what he considered to be the excessive optimism of his social gospel days. He was a respected figure in Evanston, no doubt for many of the same reasons he was in Oak Park. And yet the choice of Mills to lead a revival may have also reflected a changing mood in Evanston that was analogous to the change Mills himself had undergone.[56]

The increasingly citylike character of Evanston was thus reflected in some important ways in the life of the churches. There was significant diversity among the churches. If this did not necessarily indicate that they were divided in spirit, efforts to embody a unified spirit were nonetheless limited, partial, and often unsuccessful. Revivals did not become, as they did on several occasions in Oak Park, an occasion for renewing the specific spirit and ideals of the local community as a whole. They were either confined to a certain segment of the community or they were seen as part of a metropolitan or national effort as was the case with Dwight Moody, Gypsy Smith, the Men and Religion Movement, and Go-to-Church Sunday. Even those viewing Evanston's situation through the eyes of the church, therefore, might have been encouraged to think of Evanston more and more as a city. It may be mere speculation to think that B. Fay Mills was chosen to lead a revival in South Evanston partly because his mood of increased pessimism paralleled somewhat the mood of the ministers and churches who engaged him. There

192

were, however, more direct indications that a certain sense of powerlessness and fatalism on the part of church leaders accompanied the changes in both secular and religious life that were making Evanston appear more like a typical city and less like the kind of community it had once promised to be.

In 1904 the *Evanston Index* each week carried excerpts from several of the sermons that had been delivered the previous Sunday.[57] While these sermons naturally treated a broad range of subjects and reflected a variety of moods, the theme of failure appeared often enough to make it notable in a community such as Evanston and at a time when hopes for reform and renewal were generally high. In a sermon for the new year Timothy Frost of First Methodist said that prospects were not necessarily bright and that "everything but the kingdom may fail."[58] A week later Dr. Loba of First Congregational said that he foresaw the failure of many reforms including temperance because "people won't get together."[59] In a sermon entitled "The Game of Life," Rev. John Boyd of First Presbyterian said that people must consider the fundamental fact of life to be failure and that Christ must be looked to as the only answer to this condition.[60] Rev. B. A. Greene of First Baptist, in a sermon called "Things That Last," claimed that the Bible and American ideals were among the lasting truths that people should set their sights on, but that the rest of contemporary experience was change and decay.[61] George Craig Stewart of St. Luke's Episcopal said that there was no alternative but to have a "sense of insufficiency" for the tasks that Christians faced in the modern age.[62]

It is admittedly somewhat difficult to judge the significance of such statements or to say with any degree of certainty how deep any feelings of "insufficiency," failure, or frustration ran. In being acutely sensitive to the moral and spiritual dangers contained in their environment, Evanston clergy were not unlike their Oak Park counterparts. The mere sounding of alarms did not in itself constitute evidence that the demoralizing aspects of modern, urban life had taken a heavy toll among Evanston's religious leaders. The situation in Evanston, however, was such that one might expect to discover signs of unease among the clergy with regard to their role and the role of the churches in the community of Evanston. If the clergy were not quite so confident of their ability to tap a latent reservoir of belief and commitment as they might have been; if they were less certain that they were being looked to for leadership in recalling the community to its essential nature and purpose; and, if they were beginning to feel somewhat isolated in their desire to be both modern and faithful, the evidence for the existence of such feelings was not likely to be very often of a dramatic nature. Thus differences in the tone of language and the vocabulary employed cannot be neglected, even if they are not in itself conclusive.

The clergy in 1904 showed that they were quite aware of the subtlety with which faith and morality might be eroded.

> Sin is very patient when the forces of good are strong. Yet it lies crouching at the door waiting for a moral let-up. It is in these times of relaxation, of ungirdedness, that the evil we detest dresses itself in new garments, presents itself with a novel fascination, and leads us to another slaughter.[63]

This too was a recurring theme in the sermons that appeared in the press. It was said that anyone who indulges himself in a little "frisky liberty" so as not to appear overly pious is wrong. People whose moral sensibilities have become so dulled that they find themselves saying with frequency that they see no harm in something may be gaining the world and losing their souls.[64] Such statements were a clear indication of one important way the agenda of the clergy differed from that of the *Index*. While the *Index* devoted itself to making sure that positive signs of urban growth and vitality did not go unnoticed, the clergy were concerned instead with making sure that signs of danger did not go unnoticed, as they so easily could.

Not unexpectedly, the issues that concerned the clergy in Evanston were quite similar to those that received attention in Oak Park. Modern enthusiasms were troubling both for their inherent dangers and because of their tendency to detract from the spiritual life and the support of the church. Perhaps because of Northwestern University and its athletic teams, sports seemed to play a relatively larger role in Evanston than it did in Oak Park. Rev. Arthur Little of St. Mark's Episcopal Church called athletics and body culture a "demonic craze" that consumed the spirit and kept people from attending to their religious duties.[65] Rev. Greene of First Baptist sadly noticed that the church and religion seemed no longer capable of arousing the excitement, enthusiasm, or emotion that either football or politics produced.[66] Novelists such as Tolstoy, Zola, and Goethe might be condemned from the pulpit,[67] and even if the estimates of such people might vary among the clergy, a thirst for the modern in literature was seen as drawing people away from the reading of the Bible.[68] Society life, especially in its excesses, was described as "wicked and vicious" and condemned for its "ostentatious display of wealth."[69] On several occasions churches attempted to organize anticigarette campaigns. Lucy Page Gaston, the most renowned of the campaigners against tobacco use, was a popular and frequent speaker. On one occasion the principal of the high school, a leading layman at First Congregational, attributed the failure of the high school football team to cigarettes.[70] Temperance as both a personal and social issue was frequently discussed and a temperance pledge was a part of church covenants. Immoral amusements, gambling, certain kinds of dancing, and immodesty in dress were also among the dangers that threatened to corrupt the soul of the individual and the moral fiber of the society.

The broad social and economic problems of the society were also defined and brought before the churches in much the same way they were in Oak Park. A sermon by Rev. O. F. Jordan (Evanston Christian Church) contained a litany of many of the troubling aspects of the modern, urban age. Jordan began by stating his belief that the relation of the sexes (sexual morality, divorce, prostitution) was the most important problem confronted by the society as a whole. He went on, however, to list what he believed to be the contributing causes of the problem. They included the nature of cities, and specifically slums, poverty, and a lack of civic pride; the fact that modern life had made native-born Americans too nervous because of overwork and overplay (note being taken that the divorce rate was higher among native Americans than among immigrants); the "vicious individualism" encouraged by modern novels and the theater (in this case Hardy and Ibsen were singled out); socialism; the saloon; and an inefficient and corrupt legal system.[71] In one sermon Jordan had summarized many of the subjects that regularly found a place in the sermons of the Evanston clergy.

One of the few issues that Jordan did not address directly was the question of labor, large corporations, and strikes. Typical of the statements that might be made were two sermons inspired by a Chicago teamsters strike in 1905. At First Presbyterian Church the pastor, John Boyd, said:

> To say that a corporation has no soul is to speak sober truth. . . . A man as a member of a corporation will become a partner to enterprises which, in his private life, he would neither sanction nor tolerate. . . . Rockefeller is not peculiar in this, just conspicuous.[72]

On the other hand, Boyd went on to say, labor unions too were soulless and contributed to the root problem, which was human covetousness and greed. At First Congregational Church J. F. Loba took a slightly different approach. He reminded his listeners that discord was not necessarily bad and that often it produced creativity. Yet, he admitted, there seemed to be little creativity in the present situation. Socialism had proved unworkable, and anarchy was unthinkable. The only thing for sincere Christians to do was "to preach patiently the gospel of Jesus Christ and work for social regeneration through individual regeneration."[73] In most sermons dealing with this subject sympathy was expressed for the plight of the laborers, Christ and the church were proclaimed as the true friends of labor, and hope was held out that one day labor and management would be united in a Christian spirit. For the present, however, class-consciousness and class warfare were conceded to have the upper hand.

Just as important as the subject matter of sermons were the speakers heard and the subjects discussed at women's societies, men's clubs, adult Sunday school classes, and so forth. In this regard too Evanston church life was quite similar to church life in Oak Park. Here the concerns that appeared in sermons could be addressed regularly, directly, and at some length. Speakers with a firsthand knowledge of urban life offered their insights on conditions in factories, tenements, prisons, asylums, brothels, and saloons. The workings of the political and judicial systems were explored. The work of settlement houses, rescue missions, and institutional churches was lifted up. The perils of city life were described from many angles and a wide variety of reforms were advocated. In their general value system, the standards of personal morality and integrity espoused, and in the perspective from which they viewed the larger society, the churches of Evanston and Oak Park were quite similar. People from the two communities would have felt at home in one another's churches.

In Evanston, however, there was something missing. There was nothing in Evanston comparable to what the YMCA campaign had been in Oak Park, namely an opportunity for the churches to demonstrate their willingness and ability to provide leadership for the community as a whole and for there to be a general reaffirmation of the belief that a united Christian spirit prevailed not only among the churches but throughout the community. Ministers in Evanston did not appear as speakers before secular groups nearly to the same degree as they did in Oak Park. The appropriateness of having clergy address business organizations or of the Oak Park Club devoting an evening to a discussion of "Clubs and the Clergy" or other religious and moral issues seemed unquestioned in Oak Park. It did not seem so in Evanston. Even church organizations did not often seem inclined to address directly and specifically the needs and problems of the Evanston community.

These were perhaps signs that specialization was becoming not only a social reality made necessary by a larger and more complex community but also a state of mind that gradually circumscribed what were thought of as proper spheres of activity and influence and more narrowly defined the way people conceived of their own role and the role of others within the total community. Ministers might find themselves attacked, for instance, for venturing into matters that did not properly concern them.[74] When William McElveen, pastor of First Congregational, ran for a position on the school board and was elected on what was primarily an antifraternity platform, it was perhaps an indication that he felt his role as a minister did not provide him with a sufficient voice in the affairs with which he was concerned. In order to exert his leadership, he had to assume an additional office. Furthermore, the social life no longer revolved around the church. Perhaps out of frustration at the apparent inability of the church to fulfill this social function, Rev. Greene of First Baptist suggested that the church needed dens and sitting rooms that could provide an atmosphere for men to gather, thus offering an alternative to the home and the clubs.[75] The context of the remarks did not make it appear as though the suggestion was made tongue in cheek. By 1914 churches had been officially supplanted as social centers, for in that year Evanston became a part of what was called in the press the "social center movement." Public schools were designated as social centers for the community. They were open for various types of meetings, ran community programs, and had paid staff including social workers to administer the activities.[76] In addition to these examples, the diminished sphere of the churches' influence may be illustrated by reference to the problem of theater and especially motion pictures.

The first theater in Evanston opened in 1911 with the enthusiastic support of the press and the assurance that it would provide only the highest quality of entertainment and that it would cooperate with community groups to ensure that the performances were deemed acceptable. The Evanston Theater appeared to have some trouble "finding itself," however. It presented variously motion pictures, live "entertainments" in the form of variety acts and vaudeville, and only once in a while anything that might be called "legitimate theater." A few months after it opened, the theater agreed to cooperate with the Evanston Drama Club in an effort to establish a format that emphasized dramatic productions instead of "entertainments."[77]

For several years the effort was made with varying degrees of success. When it proved impossible to attract traveling companies on a regular basis, a stock company was formed in Evanston. By the beginning of 1914, however, the situation appeared desperate and the theater warned the community that it would have to return to vaudeville if its productions were not better attended.[78] At the same time, however, motion pictures were becoming established as the major form of theatrical entertainment in Evanston as elsewhere, and eventually the Evanston Theater too turned to the movies.

By 1915 there were five motion-picture houses in Evanston. Although it was hardly necessary, the *News-Index* was again at pains to call attention to this addition to the life of Evanston and to announce the futility of trying to prevent motion pictures from having the same impact in Evanston that they were having throughout the nation. At the same time people were asked to be discriminating in their judgments.

> The last doubt of the hold of the "movies" on popular fancy and habit is removed. There is no longer the question of whether we shall or shall not have the influence of motion pictures in the lives of our young people. The fact is established. It remains only for thoughtful citizens to do what may be done to make the new force a harmless amusement . . . to discourage by lack of patronage the demoralizing film.[79]

Not everyone was so optimistic, however, that the movies could be made into a harmless amusement merely by the personal decisions of individuals. Censorship became a public issue. The city council vacillated somewhat on the matter. It first established a board of censors for Evanston but without very definite standards. It then decided that it would be more convenient and efficient just to rely on the Chicago censors to make judgments for Evanston as to what films should be prohibited or what scenes should be excluded from movies. Finally, toward the end of the year, the council reversed itself again and established a board of censors with clearer guidelines and more authority. As this kind of debate proceeded the *Evanston News-Index* editorials shifted their emphasis. Instead of encouraging individuals to be on their guard and to act as their own censors, the *News-Index* adopted a position of staunch opposition to any form of official censorship. The efforts of the paper no longer seemed devoted to maintaining the moral standards of the community, albeit informally. Censorship, not demoralizing films, had become the enemy.[80]

There thus appeared to be a three-way contest among the leadership in Evanston over the question of censorship. Some believed Evanston's standards need be no different from those of Chicago. The major reason the *News-Index* advanced for its opposition to any form of censorship was that motion pictures were a business to be treated like any other enterprise. If the product was bad, people should not buy it. In neither of these positions was there any apparent belief expressed that Evanston had its own special set of community standards that needed to be defended. The only organized expression of this viewpoint seemed to come from the Evanston Women's Club. Although their suggestions were eventually to be written into the city ordinance, this happened without the activity of any coalition of churches and social and civic organizations such as that which had been formed in Oak Park. Both the churches and the theater owners indeed maintained a rather low profile throughout the debate.

While the question of censorship was being debated in the public area and being discussed in some church settings, a few churches began to show movies themselves. As early as the beginning of 1912 the Evanston Christian Church advertised a program of travelogues saying, "It is the purpose of the church to serve the social and educational needs of the community occasionally with such an evening."[81] Even if there could be no question as to the moral effects of the films shown, this at least gave a different look to the church. Instead of trying to control the nature of the films shown in Evanston, the church seemed to be entering into competition with the theater owners. The slight tendency in this direction went largely unnoticed, however, until 1915, when First Congregational Church introduced motion pictures into its Sunday evening worship. The films, it was announced, were to be of an "inspirational character" and would include biblical dramas, but they were to be feature films of the sort shown in theaters and not specifically educational or documentary in nature.[82] This set the stage for an ironic turn of events. In November of 1915, shortly after the new censorship law had gone into effect, the pastor was forced to announce to his congregation that the movie he had planned to show could not be shown because it had not been viewed and approved by the Evanston censors. He criticized the censorship law for being impractical, thus temporarily allying himself with the theater owners who had experienced the same difficulty on several occasions.[83] Soon thereafter movies ceased to be a part of Sunday evening worship at First Congregational.

The episode at First Congregational was notable in several ways. It demonstrated that the passing of the most recent ordinance had not satisfactorily resolved the problem of movie censorship. It revealed a somewhat distant relationship between the church and the public body, which in this case was treating the church no differently from a commercial enterprise. This was also the only time that either the church or the clergy was visible as part of the public debate over censorship. The story of the motion-picture problem in Evanston provides another example where, in retrospect, the leadership of churches can be seen to be noticeably lacking. By comparison to Oak Park, the signs that religion and the churches were still held to be the center and foundation of community life in Evanston were fewer, less convincing, and sometimes seemed almost absent. The "missing elements"—the relative absence of manifestations of widespread unity among the churches, of positive cooperation between the churches and other leadership groups, of coordinated efforts to reawaken united community support for the churches, and of a high degree of visibility of churches and their ministers in the public arena—all may suggest that the churches of Evanston had begun to act as though they felt themselves to be churches of the metropolis rather than guardians of and spokesmen for a religious, communal ideal. This impression does not rest solely upon negative evidence, however. There were a number of activities and events in Evanston that did not appear in Oak Park that would tend to confirm the idea that Evanston churches felt themselves, to some degree at least, to be in an urban environment and were patterning their behavior accordingly.

Both Evanston and Oak Park churches showed an interest in and provided financial support for settlements and institutional churches in Chicago. Jane Addams of Hull House and Graham Taylor of Chicago Commons were frequent and popular speakers, and they were only the best known of many who spoke of such work in the inner city. The Northwestern University Settlement, under the direction of Raymond Robins, provided an opportunity for church members as well as students and faculty of Northwestern to observe at firsthand and participate in the work of settlements. Individual churches had direct relationships to various institutional churches in Chicago. Both in Evanston and Oak Park churches were the backbone of support for summer camping programs provided for children of the inner city. In Evanston, however, activity of this sort was not directed exclusively toward Chicago. Both the settlement idea and the institutional church idea were experimented with as methods that might be appropriate to the city of Evanston as well.

The first effort in this direction came quite early in the period, on the heels of the untimely death of Rev. H. A. Delano, who had been the pastor of First Baptist Church. Delano had just accepted a call to an institutional church in Chicago when he became a victim of typhoid fever. It was said that the belief in the importance of such work and a personal desire to be a part of it had been growing in Delano for some time. To what extent plans may have already been made for a settlement in Evanston prior to Delano's death, and to what extent Delano may have been involved in such planning, is unclear.

But in any case a few months after Delano's death ceremonies were held to celebrate the opening of a settlement house in Evanston. It was called the Delano settlement, and the opening ceremonies were dedicated to his memory.[84]

The program of the settlement included a Sunday school, recreation and other activities for children, as well as lectures, classes, and social activities for adults. It appeared to be modeled partly after the settlement house and partly after the institutional church, and it was successful enough to be able to continue throughout the period prior to World War I and beyond. On the other hand, it was perhaps not conclusively demonstrated that settlements either were needed or would be met with great enthusiasm by those they were intended to serve.[85] There were hints that the experiment was something of a struggle. Frequent changes in the program suggested that there was some searching going on for the kinds of offerings that would attract an eager clientele. In addition, sponsorship of the program and direction passed from the hands of First Baptist to the Women's Christian Temperance Union. There were no other efforts to establish settlement houses in Evanston.

There was, however, a self-conscious effort to establish an institutional church. In 1909 the Evanston Christian Church decided to change its location. As plans for the new building were made, it was announced that the first thing to be constructed would be an "institutional church," where such things as vocational training could take place.[86] The sanctuary would follow. (It will be remembered that it was the Evanston Christian Church that undertook to provide motion-picture entertainments for the community some three years later.) Again detailed reports of these efforts were not forthcoming. Yet the mere fact that a church was thinking in this language revealed an understanding of the church's task in relation to the community that was by and large foreign to Oak Park during the same period. If it was also perhaps foreign to many of the churches in Evanston, it was nevertheless not to be discounted as a sign of the church attempting to become adapted to an increasingly urban environment.

More conspicuous than either the settlement house or the institutional church in Evanston were the Salvation Army and its offshoot, the Volunteers of America. The army was by nature conspicuous. By the time it made its appearance in Evanston, it was well known for its sensational style as well as for its work in the slum areas of large cities. When members of the Salvation Army began to beat their drums on Evanston streets and hold outdoor services, protests were raised and the city government intervened. The army was accused of disturbing the peace, attracting disorderly crowds, and being detrimental to business. In its defense the army stated that it was needed in Evanston because half of the people there were not church people.[87] Thus insult was added to injury. Indeed, the mere presence of the army in Evanston was no doubt considered an insult to the community. It placed Evanston in a category with the very worst sections of large cities, where the Salvation Army was known to have concentrated its efforts. For a group of people who were recognized for their work among paupers, drunkards, and prostitutes to single out Evanston as a city that needed their services was an insult of the highest order. The noise and eccentricity of the army may have merely provided a convenient way to rid the community of such an embarrassment.

The Volunteers of America were a slightly different matter. The volunteers had come into being when Ballington Booth, a son of Salvation Army founder William Booth, refused to obey orders to return to England and, at the beginning of 1896, split from the parent organization. He and his wife Maud then formed the Volunteers of America, which was intended to be similar to the army yet distinguished from it by being completely American in character, more closely related to established churches, and concerned with work among the respectable poor and middle class. Soon after the volunteers were formed, Ballington Booth spoke to an overflow audience at First Methodist.[88] The master of ceremonies on this occasion was Mayor Dyche, who less than a year later as head of government was to be engaged in the confrontation with the Salvation Army. A few years later Maud Booth made an equally successful appearance at First Presbyterian. On both occasions, however, the purpose was only to speak of the work that was being carried on elsewhere and to appeal for support for such work.

By 1904, however, the Volunteers of America were at work in Evanston.[89] Rev. Boyd of First Presbyterian announced in the spring of that year that there was a movement underway among the "legitimate" churches in Evanston to hold street meetings during the summer months in competition with the volunteers.[90] Nothing more was heard from this movement, but the announcement at least served notice that the Volunteers of America were not entirely free from the stigma attached to the Salvation Army. This time, though, there was no confrontation with the authorities, and the volunteers carried on with their work. The following September a huge tent was set up in South Evanston. It was described as a "beer garden without the beer," and its purpose was said to be to provide an alternative to the saloon. It was to serve as a place to socialize, to eat and drink, and to be entertained. In addition, it was to provide a means of evangelism. The social functions would take place in an explicitly Christian atmosphere. People would not only have the benefit of wholesome surroundings but would also hear the gospel proclaimed and it was hoped be brought into contact with the church.[91]

The beer garden lasted for only a season, but it was not the only effort made by the volunteers. Church members in Evanston were enlisted to aid in a program of visitation and relief among what were termed a "large number" of destitute families in the community. Evanston, it was said, was poorly equipped to deal with this problem, and thus the Volunteers of America felt called to come to the aid of the city's poor. After being initiated into such activity, a church member who wished to remain anonymous was quoted as saying: "I would never believe that so much suffering could exist in a town where there is apparently such abundance."[92] In both spectacular and quiet ways the Volunteers of America called attention to needs that it could not have been easy for many people to admit were present in Evanston. Along with the tentative explorations into the field of settlements and institutional churches, the volunteers bore witness to the notion that Evanston was not a classless society. The outlook and methods of social Christianity were gaining a foothold in Evanston, even if they were quite far from becoming the dominant mode of church life and thought. For many, no doubt, social Christianity was still something to be supported from a distance. But there were some who believed that social Christianity needed to be practiced in Evanston.

Another person who believed that the methods and concerns of social Christianity could and should be applied in Evanston was Rev. Charles Stelzle. Stelzle had grown up on the East Side in New York and had labored as a machinist for eight years before attending Moody Bible Institute and being ordained in the Presbyterian church. In 1903 he was hired to lead the newly formed Department of Church and Labor of the Presbyterian Church in the United States. From this position he gradually came to be known throughout the country as one of the chief proponents of the church taking an active interest in the problems of labor. He was active in the formation of the Federal Council of Churches and the formation of its social program, and he headed the social service division of the Men and Religion Forward Movement. In addition to being an activist within the church, he became widely known as an author and a lecturer, his best known book being *Christianity's Storm Center* (1907), in which he criticized Protestant churches for retreating from the people and problems of the city.

203

Stelzle was a resident of Evanston during the time that he was beginning his work with the Department of Church and Labor. He proposed a plan that eventually became adopted in some 125 cities across the nation.[93] It called for ministers to sit on the Central Labor Council in Evanston and for labor to send representatives to ministers' groups. In this way the aims of the church could be better communicated to the labor unions, and the problems of labor and the work of unions could be interpreted to Christian congregations. Furthermore, it might place at least some of the clergy in a position where they might effectively act as arbitrators and intermediaries in labor disputes.[94] When Stelzle proposed this plan for Evanston, it was not yet in operation in too many other cities, and in this sense it may have been premature in Evanston. It is not known how the clergy would have responded, for the Central Labor Council rejected the idea, and Stelzle withdrew his proposal.[95]

Perhaps it was only coincidence, but a week after the Central Labor Council turned down Stelzle's overture, the church and labor unions were again together in the news, this time in open conflict. The center of the controversy was John Boyd, pastor of First Presbyterian Church, who had been accused of being "an enemy to the Negroes."[96] These accusations were apparently proffered seriously and taken seriously, for on April 17 the minister's morning sermon was devoted to answering these charges. A large audience of both blacks and whites was on hand to hear what Boyd had to say.

In his sermon Boyd made no apologies. Instead of allowing himself to be placed on the defensive, he made a counterattack. He compared the racial situation in the South and in the North. (Boyd was the only minister of a central church to have been born and raised in the South.) In the South, he said, blacks did not socialize with whites, but they were permitted to work at the same jobs as whites, while in the North it was the reverse. He then presented a detailed argument aimed at demonstrating that the real enemy to black people was the labor union. Blacks, he believed, did not want or need social equality or recognition. What they needed was a chance to earn a decent living, and it was this that was being denied them by the discriminatory policies of labor unions.[97]

Boyd's sermon brought forth an immediate response from the Central Labor Council in Evanston. In a statement issued to the press, the council vigorously and categorically denied that there was racial discrimination in the unions of Evanston, and it denounced Boyd personally for making what were considered irresponsible statements.[98] Having now aroused the wrath of the labor unions as well as blacks, Boyd issued a public statement of his own that was conciliatory in nature and succeeded in quieting the voices of discord. While maintaining that he had ample facts and figures to show that there was discrimination in labor unions in the North, Boyd stated that he had not intended to make direct accusations about the situation in Evanston. He was gratified to hear that the situation that so clearly prevailed elsewhere did not prevail in Evanston. He concluded by saying, "I have never asked for the colored man anything but a chance to work at skilled remunerative labor. The leaders of labor in our community have said that it shall be granted. I am satisfied. Now, colored friends, go in and on and up."[99] Thus Boyd managed to achieve a truce with the labor unions and at the same time to reaffirm his sympathy with the cause of economic justice for blacks.

The incident involving Rev. Boyd, the labor unions, and the problems of racial discrimination was not especially notable in focusing public attention on racial problems. That a consciousness of race could threaten to divide the community was implicitly affirmed on other occasions. It was not a taboo subject in the press, even if the solution of racial problems did not yet occupy a prominent place among the acknowledged priorities of the community. The influence of the "colored vote" was referred to on more than one occasion in local elections. The alderman of the fourth ward, William Norkett, was quoted as saying that his ward was "so tough that colored people cannot live in it."[100] There were conflicts reported such as that over a billiard hall that would not admit blacks on the grounds that it would be offensive to the white clientele. It was said that the hall was "being visited daily by indignant colored citizens."[101] There were occasional public discussions carried on in the press, as for instance when a reader wrote to complain that blacks were intermixed with white students in a school musical performance. This elicited letters from both white and black readers that expressed outrage at such prejudice.[102] It was even noted at one point that there was a mysterious plan afoot to create a separate "colored town" just west of Evanston. The rumor of both white and black support for this "plan" was sufficiently widespread that Second Baptist Church felt called upon to disavow any connection with such ideas.[103] To be sure, the case of Rev. Boyd was a further example of the fact that racial divisions, like class divisions, had to be confronted in Evanston just as they did in other urban areas. It was also, however, an illustration of how the church might find itself a beleaguered party to conflicts rather than a uniting force within the community.

Earlier Boyd had been directly involved in another situation where overt conflict broke out between segments of Evanston's leadership. In 1902 he had presided at a temperance rally at First Presbyterian. In itself this was hardly an unusual event. Church meetings for the purpose of gaining support for temperance work both in Evanston and elsewhere were frequent occurrences throughout the period. On this occasion, however, Boyd's remarks transgressed the usual boundaries of such discussions. He claimed that the liquor situation in Evanston had become serious in the extreme. In support of this he cited a Chicago brewer who had told him that the people of Evanston were his best customers. The blame for this, he said, should not be placed exclusively on the shoulders of individual beer drinkers. Equally culpable, if not more so, were the city authorities and the officials of Northwestern University who were thoroughly negligent in enforcing the city ordinances and the four-mile provision of the university's charter. He condemned the casual attitude toward enforcement and asked that the public insist that the authorities do a better job on this matter.[104]

It was by no means unheard of for city officials to come under attack for inadequate enforcement. Frustration over the difficulty of controlling the sale of alcohol made charges against incumbents on the liquor question a regular part of political campaigns throughout the period. Politics was one thing, but for a minister to direct his criticism at city and university officials instead of concentrating on the practice of temperance and opposition to liquor interests perhaps connoted an attitude that was fundamentally unsympathetic to the community of Evanston and its secular leadership. One of Boyd's authorities, after all, was none other than a man who was admittedly engaged in the liquor business in Evanston. The university and city officials made no response to Boyd's charges. Perhaps it was because they had grown accustomed to hearing them and because Boyd was considered to be relatively lacking in political knowledge and influence compared to others who made such criticisms (dissident aldermen, campaign opponents, for example). In addition, the officials hardly needed to come to their own defense, for the *Index* responded immediately.

> It is a regrettable fact that a coterie of men seem to have determined to scandalize the fair name of this city by spreading the word abroad that it is a community ruled by beer politics and given up to wholesale violations of law. . . . The worst of the whole matter is that the men who deal in these denunciations pose as reformers. . . . It is time that a full stop be called to these declarations which are so perniciously false. . . . No community is more law respecting and self respecting than this, and it is about time that a strenuous halt

is called on these men who so carelessly take the name and reputation of our city and its citizens in vain.[105]

The *Index* did not attack Boyd by name, but it did make clear that its editorial was in reference to the news article in which the meeting was reported and Boyd's remarks quoted. The mention of a "coterie of men," presumably meaning all those who were on the platform at First Presbyterian plus any others they might have represented, poorly concealed the fact that strong language was being directed against a leading clergyman. To make matters worse, the issue involved was one on which the leadership of the community should, by all rights, have been united. Yet in this instance unity gave way to internecine conflict, and it was the newspaper that rose to the defense of the community, while the church seemed to be at odds with the community, albeit in the interest of temperance. Instead of assuming that the community stood united behind the church, the tenor of Boyd's statements had suggested that he felt the church's position in Evanston was similar to what it was in Chicago or other large cities where the church had to fight an uphill battle in an environment hostile to the cause of temperance.[106]

John Boyd was an outspoken man, and he experienced more than his share of controversy. He was not, however, merely an eccentric or a troublemaker. He successfully served at First Presbyterian for twelve years, a longer than average tenure. He often received favorable notices as a pastor and preacher of great ability, and indeed both the positive and negative attention he received was testimony to his stature as a man who could not be ignored. If he stood out somewhat by virtue of his background and personality, this did not make him an anomaly to be discounted in any general description of Evanston's religious leaders. Far from being a misfit, Boyd for many years was a full participant in helping to define the nature of clerical leadership in Evanston. The incidents in which Boyd was involved should not be considered untypical, although some of his actions may have helped to throw into question what the word "typical" might mean when applied to the clergy. In any case, the conflict over the temperance meeting in 1902 was not an accident caused only by the uncircumspect nature of Boyd's personality. The incident had been anticipated three years earlier, when other leading clergy had found themselves in conflict over the issue of temperance.

Only a few months after taking office Mayor Bates tried to enlist the support of the clergy in an attempt to control the liquor traffic in Evanston. He sent out personal invitations to twenty-five ministers to attend a meeting in city hall to discuss how the churches and the city administration might work together to put an end to the guerrilla attacks constantly being made on the city by the liquor interests. When the evening of the meeting came, all of the appropriate city officials were present, but twenty-one of the twenty-five ministers failed to appear, only a few having sent their regrets. (Those who appeared represented Hemenway Methodist, Wheadon Methodist, Emmanuel Lutheran, and St. Mark's Episcopal.) The mayor made no attempt to conceal his anger. He publicly condemned the clergy for being irresponsible and wondered why they had not been able to spare a few hours to discuss a matter about which they professed to be deeply concerned. The *Index* followed up this story by attempting to contact some of the pastors who had not been present at the meeting. The responses were not well calculated to restore the ministers in the mayor's good graces. Most of those contacted said simply that they had been too busy or had been detained by important business at the last minute. One was more direct. J. F. Loba of First Congregational said that he forgot and that "if Mayor Bates were a churchman he would know that Monday is a busy day for a pastor."[107]

Two months later the churches called a meeting of their own. Although city officials were invited to this meeting, it was only in a very limited sense capable of being interpreted as an effort to heal the breach between the city administration and the churches. For one thing, the meeting was specifically described as being for the purpose of supporting the Four Mile League, an independent group, and not the city administration. For another thing, only the five central churches were present, nothing like the twenty-five that the mayor had invited. And perhaps most important, the meeting was held on the terms of the churches. It was they who initiated the meeting, offered the invitations, and moderated the discussion. The place was on home ground for the churches, and the time was of their own choosing.

The symbolism of this affair, coming so soon after the debacle at city hall, was unmistakable, whether or not it was consciously orchestrated. As far as the churches were concerned, fundamental leadership on the issue of temperance was not to come from a secular source and from a mayor who was not himself a churchman. Rather there needed to be a recognition that temperance was a religious concern and that Evanston was a temperance community precisely because of the spirit, values, and beliefs of the evangelical churches. Evanston was not just a temperance community; it was a Christian community. The lack of response to the mayor's meeting and the counter meeting called two months later seemed to be an attempt to remind the administration and the people of Evanston of the proper position of the church in the community.

As if conflicts involving the church on one hand and blacks, labor leaders, the press, and the city administration on the other were not enough, there were also numerous examples of visible conflict within the church. In one instance a church was literally shut down because of conflict. Asbury Avenue Congregational Church was a mission church of First Congregational in the southwest part of Evanston. In March of 1898 the Pastor, R. K. Southgate, resigned amid rumors that his resignation had been "forced" by certain members of the congregation. It was said that he had been to a party where many members of the church were present, that there had been dancing at the party, and that he had then made explicit comments about the party in a sermon, which had caused some members to demand his resignation. These rumors were denied by the man who had hosted the party. There was, he said, no ill feeling toward the pastor.[108]

Whatever may have been the case, Southgate was succeeded by Rev. A. A. Keene, who soon found himself to be the center of a much more bitter controversy. Before the year was out Keene was asked to resign. The reasons given were that his preaching was "pessimistic," that the Sunday school attendance had dropped from 160 to 60 under his leadership, and that he had created a sensation by condemning the Spanish-American War at the south side union Thanksgiving services. When asked to resign, however, Keene refused, and the issue was put to a congregational meeting. Twenty-six members voted to support the pastor, twenty-one voted against him, and five abstained. When the vote was announced, half the members resigned, at which point the remaining half refused to grant letters of transfer unless the yearly pledges were paid in full.[109] After some efforts at mediation failed, First Congregational resumed control of the building, withdrew its financial support, and put a lock on the building to keep even the remaining members from carrying on.[110]

Asbury Avenue was not alone in being unable to keep its quarrels with clergy out of the public limelight. Emmanuel Methodist made news by seeking the transfer of its new pastor in 1894.[111] A later pastor at the same church took sharp exception to the fact that the *Index* printed remarks he had thought were off the record regarding a threatened choir strike at the church. Thus the matter escalated into a three-way controversy among the minister, the choir, and the press.[112]

The successor to John Boyd at First Presbyterian, Robert Morris, was persuaded of his lack of usefulness after a year and a half and tendered his resignation. He was defended by a leading church member who said:

> The carping and unkindly critics who sigh for a past regime were equally critical of a former pastorate, and should the angel Gabriel descend among us they would lose the music of the silver notes of his trumpet in their displeasure over the shape of his instrument.

The same person suggested that a change was needed not in the pulpit but in the pew, and Morris agreed to stay temporarily.[113]

There were, of course, other kinds of dissension reported besides those where a pastor's job was at stake. An example comes from First Congregational Church where, in 1908, the new minister, William McElveen, was said to have shocked his congregation by proposing the "open church be kept for the maids, particularly the Swedish maids, of the members of the church." Catherine Waugh McCullogh, herself a controversial figure and a woman of national reputation in connection with woman suffrage and other causes, rose immediately to support the idea in the midst of much whispering and negative shaking of heads. It was said that the motion had been put through by "Uncle Joe Cannon methods of wielding the gavel" and that there was much dissatisfaction after the fact, the opposition having been taken off guard and having had little opportunity to express itself. One woman was quoted as saying that this was a utopian idea and that "the maids will not come, and I wouldn't know what to do if they did."[114]

In addition to such intrachurch controversy, there were also occasions when an issue arose between churches. This was the case, for instance, in 1909, when Episcopalian ritual was first attacked in a sermon by Rev. Stifler of First Baptist and then defended by several members of the Episcopal church.[115]

It is not very likely that Evanston was much different from Oak Park in conflict and dissension within the church. As the John Farson affair at First Methodist in Oak Park illustrated, Oak Park churches were not immune from internal controversy. Evanston was somewhat different from Oak Park, however, in the extent to which such conflicts were reported in the press and became therefore part of the public record. In itself this was not insignificant, for to have such conflicts reflected back to the church and to the community in this way was, in a sense, to cast them as permanent features of church life instead of treating them as passing matters of little importance compared to the larger goals of the church. There was in Evanston, however, a conflict of a much more dramatic nature that was without parallel in Oak Park. Unlike Oak Park, Evanston did not manage to avoid confrontations over religious modernism, higher criticism, and the question of what constituted an orthodox interpretation of scripture.

Few people, if any, could have been prepared for the sudden need to choose sides over the issues of modernism. In the last years of the nineteenth century the existence of new trends in biblical scholarship was calmly acknowledged. The *Index*, for instance, made a veiled reference to Dwight Moody's criticisms of such scholarship:

> Mr. Moody is one of the mightiest men of the century. Many things which he says—most of his messages indeed, are freighted with a clear sense and practical teachings as to life. But it may be questioned whether some of his utterances relating to the Christian ministry are the wisest which might be spoken. Reference is had to a seeming belittling of intellectuality and ripe scholarship in the pulpit. Brains are as essential in the work of spreading the gospel as they are in any other field.[116]

Rev. William Macafee of First Methodist was a bit more direct in a sermon he delivered based on Matthew 5:17. As Jesus came not to destroy but to fulfill, he said, so should the modern Christian approach the Bible recognizing that new discoveries and new thoughts do not destroy the truths of scripture but instead enlarge and correct human understandings. Modern research and scholarship were to be accepted as long as they attempted to develop and fulfill, not destroy the revelations contained in the Bible. There was no necessity for conflict between the two.[117]

Occasional flirtations with unorthodoxy could be made without apparent repercussion, as when Rev. Waters of Emmanuel Methodist asserted in a Lincoln's Birthday sermon that "God was the Father of Abraham Lincoln as he was of Jesus Christ."[118] And when, in its first issue of 1902, the *Index* printed a front-page review of a new book by Milton Terry of Garrett Biblical Institute in which he described many of the Old Testament stories as legends and specifically said that the story of Jonah and the whale was not historical,[119] there still seemed to be little reason to think that any serious controversy was in the offing. Two weeks later, however, Professor Pearson of the English Literature Department at Northwestern dropped a bombshell, and the air of neutrality was shattered.

The headline on the front page read, "Pearson Says Bible Errs." Six full columns were devoted to a statement that Pearson intended specifically for Evanston and that was printed in both papers at his request. By way of introduction he wrote: "The article which follows is published because self respect and my conception of Christian duty forbid me to keep silence any longer." The substance of the article was not so much a defense of higher criticism as it was a broadside leveled against the church for its lack of integrity and straightforwardness in dealing with the scriptures.

> If theologians wish to regain their lost intellectual leadership, or even to possess an influence on the thoughtful part of the community, co-ordinate with of that of poets, philosophers, and men of science, they must throw aside the dogma of an infallible Bible as completely and frankly as Protestants have thrown aside the dogma of an infallible Pope.

He then went on to detail some of his reasons for saying that the Bible must not be considered infallible. The miracle stories, he said, were particularly incredible to the modern mind. He called many of them childish and crude and made clear that he was referring to the New Testament miracles as well as to those of the Old Testament. He pointed out that many of the miracles Jesus performed were nothing more than imitations or repetitions of similar actions performed by Elijah or Moses. Besides the miracles, he pointed to a number of portions of the Bible that both reason and scholarship had revealed to be legends, myths, or allegories. At the end he returned to his original theme:

> My plea is that the official leaders of the churches, those who have the necessary scholarship and the administrative responsibilities, should unite to change the prevailing policy of silence, inactivity, and obstruction in regard to the results of modern scientific and biblical scholarship into one of sympathy and encouragement for absolute freedom of inquiry and exposition. Present preaching is evasive. Present Sunday school teaching is inadequate and almost farcical.[120]

In the same issue of the newspaper there was also a highly favorable editorial that expressed general agreement with Pearson's views and commended him for his "honesty, courage, learning, reverence and piety." This was, however, the only source of support for Pearson in Evanston. Pearson's pastor, William Macafee, was in a difficult position. The day after the article appeared Macafee said from the pulpit that he had great personal affection and respect for Pearson, and that he knew him as a man of sincerity who had a love for the church. Yet he went on to denounce the views expressed in the article, dissociate himself from any connection with the article or its publication, and to aver that if Pearson were a minister he would unquestionably be tried for heresy and forced to leave the church.[121] This, however, was not sufficient. Letters poured in to Macafee that accused him of being responsible for Pearson's views or at least being tolerant of them. Thus the beleaguered minister felt it necessary to issue a statement to the press and spend the next three sermons defending his own orthodoxy and disclaiming any connection with Pearson's views or any desire to defend him.[122] Though there is no reason to doubt that Macafee still held to the views he had expressed in 1899 with regard to the compatibility of modern scholarship with a belief in the biblical revelation, Pearson had forced the issue in such a way that Macafee could not, in this context, defend such scholarship and indeed was forced to take a stand in opposition to it.

If Rev. Macafee, who was both pastor and friend to Pearson, did not find it possible to support him publicly in any way, it would perhaps be surprising to find other religious leaders who would voluntarily come forth to associate themselves with the professor, and indeed none did. Only a few days after the publication of the article President Little of Garrett Biblical Institute called the student body together so that he might make his position clear to them. He told the students that if miracles are impossible, then the incarnation and resurrection are impossible, and one cannot be a Christian and hold that view. He could therefore have no sympathy for Pearson's views. Of course Pearson's freedom of thought and expression needed to be upheld, but honesty required that if one holds such opinions he leave the church rather than attempt to get those within the church to desert their own most fundamental beliefs.[123]

Like Macafee, however, Little could scarcely avert the fallout resulting from Pearson's actions. Both Northwestern and Garrett came under attack. Although some years later the president of Northwestern was to state that it had always been the policy of the university to hire good teachers, not Methodist teachers,[124] the trustees had let it be known within two weeks that Pearson's resignation would be accepted. Pearson did not aid his cause any when, in the course of stating that he would stand by his earlier statement, he added that he believed in the divinity of Christ "as that of John Wesley, Martin Luther, or any other God-fearing, noble man."[125] The following week the trustees formally asked for Pearson's resignation, and the week after that Pearson did resign both from his teaching position and from his membership at First Methodist. In the meantime, one sermon after another was given in defense of miracles and in opposition to higher criticism. Rev. Reed of St. Paul's English Lutheran Church seemed to speak for many when he claimed that empty churches were due to "those who refused to heed truth, not to preachers who don't preach the results of higher criticism."[126] One of the more moderate statements was from J. F. Loba of First Congregational. His sermon was entitled "Is Christianity a House of Cards?," and in it he admitted that there might be honest disagreements over whether certain passages from scripture might be understood as legend or allegory, but he maintained that this must not distract from belief in the fundamental truths of the Bible. He concluded, "And in spite of all the quibbles of this learned age, I reply, 'I will arise and go to my father's house.' "[127]

With Pearson's resignation the flurry of speeches, sermons, and statements gradually abated. On the heels of Pearson's departure, five clergy did accept an invitation from the *Index* to have their views printed on the question of Jonah, one of the specific issues that had been raised prior to the Pearson affair in connection with Professor Terry's book on the Old Testament. Four of the five respondents, however, expressed an unwillingness to continue the debate on the terms that both Terry and Pearson laid down. Rev. Bristol, the predecessor to Macafee at First Methodist, said that he personally believed the book of Jonah was history, but that people should stop debating such things and concentrate on stopping the liquor traffic. Rev. Boyd of First Presbyterian said that he honestly didn't know whether the story was fact or legend and that he would take his cue from Christ who spoke of Jonah without raising such a question. Father Mooney of St. Mary's Roman Catholic said that the book was true in one sense and not in another while carefully avoiding the use of such terms as legend or allegory. Finally Rev. Brushingham stated simply that this was not an important issue and that the point of the story was the same regardless. Only one of the five, Rev. Waters of Emmanuel Methodist, clearly accepted the issue as a valid one; he aligned himself firmly with the views of Terry.[128] Indications were that on the whole Evanston clergy had no more desire to have the questions of higher criticism become a divisive issue than did the clergy of Oak Park. Yet in Evanston the issue had been forced on them early and from within the community itself. What Pearson referred to as a policy of evasion and silence was itself under attack. The same policy had served the Oak Park clergy rather well; in Evanston it was less successful.

Even as the focus of attention shifted back to other concerns, the effects of the controversy would still be observed. Charles Horswell, a professor of Old

Testament at Garrett, was forced to resign his position because he had come under fire for his teaching.[129] Rev. W. T. Euster of Wheadon Methodist delivered a bitter farewell sermon that attacked both Garrett and the churches of Evanston.

> Evanston is one of the most lovely spots upon the earth. . . . The cream of Methodism comes here to be educated. . . . There is no more important center for the Methodist Episcopal Church than this one. I have observed some things, however, that make me tremble for the great church we all love so much. I am sure that if the present trend continues for five more years we shall not have a Methodist church; it will be unitarian instead. . . . This habit of derogatory criticism of the Bible has spread a spirit of criticism all over the church here.[130]

Euster went on to say that the theater, cards, dancing, and liquor were all widespread practices of students at Garrett as well as of students at the university. After he resigned from Wheadon, he briefly edited a paper critical of Evanston as well as the university community. More than a year later it was necessary for members of First Methodist to deny that factional squabbling over this issue had anything to do with Rev. Macafee's resignation from the church.[131] And consistent with its advocacy of the "new age" in secular matters, the *Index* frequently gave favorable notices to speeches and writings of men such as Milton Terry at Garrett, and Shailer Matthews and Herbert Willet of the University of Chicago who were associated with the higher criticism.

The sight of church people experimenting with the social methods developed by city churches, quarreling with other leaders within the community, and being victimized by the debate over modernism could hardly help but spice church and community life with an urban, cosmopolitan flavor. Always in the background, and sometimes in the foreground, was a social structure that could no longer be thought of as homogeneous. The presence of the university and more or less well-defined sectional, social, and ethnic groups led to an increasing awareness that the social world of Evanston had become fragmented. But in an urban environment the private, inner world of the individual might be fragmented as well. This, at any rate, seems to have been a concern that William P. McElveen brought with him when he came to Evanston as the pastor of First Congregational in 1908.

McElveen had a varied background. He was born and raised in New York City, the son of an eighth-generation minister. As a young man he worked in New York as a newspaper reporter, gaining experiences that were both formative and useful. Only after being a reporter did he decide that his family was to have a ninth-generation minister. He entered Union Seminary, was graduated and ordained, and became the pastor of the newly formed North Congregational Church in Manhattan. Under his leadership the church established itself and prospered, but McElveen also found time to lend his investigative skills to Rev. Charles Parkhurst's anti-Tammany campaign. His friendship with Parkhurst was lasting enough that Parkhurst came to Evanston for McElveen's installation. From North Church McElveen went to New England Congregational Church in Brooklyn, which Edward Beecher, an early advocate of social Christianity, had founded and served. From Brooklyn McElveen moved to Boston, where he succeeded William Barton as pastor of Shawmut Church. Thus when McElveen came to Evanston he was well acquainted with urban church work and reform. Also he had witnessed the annexation of Brooklyn to New York and had once helped to manage one of Gypsy Smith's urban campaigns. He was no stranger to urban problems; indeed, he had spent his career dealing with them.[132]

McElveen's initial actions in Evanston, however, did not reflect the zeal for social reform that one might have expected. Instead they reflected the concerns of a movement that had been developing in Boston just prior to his departure and that was soon to gain national attention. It was called the Emmanuel movement, so named because it had originated at Emmanuel Episcopal Church in Boston.

As an outgrowth of a class on tuberculosis held at the church, the ministers, Elwood Worcester and Samuel McComb, developed what they claimed was a technique for treating many of the health problems they encountered among the people of Boston. By this time, of course, Boston was also the headquarters of Christian Science, but Revs. Worcester and McComb were careful to distinguish their movement from Christian Science. Organic diseases were to be treated only by physicians, and a practitioner of the Emmanuel technique was to accept only those patients who carried a statement from a doctor that their problem was not organic in nature. The aim of the Emmanuel movement was to treat only "functional disorders" through a specifically Christian form of psychotherapy in which the power of suggestion played a prominent role. Still the problems with which the movement dealt covered a broad spectrum, ranging from bad habits, phobias, and fixed ideas to alcoholism, hysteria, melancholia, and neurasthenia. Just as many people thought that Christianity could provide solutions to the social problems of the day, so the leaders of the Emmanuel movement thought that Christianity could heal the psychic wounds of the modern age.[133]

Soon after he took up his work at First Congregational McElveen began a series of Sunday afternoon lectures on "religious therapeutics" that quickly became quite popular and turned into a community event. The subjects of the lectures naturally varied. He spoke of Christian Science, theosophy, faith cure, and other contemporary sects or movements. He presented case studies and the results of research in psychotherapy. He interpreted scripture and spoke of the general value of religion in promoting good health. (One lecture, for instance, was on the therapeutic value of Christmas.) Through all the lectures, though, there was a common theme: Christianity itself was a religion of health and healing. Secular and sectarian approaches could be of some limited value but might also lead to distortions. Thus as a means to good health McElveen encouraged people to deepen their faith and to look within themselves, to explore the inner regions of their personality and beliefs.

By the beginning of 1909 a chapter of the League for Right Living was organized in Evanston. The notice said that the purpose of the League would be "to study and use psycho-therapy" since great interest was being shown in all forms of this phenomenon. The organizing meeting for the League for Right Living was held at First Congregational, chaired by Rev. McElveen, and addressed by Bishop Fallows of the Reformed Episcopal Church, a man prominently identified with the Emmanuel movement.[134]

McElveen was certainly not the only person to imply that Evanston's environment contained dangers to health. Both Oak Park and Evanston believed themselves to be different from Chicago in that they offered their residents healthful surroundings. Yet the *Index* kept careful watch on public health matters, reporting statistics on disease, showing concern of the purity of water, and carrying out a minor campaign to rid the community of flies. For their part, many churches moved away from the common cup at communion on grounds of hygiene. Religious therapeutics added still another dimension to the situation. It was quickly apparent that McElveen had not forsaken his concern with the problems of the modern city. Religious therapeutics was an extension, not a desertion, of such concern. The modern, urban industrial age was thought by many to produce nervousness.[135] The personal interest shown by McElveen in emotional disorders, and the interest he discovered or aroused in others, pointed to an awareness that the city threatened to become not just an outer reality but also an inner reality with destructive consequences not only physically and morally but psychologically

217

as well. The effects of urban life had perhaps penetrated even to the most intimate, deepest levels of the individual in Evanston.

In light of the many different kinds of signs of churches adapting themselves and being adapted to urban life, the decision by First Baptist to run a kindergarten during the hours of worship and adult education might have seemed insignificant. Indeed, it might well have gone unnoticed were it not for the language the church used in announcing the plan. It said, "This plan has been worked out very satisfactorily in Chicago and it has been urged that Evanston, with its growing metropolitan character, should be able to offer just as much." The *News-Index* was quick to pick up on this brief statement and to elaborate its significance.

> It is in the "growing metropolitan character" of Evanston that the Sunday morning kindergarten is to be instituted at First Baptist. . . . Evanston is assuming more and more the metropolitan character. Her people are largely entirely urban in their likes and dislikes. . . . Considering our proximity to Chicago, whose metropolitan character is recognized, we do well to change our habits to accord with metropolitan demands when it is practicable. The possibility of finding urban conditions on the other side of an invisible boundary line imposes upon us a submission to conditions there.[136]

The last sentence was perhaps a bit mysterious, but also suggestive. The boundary line that mattered most in Evanston had to do much more with the imagination than it did with geography. Church leaders, like many others, had begun to perceive that Evanston was a city and that its churches were churches of the city.

"But What Shall Dominate the City?"

At the end of its editorial pointing out the significance of the Sunday morning kindergarten at First Baptist, the *News-Index* unobtrusively and matter-of-factly suggested that perhaps the time had come for Evanston to give up the idea of a rest day Sabbath. This certainly went beyond anything that First Baptist had stated or implied, but the *News-Index* perhaps felt that the church had itself opened the way for such a thought by officially acknowledging, as it were, the "growing metropolitan character" of the community. It was not the first time that the paper had expressed its opinion on the issue by any means. But if the *News-Index* sensed that there were some new developments in the offing with regard to the question of Sabbath observance, it did not have to wait long for its intuition to be borne out. Within a few months the issue was being confronted more directly and publicly than ever before. In the process additional light was shed on the nature of the community and the state of mind of the clergy.

Certain specific concerns with regard to the Sabbath had surfaced sporadically in the years prior to 1915. In 1895, for instance, an ordinance was passed forbidding the operation of barbershops on Sunday. Most of the barbershops, it seems, were accustomed to closing on Sunday and had asked that the custom become a matter of law in order to prevent their competitors from taking advantage of the situation. The minority of barbershop owners who wished to remain open objected to having this law forced on them merely because others had freely chosen to close on Sundays. They also protested vigorously the idea of a law that applied only to barbershops and not to other businesses. The *Index* noted this protest and went on to say, "The preachers hail the law with delight, calling it an entering wedge, looking eventually to the closing of all occupations on Sunday."[137] The language was revealing, for the ministers were described as feeling that it was they, not the enemies of Sabbath observance, who needed the "entering wedge" in the situation. The law did not last, however, and by the time the issue was raised again in 1906 things had changed. Again the barbers approached the city council requesting a Sunday closing law specifically for barbershops. They had managed to obtain an agreement to close from every owner except one. This time the response was different, though. The corporation counsel said that such a law would be unconstitutional. He refused to even draft such a law, and the city council refused to consider the matter.[138]

In the meantime another effort to suspend the operation of business on Sunday had been initiated by the clerks of Evanston stores. They requested that their employers close so that they might have the day off, and the owners in general responded that they would do it if the public would stand for it. Editorializing on the subject, the *Index* said that the public was duty bound to support the clerks' request and noted in passing that there were some who believed that the Fourth Commandment ought to be taken more seriously.[139] There was, however, no attempt to solicit public opinion on the matter until seven years later when the postmaster in Evanston conducted a poll on whether the post office should be closed on Sunday. The response was overwhelmingly in favor of the idea, and the post office was duly closed.[140] Finally, in 1912, the churches entered the picture. It was reported that "interdenominational churches" had united with the Evanston Women's Club to make a formal proposal to the Commercial Association. The proposal was that businesses be closed a half day each week during the summer for the benefit of employees, that stores close every night at 6:00, and that there be no business conducted on Sunday. The Commercial Association was reported to be severely divided over the proposal. The half-holiday during the summer was approved, but the other two ideas were tabled and referred for further study.[141]

The fact that the proposal made to the Commercial Association combined a proposal for Sunday closings with two other ideas aimed at benefiting the employees of the businesses in question gave the appearance that the primary concern of the Women's Club and the churches involved was more with the welfare of working people than with any attempt to reinstate the Sabbath on explicitly religious grounds. This may have been a move strategically calculated to promote Sabbath observance in any way that might gain the widest support and encounter the least resistance. Without speculating on the motives involved in this instance, however, it can be said that prior to 1915 those who may have believed that Evanston's identity and integrity depended on the keeping of a Christian Sabbath did not find their views clearly or strongly articulated in the public arena.

There were some indications that the churches were aware of having to compete with both business and recreational activities for attention. George Craig Stewart of St. Luke's Episcopal Church, for instance, wrote an article for the church newsletter that found its way into the *Index* and thus became available to the general public. It was entitled "God and Golf."

> This is a plea, not for total abstinence from golf, but for temperance. When you neglect God and His church for the game, you are not engaging in innocent recreation; you are guilty of committing sin. Most of our men can play on weekdays. They shall spend Sunday in some other way. . . . If you can't play during the week, the church sets no ban on a game on Sunday—it is the Lord's day and golf can be played to His glory—only remember that she does make it a duty to be present every Sunday at the great act of worship when the holy eucharist is offered.[142]

Although the statement was firm in defending the obligations Christians owed to God and to the church on Sunday, it made no reference to any obligations the people of Evanston might owe to the community with regard to Sabbath observance. In fact a kind of sanction was granted to Sunday golf so long as it did not interfere specifically with worship. Similar in nature was a sermon delivered at First Presbyterian on "Go-to-Church Sunday" in 1914. It was entitled "Puritan Error and Pagan Reaction," and as the title implied, both the rigidity of strict Sabbatarians and the total disregard on display in modern society were held to be wrong. The preacher said that the approach of the church should not be to place restrictions on people but to promote their growth and fulfillment, and that this should apply to the Sabbath as well as anything else. On the other hand he said he was saddened when he saw churches closed on Sunday evenings while other activities were flourishing.[143]

Concern over how the church was affected by relaxed standards of Sabbath observance could only have been heightened when, in 1915, the *News-Index* innocently announced that it had decided to sponsor a twelve-week series of high class musical entertainments at the Evanston Theater on Sunday evenings, members of the Chicago Symphony having been engaged for the first performance. The paper said it had arrived at this plan after making a careful study of social conditions in Evanston and finding that many people, especially young people, were going to Chicago to be entertained on Sunday evenings. It was hoped that by providing these programs in Evanston some of these people could be persuaded to stay in the community where the entertainment would be of higher quality and where the surroundings were less dangerous. Mayor Small, former Mayor Dyche, and several prominent businessmen were quoted in support of the idea.[144]

Not everyone, however, was inclined to see this plan only as an attempt to offer competition to Chicago entertainments. The more cynical view was expressed in a letter to the editor that appeared in the paper two days later.

> I know nothing of your personal or religious opinions, but this action of yours looks very much like a quiet sneer at the church life and action of the city, struggling as some of them are to maintain a Sunday evening service. And would it not occur to you that your proposition has no sympathy with those who have some regard for the sacredness of the Lord's Day? You are doing your best to introduce what most surely will break down the all too feeble safeguards of our sacred day of rest, for of course, if you are permitted to give Sunday performances, soon every theater in town will claim the same right and other things will follow. Some of us have certain rights in this community and have chosen this place to live because of its high religious ideals.[145]

It was perhaps symptomatic that even such a spirited appeal on behalf of the churches and the Sabbath contained a tone of defensiveness, almost of despair.

The churches were struggling; those who had even "some regard for the sacredness of the Lord's Day" were being ignored; the safeguards of the Sabbath were "all too feeble"; and the statement that "some of us have rights in this community" sounded much more like the plea of a besieged minority than a call to rededication from a group that believed itself to represent the essential faith and purpose of the community. The *News-Index* did little to relieve any sense of woundedness. On the contrary, it introduced the letter with an editor's note stating that the letter was an example of intolerance that was no longer appropriate in Evanston. A week later the paper defended its Sunday programs by saying that the intent was to save souls and was thus nothing more than what the churches claimed to be interested in. The *News-Index* portrayed itself as having become the guardian of the community's welfare and ideals while the church, by implication, had failed or abdicated its leadership in this area and was involved only in efforts on its own behalf.[146]

In spite of extensive promotional efforts, the *News-Index* scheme proved to be something less than a smashing success. By the end of the twelve weeks it was admitted that the attendance had been less than anticipated, that a financial loss had been incurred, and that those who did attend were not those whom it had been hoped would be reached. "While it has been our pleasure if not our profit, to afford these twelve evenings of really excellent music, we must admit, and do freely, that as a venture in social work it failed."[147] Scarcely had the *News-Index* laid its plans to rest, however, when the issue of Sabbath observance was raised again in a new way.

It was hardly any secret that Sunday baseball of an organized variety had established itself in Evanston. When the Evanston team met the team from Rogers Park (a Chicago neighborhood just south of Evanston) in the season opener in 1915, there were 2,000 people in attendance. Among them was the newly elected mayor, Harry Pearsons, along with the city treasurer and three aldermen. The mayor was there to participate in opening day ceremonies and throw out the first ball. He was not unmindful of the symbolic significance of the occasion; instead of being quietly tolerated, Sunday baseball for the first time was being given official recognition. In a front-page article under the headline "Mayor Gives Sunday Ball His Sanction," the mayor was quoted as saying:

> Times change, but some of our people do not realize that we are no longer a country village. Rational amusements of this sort keep people out of doubtful places, where they were in the habit of going when nothing better was offered,

and is an excellent thing. There is no more reason why Sunday baseball should be condemned than Sunday golf or Sunday tennis. They are playing tennis now on the Ashland Avenue courts and at the Country Club. Why should not a great number enjoy a game of ball?[148]

On the same Sunday the current events class at First Congregational happened to be discussing the topic of playgrounds and recreation. Word of the mayor's plans had apparently already gotten out, for after some general presentations had been made the discussion turned to the issue of the day, and a heated debate ensued. Some said that Sunday baseball should not be permitted on publicly maintained playgrounds and that in any case the mayor should not be placing his stamp of approval on the practice even if he did not wish to prohibit it. Two aldermen, as well as others, defended the mayor, saying there were worse things than Sunday baseball and that if it were stopped baseball fans might start making citizens arrests of golfers.[149]

A week later it was reported that the theater owners had requested the city council to permit movie theaters to be open on Sundays. When the same issue arose in Oak Park, it had been the theater owners and those who favored Sunday movies who had been forced to plead their case by gathering signatures on petitions. In Evanston it was the religious leadership that at least gave the impression of feeling that its hands needed to be strengthened by offering lists of signatures as evidence. Petitions were circulated, not in front of the theaters, but in the churches. Even this petition drive, however, was not well coordinated. A. B. Dale, director of the YMCA and secretary of the Ministers' Association, said that the Ministers' Association was not responsible for the antimovie campaign and that the matter was "in the hands of the ministers themselves."[150] Nevertheless, the opponents of Sunday movies achieved a victory of sorts, for within a few weeks the theater owners had, without explanation, withdrawn their request. On the other hand, the "victory" might have had something of a hollow ring to it. There had been no real test of the influence of religious leadership or the state of public opinion, no public reaffirmation of the principle of Sabbath observance in the form of either a city council vote or a popular referendum.

Although the threat of Sunday movies had been removed and there seemed to be no possibility of eliminating Sunday baseball, there was no evidence that the question of Sabbath observance had been resolved to anyone's satisfaction, and the discussion continued. Rev. McElveen declared in a sermon that although he was in favor of liberalizing the Sabbath, he was concerned lest it

223

be lost altogether. The Sabbath, he said, had been and continued to be a "pillar of the republic" and could not be deserted. What was needed instead was a New Testament attitude, one that was not legalistic. Specifically this meant that "anything that renews and gives health to the mind, body, or spirit" should be countenanced. That included baseball if played for fun and not profit. But anything that was based on a commercial spirit must continue to be prohibited.[151] Shortly after it printed McElveen's sermon, the *News-Index* took what was, for it, an unusual step and extended an invitation to Evanston's clergy, both in print and by mail, to express their views on the question of Sabbath observance in Evanston.

Seven ministers accepted the invitation and submitted statements for publication. One of them was H. P. Smyth, pastor of St. Mary's Roman Catholic Church. Perhaps out of an awareness that his attitude would be different from the majority of his colleagues, he began by admitting that his first inclination had been to withhold comment and that he wished it understood that he had an "absolute respect" for the conscience of others on this matter. Having determined, however, that it would be more courteous to reply, he would state his opinion frankly:

> In my judgment we are face to face not with what is best but with what is practicable. Sunday perhaps ought to be spent in church—all day. Well, I am altruistic enough to leave the glory of doing that to someone else. It is too much for me. . . . People, and Evanstonians are people, will seek amusement on Sunday afternoons, if not in Evanston, then elsewhere.[152]

Smyth went on to say that he preferred to see people stay in Evanston, that he preferred outdoor sports and recreation as a form of amusement, but that something was certainly needed for bad weather and the winter months. He stopped just short of endorsing Sunday movies and theater, saying that he would graciously leave that question to the mayor and the city council. In the general tone of his remarks, and specifically in leaving the door open for Sunday movies, Smyth did differ, to be sure, from his Protestant colleagues. Yet as the other statements appeared, it could be readily observed that the convictions of the Protestant clergy were also being framed in such a way as to be more in accord with the attitudes and behavior of people who lived in an urban society.

There was undeniably a drift away from the Sabbath, as it had once been understood, in both Evanston and Oak Park. In Evanston, however, the drift was more visible, more organized, and had finally received official sanction from the mayor. To some it appeared that the ministers too were "drifting."

> Ministers of the Gospel, the Christian's Sabbath is in danger, and it is up to you to defend it. . . . What are you ministers and bishops going to do about it? Are you going to fold your hands and take your ease and let your Master's business go to naught?[153]

It was not clear whether the writer of this letter was expressing frustration over what he considered to be a general lack of leadership or whether his statement had been prompted specifically by the nature of the statements presently being made. More than likely it was both.

The six Protestant ministers who responded to the invitation to express their views all, to varying degrees, supported a broader, more modern interpretation of the Sabbath and dissociated themselves from the restrictive attitudes of the past. In so doing they distinguished themselves somewhat from their clerical brethren in Oak Park, who indicated that they wished to preserve the substance of the Sabbath without being heavy-handed, severe, or dictatorial. Evanston ministers took a position that Oak Park ministers by and large would not take. They offered their positive approval of many activities once thought to be detrimental to the Sabbath. Golf, as George Craig Stewart had said, could be played to the glory of God, and so now, most of them seemed to believe, could baseball. Yet all six of the respondents did agree that the Sabbath was in danger, and it was easier for them to state that a line must be drawn, and where they would draw it, than it was actually to prevent the drift from continuing once it had gained momentum. Thus while offering their support for a more liberalized Sabbath, the ministers pleaded to retain some form of Sabbath observance, even if its meaning had admittedly been significantly altered.

A. S. C. Clarke of Second Presbyterian offered as a general principle that Sunday ought not to be a time for "secularizing our minds or lowering our finer natures." Specifically this meant there should be no movies and no drama on Sundays. Such things, he said, "are not in the best interests of our city or its people," but he went on to place the issue in a larger context. He said that neurasthenia (anxiety, nervousness) had become a national disease and that a quiet Sabbath was needed to combat the effects of the modern age. "It may be that our Puritan forbears erred on the side of sobriety, but the pendulum has surely swung to the opposite side of the clock in our day."[154] George

225

Whiteside of United Presbyterian, though expressing disapproval of sports as well as motion pictures and theater, took a position quite similar to Dr. Clarke's.

> So far as the young people of Evanston having a good time on Sunday I can go a long way with you. . . . While there were many good things about the old Puritan Sabbath, at the same time I think there were many things very much overworked. But as I see it the contention is not so much between the Old Puritan Sabbath and our Sabbath, as between our Sabbath and no Sabbath at all.

Like Clarke, Whiteside said that he believed that the health of society depended on preserving the Sabbath and that this should be sufficient grounds for some regulation of Sabbath activities, even though he fully understood that laws could not be enacted from a "religious standpoint." Beyond that he could only "beg for the Sabbath day to be observed in a way conducive to the highest morals and the cultivation of true religion among our people."[155]

Two statements centered, as McElveen's sermon had, on commercialism as the decisive factor. George Craig Stewart repeated that he would favor any kind of wholesome recreation that did not interfere with worship. He added, however, that wholesome recreation did not include anything that involved the forced labor of another or that involved businesses operated for profit. He was thus vigorously opposed, he said, to "professional games, theater, motion pictures, and the like."[156] (No mention was made of businesses of other sorts.) Lloyd Walter of St. Paul's English Lutheran Church dealt exclusively with the question of motion pictures and said that he was firmly opposed to Sunday movies on the grounds that a profit motive was behind the idea. In the course of his argument he said, "I had hoped that the population of this city was of such a character that such a matter could not nor ever would come to an open issue."[157] There were, however, only two of the six statements from Protestant clergy that brought the character of Evanston and its people directly into the center of what was at stake.

Timothy Frost, the pastor of First Methodist, said that recreation, defined as activities that renewed the body and spirit, must be distinguished from mere entertainment and that he could approve of the former but not the latter. He then went on to describe his concern in forms that would have been more familiar to people in Oak Park. Evanston, he said, had been marked from the beginning by a spirit and practice that made it different from other places, and especially different from Chicago. Some of these qualities could be easily specified, but others had become "so fine and elusive as to defy precise definition." It was therefore extremely important to the community not to allow Sunday movies, for

> such an innovation would be a movement toward making Evanston the kind of city Chicago is. . . . And it is at least an open question if it might not be as well for some young people to go to Chicago as for Chicago to be brought to Evanston on Sunday nights.[158]

Orvis Jordan of the Evanston Christian Church was the other minister to take up this theme in a more than passing manner. Jordan addressed the issue of Sabbath observance from three standpoints. The humanitarian question was dealt with simply; there should be no forced labor on Sunday. Second, there was the community standpoint, and here Jordan joined forces with Frost in stating that Evanston still had a distinctive character that must be preserved.

> Believing as I do—and shall continue to believe until there is a referendum to the contrary—that Evanston is true to her past history and ideals, and that people have moved here to get away from the noisy continental Sunday of other sections of Cook County, I resist every innovation that would destroy Evanston's distinctive character.[159]

Both Frost and Jordan reaffirmed their belief in Evanston as a community with a special identity, yet each statement contained a note of awareness that their belief was now open to challenge. Frost had referred to qualities that had become "so fine and elusive as to defy precise definition," while Jordan had implied the shadowy presence of opposing views and contrary evidence by insisting that only a referendum would dissuade him from his faith that the community had not lost touch with its past. The slight edge of defensiveness in Jordan's statement might have slipped by unnoticed, however, had his tone not shifted considerably when he came to considering what he called the "religious aspect."

> The church has been crowded and jostled on every hand in the city life. The Protestant churches have given up their children to the public school. They have given up the young people in large measure to many secular movements through the week that are excellent in character. If the church gives up Sunday what is left? Does not Evanston still care what happens to the churches?

227

It was perhaps fitting that the debate over Sabbath observance should temporarily be brought to an end by the plaintiveness of Jordan's final question: Does not Evanston still care what happens to the churches? It was a question that in a sense had been quietly taking shape in the interstices of daily life for many years, until finally the words could be spoken. It was a question too for which there was and could be no definitive answer. On the one hand, there were still many ways Evanston was manifestly different from Chicago and the least of these was the obvious presence and strength of the Protestant churches. It was by this time well documented that in vast areas of cities throughout the nation the mainline Protestant churches were all but invisible. People had abandoned the churches and the churches had abandoned the city and its people. Such was not the case in Evanston. But this would have been a sufficient answer to Jordan's question only for those who had given up or had never harbored a vision of Evanston as a covenanted community. That vision had once nourished a hope that Evanston could demonstrate the possibility of a city becoming a holy commonwealth, in which Christian unity would conquer divisions and the love of God reign in both private and public affairs. In such a city the churches would naturally be looked to for leadership and would visibly represent the underlying spirit and ideals of the community. If the vision of a redeemed city was to be made a reality, the churches could not, any more than others, try to preserve a village past. Yet as the community in fact moved toward becoming a city, the churches found themselves variously slighted, ignored, attacked, divided, and powerless to fulfill their own expectations. It was within this context that Jordan had asked: Does not Evanston still care what happens to the churches?

At just about the time that Evanston voted to adopt a city form of government, a "White City" was being constructed on Chicago's lakefront. The Chicago World's Fair was to capture the imagination of many thousands of people as a dream of the future come to life. It was a huge canvas showing an artist's conception of the rich possibilities inherent in the city, an illustration of what the American city could be and was meant to be. Technology was celebrated. So was art. Nations and cultures from all over the world set up exhibits. There were exhibits too that represented the pursuits and aspirations of the American people from education and philanthropy to agriculture and business. Leaders of many of the world's religions met in a show of a new spirit of tolerance and desire for understanding in the Parliament of Religions. The city was being revealed as a place that could foster hope instead of despair.

228

From Evanston's viewpoint it was perhaps only right and proper that the chief architect of the World's Fair should be Daniel Burnham, a prominent and established resident of the community. Also a resident of the community was Lorado Taft, whose sculptures occupied positions of honor of the "White City."[160] This connection between the "White City" and Evanston was appropriate because Evanston itself had come to the point where it could imagine itself as a "city beautiful," an "ideal city," a "model city." There were some, however, who were not totally enchanted by the vision offered by the World's Fair. Some, for instance, saw in the Parliament of Religions the possibility of Christianity being compromised and losing its identity in a misguided quest for understanding and unity."[161] Individuals and denominations raised strong objections when it was decided that the Fair should remain open on Sundays. Meetings intended to coincide with the Fair were canceled, and there was some talk of boycott. Perhaps this grand vision was after all only a secular vision. The same question may have haunted religious leaders in Evanston, for in the years that followed it was the press and occasionally political figures in Evanston who referred to Evanston as the "ideal city" and the "city beautiful," not the religious leaders. And in 1915 in Evanston it was once again the problem of the Sabbath that raised the question of whether an ideal city had been built that had nevertheless lost its soul.

The city as the kind of place that by its very nature fostered illusions and hence, ultimately, disillusionment was the theme of a sermon by Dr. McElveen in 1916 called "The Tragedy and Comedy of American Cities."[162] The comic dimension of cities was that they seduced people into believing visions of grandeur and then mercilessly ridiculed or destroyed the very pretentiousness they had helped to create. High ideals and noble aspirations were constantly being mocked by reality. The idea of the city as a giant meeting place, center for social intercourse, and a means of bringing people together, for instance, was betrayed by the fact that in spite of physical closeness, isolation and loneliness were the fundamental realities for many people living in the city. Likewise, cities were often held to be centers of refinement, culture, and sophistication, places where human creativity and genius could come to full expression. Yet in reality cities were controlled by forces of quite a different order: "Boston is called the Athens of America, but her streets were laid out by a cow." Beginning with this jest, McElveen went on to discourse at some length on the role cows had played in the history of American cities, noting that many cities of the Midwest had begun as cow towns, places where the gathering of cattle rather than the gathering of people had been the primary motivation, and that Chicago had been very nearly destroyed by a cow. The lighthearted analysis hinted at the more serious thought that it was the bestial side of human nature that in fact defined and determined the city, whatever thoughts to the contrary there might be.

There was also, however, a tragic dimension to cities. Human pretentiousness deserved to be mocked, but it was not a laughing matter when human beings disregarded the will of God, and cities had a definite place in providential design. This could be seen by viewing cities within a scriptural framework. "Man's first home," McElveen said, "was a garden; man's final home is to be a city." The reference of course was to the vision of a New Jerusalem in the book of Revelation. That the contemporary growth of cities was in accord with the divine plan, that it was God's intention for cities to play a central role in the drama of salvation and for history to be consummated in the New Jerusalem was not an original insight on McElveen's part. Josiah Strong, for instance, had stated the same in his popular books *The Twentieth Century City* and *The Challenge of the City*. It was simply McElveen's purpose, as it had been Strong's, to awaken people to the urgency of the questions that confronted them. McElveen closed his sermon with such a question: "The city is to be the master fact of the twentieth century. In 1920 the cities of America will dominate the nation. But what will dominate the city—the church or the saloon?"

Many people in Evanston had once hoped that their city, by its example, could lead the way to a lasting resolution of this question. No doubt many continued to hope. In 1916 Evanston was still quite clearly not dominated by saloons. But it was not clear that it was or could be any longer dominated by the church. Far away from Evanston war had already shattered peace in Europe, and in the United States an age was brought to an end when in April 1917 the nation declared war on Germany. A few months later the early-morning peace of Evanston was shattered by a unionist's bomb; the barbershops of Evanston had been resisting unionization. No one had seen the bomb being made or planted. Few had even heard the explosion. But the results were there to be observed. The faith of those who believed in the communal ideal as well as those who believed in the promise of the city could not be destroyed by such an event, but neither could such faith be unaffected. The question of whether the tragedy of American cities could be avoided still awaited an answer.

The Communal Ideal
and the City

Time, it would seem, has discredited much of what the communities of Oak Park and Evanston stood for. A bitter experience with national prohibition has cast the temperance fervor of the pre-World War I era in a kind of sinister light as well as called into question the wisdom of any attempt to regulate personal morality. Scruples against such things as the Sunday newspaper, Sunday baseball and motion pictures, the tango, and the theater now seem to be quaint relics of a bygone era. The various forms of exclusiveness practiced consciously or unconsciously in Oak Park and Evanston seem, to put it kindly, ungenerous. The sense of confidence that many Oak Parkers and Evanstonians had in the rightness of their standards can be seen as merely an expression of class or religious pride. And the optimism of many in the ultimate, and not too distant, triumph of righteousness and the redemption of the social order can now be seen to be misguided and superficial, even if memories of that period may occasionally produce a wistful desire to recapture something of that optimism.

It would be a mistake, however, to let such things lead toward an attitude of mere condescension or condemnation. At a time when the growth of cities was bringing about major dislocations at all levels of American life, Oak Park and Evanston attempted to provide an answer. They brought indirectly into the urban milieu ideals of community life that they believed offered hope of both restoration and renewal. At the same time, they were ideals that ran the grave risk of being considered already obsolete.

It is not necessary to extend the stories of Oak Park and Evanston beyond World War I in order to see the beginnings of significant challenges to the communal ideals that had been articulated by founders and leaders of the two communities. These challenges arose even while people were still trying to give tangible reality to their beliefs and visions. Though people in both Oak Park and Evanston were able to remember simpler times when the villages more nearly approximated their communal ideals, the hopes involved were of such a nature that they could not be fully realized before signs of disintegration began to appear. It was somewhat difficult to discern whether movement was forward or backward, since the process of realizing ideals and having them undermined proceeded simultaneously on different fronts. Evanston moved much more quickly away from the communal ideal both in its actual life and in the statements of its leaders. The story of a community founded around what was soon to become a major university inevitably differs considerably from that of one without such a major institutional presence. Even as Evanston moved away from the communal ideal, however, there were unmistakable signs that the ideal was still an important point of reference for people of differing opinions on the future course Evanston would, or should, take. The comparison of the two communities serves perhaps to highlight the tenacity with which people in Oak Park held on to the communal ideal. It also reveals that the two stories were in many respects similar.

In both communities, though more noticeably in Evanston, dissenting voices arose to question assumptions and accepted practice. Once such voices were heard, it was much more difficult to assert with credibility that a unified spirit prevailed. Even if it could be shown or assumed that the dissenting voices represented only a minority of opinion, this poorly compensated for the damage done to the image of consensus. More often, though, the challenges were of a more subtle, but also more pervasive, nature. Modern, urban life offered people many things to choose from, and as individuals quietly made their choices, it became apparent that people no longer "practiced one truth," to use the words of the Dedham covenant. The judgments implicit in the situation of the two communities prior to World War I are perhaps, in this instance, more to the point than critiques too easily made from the superior wisdom of hindsight. By its very presence the city stood in judgment upon Oak Park and Evanston, just as by their presence Oak Park and Evanston stood in judgment upon the city.

Whether the stories of Oak Park and Evanston were unusual or whether they were paralleled in other communities of a similar nature can, of course, be determined only by detailed investigations of other American suburbs during this period. Whatever the results of such investigations may be, however, the stories of Oak Park and Evanston must be considered as a part of the story of cities in the United States. They were prestigious suburbs of Chicago, contiguous to the city. They were not isolated towns quietly witnessing a nonurban way of life while the city pursued a separate course. Their people were participants in, not merely remote witnesses of, the process of urbanization. The ideals they proclaimed they believed particularly appropriate to a metropolitan setting. It is one of the ironies of the story of Oak Park and Evanston that the idea of being a model community could, in both cases, produce a distinctly antiurban flavor while at the same time inspire sympathy for the city and actions on its behalf.

Oak Park and Evanston in the years prior to World War I dramatized many of the tensions and ambiguities of the time. Unable to embrace urban life, people found that they could neither turn their backs on the city nor escape its influence. Unable to discard basic assumptions about the nature of community life that were rooted in a distant New England past, they also desired to affirm their modernity, and in so doing found themselves being separated from that past even as they attempted to preserve it. That the basic ideals of the covenanted community could be professed and practiced even to the extent they were almost three hundred years after the establishment of the first Puritan settlements in New England, and in a place as unlikely as metropolitan Chicago, is testimony to the powerful appeal of the Puritan vision. This may suggest that visions similar to those that Oak Park and Evanston attempted to embody may have silently informed the attitudes and behavior of many individuals during this period. Nor can it be assumed that such visions do not still inform people today, for the question of what the proper foundations are for life in urban communities is still very much with us.

Notes

INTRODUCTION

1. Josiah Strong, *The Challenge of the City* (New York: Young People's Missionary Movement, 1907), p. 3.

CHAPTER ONE

1. Richard Wade and Harold Mayer, *Chicago: Growth of a Metropolis* (Chicago: University of Chicago Press, 1969), p. 152.
2. Frank Lloyd Wright was at one time a resident of Oak Park and many early examples of the "prairie school" of architecture may still be seen there.
3. Quotations here are taken from the text of "A Model of Christian Charity" as printed in Perry Miller and Thomas Johnson, *The Puritans*, 2 vols. (New York: American Book Company, 1938), 1:195-98. I have adapted spelling and punctuation to modern usage.
4. Kenneth Lockridge, for instance, whose description of Dedham is relied upon to provide an example of how the covenant was written into the life of a town, characterizes the covenanted community as a "Christian, Utopian, Closed, Corporate Community." See Kenneth A. Lockridge, *A New England Town: The First Hundred Years* (New York: W. W. Norton and Company, 1970), p. 16. The issue is raised here in order to avoid a possible confusion in the argument. Later towns, which could not be described as utopian experiments in any ordinary sense of the term, were sometimes more direct heirs of the covenanted community than were the various, specifically utopian ventures. The utopian impulse continued to play an important role, but it may also be somewhat misleading to emphasize the word "utopian" in regard to the Puritan covenant.
5. For a description of the intellectual ties between old and new England, see Miller and Johnson's introduction to *The Puritans*. A close look at the continuities and discontinuities in economic, political, and legal customs can be found in Sumner Chilton Powell, *Puritan Village: The Formation of a New England Town* (Middletown: Wesleyan University Press, 1963).
6. This does not mean, of course, that the Puritans viewed their success or failure in keeping the covenant as anything less than a matter of the utmost importance. For one thing, God's judgment would be visited on a people who

entered into such a covenanted relationship with God and then failed to live up to the contract. The shame of such failure and the terror of God's wrath could little be compensated for by a presumption that the idea of the covenanted community would not die. But beyond this point, the repeated attempts to re-create the covenanted community were not a part of the Puritan vision. For all the Puritans knew, the fate of humanity might rest on how well or poorly they held to the covenant.

7. The ways covenanted communities viewed nature and the wilderness are handled at a later point in the discussion. But for the argument that Puritans originally viewed their new environment as a "void," see Peter Carroll, *Puritanism and the Wilderness* (New York: Columbia University Press, 1969), pp. 194-95.

8. For an analysis of the ambiguity involved in the use of the term "errand" to describe the Puritan task, see the title essay in Perry Miller's collection, *Errand into the Wilderness* (New York: Harper and Row, 1964). Miller argues that it was not so much the possibility of failing to live out the obligations of the covenant that threatened the Puritans as it was the possibility that they would succeed in all the essentials of establishing covenanted communities and it would turn out not to make any difference.

9. Quoted in Lockridge, *A New England Town*, p. 6.

10. Ibid., pp. 4-5.

11. Ibid., pp. 24-25.

12. Ibid., p. 26.

13. Lockridge estimates that at its peak, around 1648, the church claimed approximately 70 percent of the adult males of the town and baptized 80 percent of the children, one parent's membership being sufficient to qualify a child for baptism. Since the population of the town throughout the seventeenth century was about five hundred, this meant that something in the neighborhood of one hundred people remained outside the communion of the church. Ibid., p. 31.

14. The relevant sections in the Dedham covenant are:

"Two: That we shall by all means labor to keep off from us all such as are contrary minded, and receive only such unto us as may be probably of one heart with us, and such as that we either know or may well and truly be informed to walk in peaceable conversation with all meekness of spirit, this for the edification of each other in the knowledge and faith of the Lord Jesus, and the mutual encouragement unto all temporal comforts in all things, seeking the good of each other, out of which may be derived true peace.

"Three: That if at any time differences shall rise between parties of our said town, that then such party or parties shall presently refer all such differences unto some one, two, or three others of our said society to be fully accorded and determined without further delay, if it possibly may be." Quoted in ibid., pp. 5-6.

15. Page Smith, *As a City upon a Hill* (New York: Alfred A. Knopf, 1966), chapter III. Smith's line of argument should not be thought of as a total interpretation

of westward expansion. It is perhaps overly ambitious and therefore too much given to generalization. Nevertheless, it does call attention to the potential for productive interpretations of specific towns that might otherwise be ignored.

16. For Smith's own discussion of his typology see chapter II, ibid. The fact that it is a typology means, of course, that the terms must be used somewhat loosely when applied to specific communities. While some towns may fall clearly into one category or the other, many towns that began in a cumulative fashion later attempted to achieve some of the characteristics of colonized towns while towns that began as colonized ventures might gradually lose the defining traits with which they began. The distinction remains useful, however, and is used occasionally with reference to Chicago, Evanston, and Oak Park,

17. Even towns established by speculators, however, might take on a number of qualities associated with New England towns. See Ray Billington's discussion of the Ohio Company and the establishment of Marietta, Ohio in *Westward Expansion: A History of the American Frontier*, 3rd edition (New York: Macmillan Company, 1967), pp. 212ff.

18. Again Lockridge supplies valuable detailed information and analysis of how the broad concerns of New England culture combined with local dynamics to produce the process here described in general terms. See *A New England Town*, chapters 6-8. It is beyond the scope of this work to review the extensive literature on New England towns, and the discussions on such issues as the role and importance of ideology and factors contributing to stability and change. Many of the issues are summarized in Rhys Isaac, "Order and Growth, Authority and Meaning in Colonial New England," *American Historical Review* 76 (June 1971): 728-37. This is a review article of four community studies. Other works that have informed my treatment are cited in the bibliography.

19. Russel B. Nye, *Midwestern Progressive Politics* (East Lansing: Michigan State University Press, 1951), p. 6.

20. Billington, *Westward Expansion*, p. 308.

21. This approach to the Great Awakening in New England is based on Perry Miller's analysis in "Jonathan Edwards and the Great Awakening," *Errand into the Wilderness*, pp. 153-66.

22. Smith, *As a City upon a Hill*, p. 41. Also p. 198.

23. Statistics are unavailable that would prove that a higher proportion of Oak Park and Evanston residents had experienced revivalistic fervor than had residents of Chicago at the time, and in any case statistics would be relatively unimportant since merely having attended revivals tells nothing of the experiences and attitudes derived from them. It is, however, striking that what biographical information is available on residents of Evanston and Oak Park so often mentions that the person experienced conversion in a specific revival. Since much of the information was presumably contributed by the people themselves, it is an indication of the meaning that such experiences held for them. The ways "popular" denominations held to the corporate ideal, thus making possible cooperation between themselves and more exclusively New England traditions, is discussed in T. Scott Miyakawa, *Protestants and Pioneers* (Chicago: University

of Chicago Press, 1964). In addition to the sources on revivalism mentioned in the bibliography, Hugh Dalziel Duncan's *Culture and Democracy* (Totowa, New Jersey: Bedminster Press, 1965) contains a suggestive chapter on revivalism in the Chicago region entitled "The Search for Community in Religious Expression."

24. C. Dana, *The Garden of the World, or the Great West* (Boston: Wentworth and Company, 1856), p. 13.

25. The various meanings attached to the West as garden in popular culture, literature, and politics are well and extensively explored in Henry Nash Smith, *The Virgin Land: The American West as Symbol and Myth* (New York: Random House, Vintage Books, 1950). Leo Marx, *The Machine in the Garden* (New York: Oxford University Press, 1967) and R. W. B. Lewis, *The American Adam* (Chicago: University of Chicago Press, 1958) are also useful studies of this theme from a narrower perspective. David Noble in *Historians Against History* (Minneapolis: University of Minnesota Press, 1965) argues that a "covenant with nature" has been implicit in American historiography.

26. Dana, *The Garden of the World*, p. 14.

27. Daniel Boorstin, *The Americans: The National Experience* (New York: Random House, Vintage Books, 1967), pp. 113-68.

28. *Chicago Tribune*, 30 March 1873. This statement is highly similar in tone, and even in some of its language, to statements later to appear in the newspapers of Oak Park and Evanston.

29. Theodore Dreiser, *The Titan* (New York: New American Library, [1914] 1965), pp. 60-61.

30. Bessie Pierce notes that in 1837 the males in Chicago outnumbered the females by more than two to one. Although the ratio evened out somewhat as time went on, males still predominated throughout the period prior to the Civil War. Bessie Pierce, *History of Chicago*, 3 vols. (New York: Alfred A. Knopf, 1937), 1:172.

31. Ibid., p. 76.

32. Ibid., p. 174. Also Jeremiah Porter, "The Earliest Religious History of Chicago," address read before the Chicago Historical Society in 1859, reprinted in Fergus Historical Series, no. 14 (Chicago: Fergus Printing Company, 1881), p. 56.

33. Pierce, *History of Chicago*, 1:231-32.

34. Ibid., p. 261.

35. Bessie Pierce, *As Others See Chicago* (Chicago: University of Chicago Press, 1933), p. 164. Quotes are from an article entitled, "Chicago in 1856," *Putnam's Monthly Magazine*, June 1856, author unknown.

36. Ibid., p. 120.

37. Much of the discussion of Ogden is based on Daniel Boorstin's treatment of him in *The Americans: The National Experience*, pp. 116-18. But see also the estimate of Ogden by one of his contemporaries, Isaac N. Arnold, *William B.*

Ogden and Early Days in Chicago, Fergus Historical Series, no. 17 (Chicago: Fergus Printing Co., 1882).

38. From the *Weekly Chicago Democrat*, 1 October 1853, quoted in Pierce, *History of Chicago*, 2:150.
39. Quoted by Wentworth himself in a speech before the Sunday Lecture Society, April 11, 1875 and reprinted in the Fergus Historical Series, no. 8 (Chicago: Fergus Printing Co., 1876), under the title "Early Chicago."
40. Joseph Balestier, *The Annals of Chicago: A Lecture Delivered Before the Chicago Lyceum, January 21, 1840* (Chicago: Edward H. Rudd, 1840), pp. 18-19.
41. Evanston congressman George Foss, quoted in *Evanston Index*, 26 January 1895.
42. Pierce, *History of Chicago*, 2:440.

CHAPTER TWO

1. Residents' own consciousness of time as it affected the way they understood themselves and their communities is discussed in the following chapter.
2. For data on the original purchases of land in the Oak Park area see Arthur Evans LeGacy, "Improvers and Preservers" (Ph.D. dissertation, University of Chicago, 1967), pp. 12-13.
3. May Estelle Cook, *Little Old Oak Park* (privately printed, 1961), p. 33.
4. Robert St. John, *This Was My World* (Garden City: Doubleday and Company, 1953), p. 14.
5. The most important of those in Oak Park who came from Onondaga County are: Henry W. Austin, early resident of Oak Park and the man for whom the community of Austin just east of Oak Park was named; O. W. Herrick, an early schoolteacher and later important in business and politics; Augustin Porter, along with Austin and others responsible for the victory of temperance forces and an important community figure; James Wilmarth Scoville and relatives, discussed in some detail below. All these and others as well were born and raised in either Pompey or Skaneateles. I have been able to find no direct evidence, with the exception of the Scoville family, that these people knew one another or influenced one another to come to Oak Park. Nevertheless, they are all from the same region in Onondaga County, were roughly the same age, all being born in the late 1820s, and many had some connection with Skaneateles Academy. The scattered information available on these people can be found in the biographical files in the Oak Park Public Library.
6. Smith, *As a City Upon a Hill*, p. 32.
7. A. T. Andreas, *History of Cook County, Illinois* (Chicago: Andreas, 1884), p. 782.
8. Ibid.
9. Elizabeth Porter Furbeck, "Personal Reminiscences of Pioneer Life," typed copy of speech delivered before the Society of Pioneers of Chicago, 25 May 1898,

available in Oak Park Public Library, p. 2. William Halley, newspaperman and Oak Park historian, says that the name was suggested by John Wentworth. The point is significant only in that it indicates something of the sentiments held by some of the early settlement, the name Proviso having been proposed in honor of the Wilmot Proviso. Since Porter and Wentworth were friends and both were abolitionist in their sympathies, the suggestion could well have originated with either.

10. First Congregational Church (Oak Park), *The Red Book* (1924), p. 13.

11. Information on these men comes from a number of sources: scattered pieces of data compiled in the biographical files of the Oak Park Public Library; the standard histories by Oak Park residents listed in the bibliography; and the material in Andreas's *History of Cook County*. Unless sources disagree on points of some significance, footnotes for basic factual material are avoided.

12. The founding members of the Union Ecclesiastical Society of Oak Ridge included Niles, Austin, Kettlestrings, Herrick, and George and James Scoville. Niles, Austin, and James Scoville were the first trustees of the Oak Ridge Ecclesiastical Society, later to become First Congregational Church, while Herrick was secretary-treasurer. Dunlop was the first to organize a banking facility but Austin, Scoville, and Herrick were involved in the creation of banks at a later date. The development of community institutions was a major concern of all these people.

13. The quote is taken from an interview with Walter Kettlestrings reported in *Oak Leaves*, 28 March 1930.

14. Cook, *Little Old Oak Park*, p. 45.

15. Whitney R. Cross, *The Burned-over District* (Ithaca: Cornell University Press, 1950), provides an interesting analysis of this region that was to contribute much to the settling of the Northwest Territory. The utopian experiment near Skaneateles is described briefly on p. 332.

16. Augustin Porter's daughter wrote: "It is not uncommon for people when they leave their old homes and religious privileges to seemingly leave their old Bibles and the Sabbath; there is nothing I feel more grateful to my parents for than that they did not." Furbeck, "Personal Reminiscences of Pioneer Life," p. 8.

17. Cook, *Little Old Oak Park*, p. 43.

18. The origin of the custom of town meetings is not mentioned in any of the sources. An early historian of Oak Park, however, noted: "There were annual town meetings at which officers were elected, taxes voted, and the general business of the town transacted." Apparently such assemblies were discontinued in Cicero Township with the coming to power of the McCaffery ring in 1867. John Lewis, *Chapters in Oak Park History* (privately printed, n.d.), p. 7.

19. Information on Scoville's life and character is taken from Dr. Simon James Humphrey, *James Wilmarth Scoville: A Memorial* (n.p., n.d.), Oak Park Public Library.

20. Scoville's presentation speech at the dedication of Scoville Institute, as quoted in ibid., p. 66.

21. The scale of Scoville's activities is indicated somewhat by the estimate that he gave away approximately $300,000 during his lifetime. He apparently always lived comfortably but not in luxury.

22. Humphrey, *James Wilmarth Scoville*, pp. 23-25.

23. Kettlestrings also was remembered in this way. Generous in lending money to those in need with little or no security from them and often undertaking to provide work for people, he nevertheless was strongly opposed to outright gifts, which he felt were demeaning and destructive of character. See Edwin O. Gale, *Reminiscences of Early Chicago and Vicinity* (Chicago: Fleming H. Revell Company, 1902), p. 420.

24. The major source of information on the McCaffery ring is Lewis, *Chapters in Oak Park History*. Lewis was a lawyer who came to Oak Park in 1873, just after the battle with McCaffery had been won. Later he was a leader in Oak Park's successful fight to separate from Cicero Township and to avoid annexation to Chicago. The importance of the McCaffery episode is corroborated by various incidental references to it in newspapers of a much later date. Apparently the affair became a part of the common memory of the village.

25. Gertrude Fox Hoagland, *An Historical Survey of Oak Park, Illinois* (compiled under Federal W.P.A. Project #9516, 1937), p. 10; gives the following figures: 1835, $1.25 per acre; 1850, $200 per acre; 1857, $400 per acre; 1876, $1,000 per acre; 1877, $4,000 per acre.

26. First Congregational Church (Oak Park), *The Red Book*, p. 9.

27. Information on some of these is unavailable. The three most important were Goodrich, Lunt, and Evans. Goodrich was an important figure in the early history of Chicago as a lawyer and friend of William B. Ogden, Hubbard, and others. His involvements included the Chicago Lyceum, the first temperance society in Chicago, the Chicago Bible Society, the American Bible Society, and the Whig and Republican parties. Information on him can be found in the Evanston Historical Society Biographical files. See especially the obituary in *Chicago Inter-Ocean*, 16 March 1889. Several biographies of Evans are available and are noted in the bibliography. He was an abolitionist and crusader for humane treatment of the mentally ill as well as an important figure in railroads and real estate in Chicago. As alderman he was instrumental in the upgrading of the Chicago school system. Lunt was apparently active on a much smaller scale and his name does not appear in the major references on early Chicago, but he was related through marriage to both Gurdon Hubbard and Evans and lived next door to Scammon. A family portrait of him may be found in Cornelia Gray Lunt, *Sketches of Childhood and Girlhood* (Evanston: privately printed, 1925): "It was far-reaching philanthropies, splendid self-effacement, devotion to the highest standards, love of church and state, that made my father's life so worthy and wonderful. To him it was always causes that appealed," p. 25. Lunt was connected with the YMCA, the Chicago Bible Society, and the Chicago Orphan Asylum. His vocation was grain merchant and he is said to have enjoyed the reputation of being the most honest of those engaged in the trade.

28. Quoted in Harvey B. Hurd and Robert D. Sheppard, eds., *History of Evanston*, Vol. 2 of *Historical Encyclopedia of Illinois and the History of Evanston*, Newton Bateman, ed. (Chicago: Munsell Publishing Company, 1906), p. 54.
29. Ibid., pp. 55, 57.
30. Quoted in ibid., p. 56. Joseph Kettlestrings was among those named as original trustees in the charter, but he apparently dropped out of the picture after he returned to Oak Park.
31. Quoted in ibid, p. 65.
32. See for instance issues of the *Evanston Index*, 10 and 31 January 1874. Some of the tavern owners were attempting to avoid the four-mile limit by building a zigzag road to their places of business. Evanstonians thus found it necessary to go to some lengths to prove that "as the crow flies" these places were within the four-mile limit. These were only a few of many instances, however. A brief summary of litigation relating to enforcement of the charter provision and the nature of continuing violations appears in ibid., pp. 317-21.
33. The *Evanston Index* of September 6, 1873 wrote: "We do not recognize any antagonism, even in the slightest degree, between our people and the University. On the contrary, whatever is for the interest of one is for the interest of the other." The very need to make such a statement, however, is an indication that the opinion was not unanimously shared.
34. In 1855, at the same time the temperance amendment was added to the charter, another amendment was included that declared the university exempt from taxation. Also in this year John Evans advocated a policy of retaining lands owned by the university that were not needed in the immediate future rather than selling them. At the time this policy was tabled, but it was apparently later adopted, for in 1874 the *Evanston Index* wrote that it was looking forward to a change in university land policy by which it retained control of its lands and used them as rental properties. This had given rise to significant opposition because such lands were not being taxed and some claimed that the quality of housing was poor. In 1869 a group of townsmen had petitioned the university for a change in policy, but the petition was denied with Grant Goodrich reminding the people of the university's important contributions to the town. In 1876 the issue was taken to court with the village requesting that those lands not being used for educational purposes be subject to taxation. The Supreme Court decided in the university's favor, but the legal decision did not put an end to the political issue. See Hurd and Sheppard, *History of Evanston*, pp. 65-66, 79, 85 and *Evanston Index*, 27 June 1874. An example of other issues that arose between the village and the university occurred in 1874 when the right of college students to vote in village elections was contested. See *Evanston Index* for March and April 1874.
35. Accurate figures on land values in terms of acres are difficult to determine because the land was most often sold by lots or by front footage, but a choice piece of land of 14,050 square feet in 1855 sold for $350 or roughly $1,000 per acre. By 1865 the same lot sold for $600, while by 1870 the lot, now reduced to 8,000 square feet, sold for $2,000 or about $10,000 per acre.

Prices, of course, fell radically after the Panic of 1873. Hurd and Sheppard, *History of Evanston*, p. 297.

36. Though both village and university were predominantly Methodist, the intention was not to exclude in any way members of other Protestant denominations. Northwestern had written into its charter that membership in the Methodist denomination was not to be a requirement for either faculty or students. The university also donated the land for churches of other denominations.

37. It is more difficult to generalize about the points of origin for Evanston residents than for Oak Park residents. Still, a large number of people came from New England or western New York. Almost by definition they were not frontier Methodists with an anti-intellectual attitude. They were Republicans, though some may have come from the antislavery wing of the Democratic Party. And though not all were Methodists, the Methodist code of discipline probably formed an implicit basis for judging what behavior would be acceptable.

38. The circular advertising the meeting read as follows:
"Whereas, The present stringency of the money market affects with more or less severity the entire community, but with much more severity the poorer and laboring classes who have but partially paid for their little homes, and
Whereas, It is as likely to continue as to cease, and a considerable number of the residents of the village of Evanston, although the owners of small homesteads are, through their inability to obtain employment, without any incoming means to pay heavy taxes, or even to obtain bread for their families, and
Whereas, A tax is about to be levied and assessed upon all the real property in the village of Evanston for the purpose of building what is called the water works,
Therefore, It is desirable that a public meeting be held of the taxpayers, voters, and property holders of the village of Evanston that are opposed to the present levy of excessive taxes, to meet at Jennings Hall on Saturday evening at 7½ o'clock to devise means to arrest the immediate levy of oppressive assessments, but not to oppose the final desired object of obtaining good water." Quoted in the *Evanston Index*, 3 January 1874.

39. The account of the meeting is taken from the *Evanston Index*, 3 January 1874.

40. Kedzie letter replying to a letter by Philo Judson, *Evanston Index*, 14 March 1874.

41. *Evanston Index*, 11 April 1874. The *Index* was a paper which had begun in the summer of 1873 and was at this time owned, published, and edited by Alfred Sewell, who had previously been in partnership with Samuel Dunlop of Oak Park.

42. See for instance, ibid., 7 and 14 March 1874. The problem receives incidental mention in the *Index* throughout the later years of the 1870s.

43. Ibid., 9 May 1874.

44. Ibid., 3 February 1877.

CHAPTER THREE

1. Anselm Strauss, *Images of the American City* (Glencoe, Illinois: Free Press of Glencoe, 1961), pp. 230ff.
2. Strong, *The Challenge of the City*, p. 3.
3. Henry J. Fletcher, "The Doom of the Small Town," *Forum* 19 (April 1895): 214.
4. *Oak Leaves*, 30 January 1903.
5. Ibid.
6. Ibid.
7. Ibid.
8. Notices of the secessionist meetings and references to the uncertainty about Oak Park's future may be found in nearly all the issues of the *Oak Park Reporter* from January through May 1900.
9. "Civic ideal" was used in the editorial already quoted. References to Oak Park as a model will appear in statements quoted below in connection with other elements of Oak Park's self-concept. The earliest use of "model" that I have found was in the title of a Fellowship Club meeting at Unity Church in January 1899. Significantly this was at a time when Oak Park had voted itself into separate existence as a village and had not yet been denied independence by rulings of the courts. Previous to home rule Oak Parkers could refer to their community as "Chicago's finest suburb" but independence was apparently a prerequisite for the idea of Oak Park as a model community.
10. *Oak Leaves*, 6 February 1903.
11. Quoted in ibid.
12. Quoted in *Oak Park Reporter*, 1 June 1899.
13. Furbeck, "Personal Reminiscences," pp. 1, 9.
14. Quoted in *Oak Leaves*, 1 May 1903.
15. William E. Barton, "The Secret Charm of Oak Park," Introduction to *Glimpses of Oak Park*, by Frank H. June and George R. Hemingway (Oak Park: June and Hemingway, 1912).
16. Ibid.
17. Ibid.
18. There are no full-length interpretive histories of Oak Park. A few brief statements appear as parts of books that were basically promotional in nature. With the exception of these, the material quoted in this section is intentionally restricted to the years just before and after Oak Park gained its independence. This was a time when attempts to be self-conscious about "who we are" were frequent.
19. Quoted in *Oak Leaves*, 16 January 1903.
20. Quoted in ibid., 20 November 1903.
21. The arguments for and against separation appeared in the local press during the last half of 1898 and again in the several months preceding the election of November 1901. There were a few dissenting voices who felt either that

sectionalism was not a major problem in the township or that sectionalism would not be eliminated by making Oak Park a separate municipality. These were not, however, likely to be the most effective arguments against annexation, for the antagonism between North and South Cicero was a matter of long standing.

22. *Oak Leaves*, 25 April 1902.
23. William Halley, *Pictorial Oak Park* (Oak Park: Halley, 1898), p. 4.
24. Lewis, *Chapters in Oak Park History*, p. 48. The conflict between the two tickets was carried on in the local press throughout December 1901.
25. Quoted in *Oak Leaves*, 20 November 1903.
26. Ibid., 16 May 1902.
27. Barton, "The Secret Charm of Oak Park."
28. "Oak Park: Chicago's Leading and Largest Western Suburb," *Oak Park Reporter*, 23 December 1887.
29. *The Vindicator*, 13 January 1883.
30. Halley, "What our History Consists of," in *Pictorial Oak Park*, pp. 2ff.
31. Because Oak Park had a north-south ridge at approximately its center, the onetime shore of Lake Michigan, which made the land relatively dry and therefore attractive to early settlers; thus the name Oak Ridge. Oak Parkers became fond of referring to the "fact" that when it rained waters from one side of the ridge eventually found their way into the Des Plaines River and eventually into the Gulf of Mexico while waters from the other side would find their way into Lake Michigan and hence to the Atlantic Ocean. When Oak Parkers made use of this tale, perhaps with tongue in cheek, they meant to indicate that they were no out-of-the-way place. In a variety of ways they were indeed a bridge and a watershed. Oak Park's ridge was a continental axis point.
32. See, for instance, the speech of Jesse Baldwin in *Oak Leaves*, 20 November 1903.
33. In addition to other sources that have and will serve to illustrate the point, the importance of the prairie to Oak Park's continuing sense of identity can be discerned in Edwin O. Gale, *Reminiscences of Oak Park, Galewood, and Vicinity* (Oak Park Public Library, n.p., 1898), and Furbeck, "Personal Reminiscences."
34. For instance, when Waukegan began to consider seriously the question of internal improvements after Evanston had finally determined to build its waterworks, the *Evanston Index* commented: "Thus is Evanston doing a missionary work among her older and slower sisters." *Evanston Index*, 4 April 1874.
35. When the custom of providing organized outings for poor children of Chicago began in Evanston, the *Index* said: "These are regular New Testament excursions. We remember that we are there commanded by the Master, when we make a feast, not to bid the rich who can reward us, but the poor, the lame, the halt, and the blind from the highways and hedges, and the reward shall come from above." Ibid., 5 July 1873.
36. Frances Willard, *A Classic Town: The Story of Evanston* (Chicago: Women's Temperance Publishing Association, 1891), p. 15.

37. The difference is, of course, one of degree. Oak Park was proud of those residents who received national recognition. Yet if such recognition carried an individual away from Oak Park his stature in Oak Park might well be reduced, while for Evanston the opposite was often true. It is also perhaps more than accidental that the most renowned of Oak Parkers, Ernest Hemingway and Frank Lloyd Wright, encountered some difficulty in finding full acceptance within their own community. William E. Barton affords another example. Though achieving national recognition, Barton lived in Oak Park for twenty-five years, immersed himself in its history, and acted as its spokesman and interpreter. He remained essentially a "local boy."

38. This attitude appears, for instance, in the biographical sketch of Evans in Viola Crouch Reeling, *Evanston: Its Land and Its People* (Evanston: Daughters of the American Revolution, Fort Dearborn, 1928), pp. 458ff.

39. *Evanston Index*, 3 March 1900.

40. Ibid., 28 July 1900.

41. This is perhaps a major reason why it is more difficult to find statements of any length at all in which Evanstonians try to articulate their identity. Occasionally revealing statements may be discovered in unlikely contexts, but most often the sources simply assume a fundamental understanding of communal identity.

42. "Consider, too, the wise adaptedness of the university's cognomen. It was then embodied prophecy; it is embodied history now. Men of more restricted vision planned a 'Chicago' and 'Lake Forest' University, but our trustees looking with prescient gaze down the future's mystic maze, saw 'all the wonder that should be' in the 'long result of time,' of which we have seen nearly forty years, and wrote, not 'Excelsior' but 'Northwestern' on their banners. Mighty as the word was then, it is a hundredfold more mighty now. The old Northwest stopped with Minnesota, Iowa and Kansas; the new Northwest stretches to Puget Sound and the Pacific Sea." Willard, *A Classic Town*, pp. 14-15.

43. *Evanston Index*, 28 July and 8 December 1900.

44. Ibid., 15 December 1900.

45. Willard, *A Classic Town*, p. 57.

46. *Evanston Press*, 2 January 1892.

47. For reasons not immediately discernable in the sources, the *Evanston Index* and a group of men who had previously spoken in favor of both the annexation proposal and a city charter switched their positions at the last minute and advocated a vote against the propositions. They stated merely that it was not in the best interests of Evanston, economically, and otherwise, to follow the proposed course at that time. Though bitterly denounced by the *Evanston Press*, the turnabout obviously had little or no effect on the final tally, and the issue seems to have been quickly forgotten.

48. *Evanston Press*, 2 January 1892.

49. Ibid., 30 January 1892.

50. Ibid., 6 February 1892.

51. Speech by James Raymond quoted in *Evanston Index*, 28 July 1900, p. 1.

52. This is not to say that Evanstonians were incapable of taking pride in their association with Chicago. There were occasions, such as the World's Fair, when Chicago appeared in a different light. "And as in this great Northwest wealth and plenty come teeming from the soil, as its giant city is the synonym of progress, enterprise, and energy, so shall the future city of Evanston be no secondary feature in the grand aggregation that makes the World's Fair City one of the wonders of the world." Quoted in *Evanston Press*, 9 January 1892.
53. Speech by W. E. Church at a mass meeting held in opposition to consolidation as reported in the *Evanston Index*, 8 December 1900.
54. Ibid., 12 July 1873.
55. Quoted in ibid., 8 July 1876.
56. *Evanston Press*, 5 January 1889, p. 4.
57. *Evanston Index*, 18 August 1900.
58. Frances Willard quoting a Mrs. Bragdon, *Evanston Press*, 9 February 1889.
59. A final way Evanston appropriated an image from Chicago may be noted here. The speed with which Chicago had grown into a major city had been often noted as evidence that it was a city of destiny. Writing in 1898 Harvey Hurd said of Evanston: "Unlike some of the historic towns of the United States, whose history has been written covering two centuries or more . . . this tidy suburban town has developed quickly within itself all the forces that make up our active, advanced American life . . . it is an epitome of distinctly modern progress." Hurd and Sheppard, *History of Evanston*, p. 15.
60. *Evanston Index*, 12 July 1873, p. 2.
61. *Evanston Press*, 2 January 1892, p. 1.
62. Ibid., 9 February, 1889.
63. Willard, *A Classic Town*, p. 44.
64. Hurd and Sheppard, *History of Evanston*, p. 19.
65. Willard, *A Classic Town*, p. 88.
66. *Evanston Index*, 24 February 1900.
67. Hurd and Sheppard, *History of Evanston*, p. 338.
68. Willard, *A Classic Town*, p. 25.

CHAPTER FOUR

1. *Oak Park Reporter*, 5 December 1901.
2. Speech of Edward Steiner reported in *Oak Leaves*, 3 April 1915.
3. Ibid., 22 November 1913.
4. Reported in ibid., 4 April 1911.
5. Allen F. Davis, *Spearheads for Reform: The Social Settlements and the Progressive Movement* (New York: Oxford University Press, 1967), p. 13. The author notes that in 1891 there were 6 settlements in the United States, that by 1900 there were over 100, and by 1905 more than 200. This is an indication of the

significant growth of the movement during the early years of home rule in Oak Park.

6. Sermon by Cornelius Dickinson, printed in *Golden Jubilee Booklet of First Congregational Church*, 1913.

7. Sermon by Dr. Burns of First Methodist, printed in the *Oak Park Reporter*, 27 January 1899.

8. *Oak Leaves*, 29 April 1916.

9. Hoagland, *An Historical Survey of Oak Park*, p. 13.

10. *Oak Leaves*, Fifth Anniversary Edition, 1907.

11. Ibid., 3 July 1915.

12. Humphrey, *James Wilmarth Scoville*.

13. *Oak Leaves*, 15 February 1913.

14. First Congregational Church, *Golden Jubilee Booklet*.

15. A small indication of this is that Universalists and Episcopalians were not mentioned in the above quotation referring to the people of "kindred covenanter blood" who reinforced the early Congregationalists. The reason Universalists might be considered something of a special case is somewhat obvious. One Congregational minister referred to them as "worthy and lovable a lot of heretics as ever were born." At the time of the founding the Universalists had expressed their desire to separate from the union church in order to "have the Word of God interpreted according to our own conscientious belief and power to accept." (*Oak Leaves*, Fifth Anniversary Edition, 1907) It was also said in 1907 that, "The attitude of suspicion and mistrust which was more or less pronounced for a number of years has given way to one of complete fraternity." In the case of Grace Episcopal Church, there was no public acknowledgment of differences, but the church's own publication often struggled to maintain a historical and ecclesiological identity, while affirming a spirit of cooperation.

16. The pattern of religious affiliation in Oak Park may be indicated somewhat by the results of a religious census taken in 1900. Of active church members, it showed the following breakdown: Congregationalist, 32.6%; Methodist, 11.5%; Presbyterian, 10.6%; Baptist, 10.5%; Episcopal, 11.4%; Lutheran, 9%; Roman Catholic, 5.5%; Universalist, 4.1%. It also showed church membership to be 3,875 adults and 354 children, average attendance at 4,424 adults and 999 children, and Sunday school enrollment at 1,287 adults and 1,797 children. The total population of Oak Park at the time was slightly less than 10,000, but it is difficult to draw accurate conclusions from the figures, since, for instance, there is no indication of whether people belonging to churches outside Oak Park were included in the membership figures. Reported in *First Congregational Church Bulletin*, 16 December 1900.

17. *Oak Leaves*, 15 February 1913.

18. Specifically the breakdown was as follows: 38 church related; 27 connected with government or public affairs; 20 educational or cultural; 9 related to fraternal or social organizations; 6 "human interest."

19. *Oak Leaves*, 27 April 1907.

20. Interview with Arthur Amacker, Oak Park, Illinois, 3 May 1973.
21. *Oak Leaves*, 3 October 1914.
22. Ibid., 7 August 1915.
23. Ibid., 22 January 1910.
24. Ibid., 23 July 1910.
25. Ibid., 16 May 1902 (my emphasis).
26. *Chicago Tribune*, 9 October 1903. Unless otherwise indicated, background information on the issues involved also comes from this extensive article.
27. Ibid.
28. Ibid.
29. *Oak Leaves*, 23 October 1903.
30. *Chicago Tribune*, 9 October 1903.
31. *Oak Leaves*, 18 April 1902. The names attached to the initial call were from several churches and were, no doubt, recognizable as leaders in their respective churches. One of the names was N. M. Jones, already mentioned as the leader of the "conservatives" at First Methodist. Another was Edson Lyman, who had been a deacon at First Congregational since 1876.
32. Ibid., 25 April 1902.
33. Laymen and -women were identified either by their occupation or by their connection with other organizations. While many of the names can be identified in connection with a specific church, it has been impossible to get a completely accurate picture of which churches were being represented by the laypeople. The pastors who contributed statements were the following: Barton, First Congregational; Strong, Second Congregational; Armstrong, Third Congregational; Hill, First Methodist; Youker, Euclid Avenue Methodist; McCaskill, Third Methodist; Soares, First Baptist; Shayler, Grace Episcopal; Hintze, German Evangelical; Creighton, River Forest Methodist; Johnstone, River Forest Presbyterian; Brown, state secretary of the YMCA. Those missing were only the four most newly formed congregations, First Presbyterian, which was in the process of seeking a new minister, and Unity. Unity heard speakers on the YMCA, but appeared not to be officially involved in the campaign. The German Evangelical church had only recently added its support.
34. *Oak Leaves*, 9 January 1903. Other phrases appearing in quotation marks come from various of the statements that appeared in the three issues of January 9, 16, and 23.
35. Ibid., 9 January 1903.
36. Mrs. Sidney Niles, ibid., 18 March 1911.
37. *St. Edmund's Parish Monthly*, February 1914.
38. *Oak Leaves*, 25 October 1913.
39. Ibid., 24 January 1914.
40. Ibid., 17 March 1917.
41. Ibid., 29 October 1910.
42. Gambling was a favorite theme of *Grace Church Items*, the newsletter of Grace Episcopal Church, which contained this quote (12 December 1907).
43. *Oak Leaves*, 8 January 1910.

44. Ibid., 4 July 1914.
45. Reported in ibid., 1 May 1903.
46. *St. Edmund's Parish Monthly*, August 1912.
47. PTA talk given by a teacher, Id Windate, reported in *Oak Leaves*, 11 May 1907.
48. A personal account that communicates a feel for the religious ethos at work in one family is Marcelline Sanford, *At the Hemingways: A Family Portrait* (Boston: Atlantic Monthly Press, Little, Brown and Company, 1961).
49. Quoted in *Oak Leaves*, 19 February 1916.
50. Lindsay's book, *The Art of the Moving Picture*, is excerpted in Roderick Nash, ed., *The Call of the Wild* (New York: George Braziller, 1970), pp. 158-71.
51. Interview with Arthur Amacker.
52. *Oak Leaves*, 7 December 1907.
53. Ibid., 18 March 1911.
54. Ibid., 18 January 1908.
55. Ibid., 23 January 1912.
56. Lecturer to the Nineteenth Century Club quoted in ibid., 9 December 1911.
57. Ibid., 8 June 1912.
58. Ibid., 7 March 1914.
59. Ibid., 28 February 1914.
60. Ibid., 15 April 1916.
61. Ibid., 16 May 1916.
62. Ibid., 25 November 1916.
63. A somewhat impressionistic survey of attitudes toward the Sabbath during this period is presented in Francis Weisenburger, *Triumph of Faith* (Richmond: William Byrd Press, 1962), pp. 118-33.
64. Interview with Robert Heald, River Forest, Illinois, 20 October 1972.
65. Interview with Arthur Amacker.
66. Quoted in *Oak Leaves*, 1 May 1903.
67. Quoted in ibid., 4 May 1907.
68. Ibid., 8 July 1911.
69. Ibid., 27 April 1907.
70. Ibid., 26 April 1913.
71. Ibid., 14 November 1914.
72. Julius Ward, "The New Sunday," *Atlantic Monthly*, April 1881, quoted in Weisenburger, *Triumph of Faith*, p. 130.
73. Rev. B. I. Bell, quoted in *Oak Leaves*, 7 September 1912.
74. Kenneth Lockridge shows how, even in seventeenth-century New England, the covenant and the communal ideal depended heavily on the intangible, voluntary participation of town residents. The need to enforce the "covenant" was a sure sign of decline, the failure of the hopes of the founders. See *A New England Town: The First Hundred Years*, chapter 5.
75. *Oak Leaves*, 13 January 1917.
76. Ibid., 10 May 1913.
77. Quoted in ibid., 31 March 1917.

78. Ibid.
79. Ibid.
80. Ibid.
81. Ibid., 7 April 1917.
82. Ibid., 25 January 1908.
83. Ibid., 16 July 1910.
84. *First Congregational Church Bulletin*, 1 July 1894 and 16 December 1900.
85. *Oak Leaves*, 26 November 1910.
86. Ibid., 16 May 1914.
87. Ibid., 26 September 1914.
88. Ibid., 30 December 1911.
89. Ibid., 28 December 1907.
90. Ibid., 27 December 1913.
91. Ibid., 20 March 1915.
92. At First Congregational, for instance, Rev. Barton was admired for his dignity and learning, the music was judged by the highest artistic standards, and formal dress was required for ushers. Such things conspired to give the impression that whatever else worship may have been, it was also an event of "high culture."
93. Henry F. May, *Protestant Churches in Industrial America* (New York: Harper and Row, Harper Torchbooks, 1967), p. 253.
94. William McLoughlin, *Modern Revivalism* (New York: Ronald Press, 1959), pp. 336ff.
95. *Oak Leaves*, 19 June 1915.
96. William E. Barton, *Autobiography* (Indianapolis: Bobbs-Merrill Company, 1932), p. 250.
97. Pastors invited to lead the services were, in order: Luccock, First Presbyterian; Ward, Euclid Avenue Methodist; Denman, First Baptist; Barton, First Congregational; Montgomery, Second Presbyterian; Jones, Fourth Congregational; Williams, First Methodist.
98. Unless otherwise noted, all quotations concerning the revival come from the 1 January 1910 issue of *Oak Leaves*.
99. Quotations are from Charles Howard Hopkins, *The Rise of the Social Gospel in American Protestantism* (New Haven: Yale University Press, 1967), pp. 296-97.
100. *Oak Leaves*, 28 October 1911.
101. Ibid., 4 November 1911.
102. Ibid., 13 April 1912.
103. Ibid., 31 January 1914.
104. Ibid., 3 January 1914.
105. Ibid., 4 February 1914.
106. Ibid., 11 February 1914.
107. Election results printed in *Oak Leaves*, 12 November 1904 and 7 November 1908.
108. For a discussion of the events surrounding the formation of the Progressive Party and a description of the convention itself see George Mowry, *Theodore*

251

Roosevelt and the Progressive Movement (New York: Hill and Wang, 1960), chapter IX.

109. The Progressive Party in Oak Park emphasized this theme in their advertisements. See, for instance, *Oak Leaves*, 2 November 1912.

110. Ibid., 9 November 1912.

111. One issue that did come to a direct vote in Oak Park was the initiative and referendum. The results showed 2,372 in favor and 182 opposed. Ibid., supplement 15, 1910.

112. The relationship between prohibition and Progressivism is treated in James H. Timberlake, *Prohibition and the Progressive Movement* (Cambridge: Harvard University Press, 1963). Briefer treatments may be found in Richard Hofstadter, *The Age of Reform* (New York: Random House, Vintage Books, 1955), pp. 283ff., and Paul Carter, *The Decline and Revival of the Social Gospel* (Ithaca: Cornell University Press, 1956), pp. 31-36.

113. *Oak Leaves*, 4 May 1907.

114. The various approaches were debated, for instance, at a meeting at First Baptist Church reported in ibid., 5 October 1912.

115. Letter to the editor, ibid., 28 May 1908.

116. Ibid., 12 July 1919.

117. Ibid., 14 June 1913.

118. Ibid., 26 February and in April 1916.

119. *St. Edmund's Parish Monthly*, August 1910 and December 1912. In the latter issue Code wrote: "We turn with loathing from the 'new woman' who, forgetting her sex and throwing aside the veil of modesty, assumes with brazen face the platform or even the pulpit . . . and advocates rights which, if granted, would be the very undoing of her social standing."

120. Speech quoted in *Oak Leaves*, 3 June 1916.

121. Ibid., 19 October 1907. Such differences in the woman suffrage movement are discussed in Aileen Kraditor, *The Ideas of the Woman Suffrage Movement 1890-1920* (New York: Doubleday and Company, Anchor Books, 1971), especially chapter 3.

122. *Oak Leaves*, 27 April 1907.

123. Ibid., 20 January 1912.

124. Quoted in ibid., 4 December 1915.

125. Reported in ibid., 18 November 1914.

126. Reported in ibid., 16 November 1912.

127. Ibid., 18 November 1911.

128. Ibid., 20 July 1912.

129. Strong later went to Seattle, where he became well known for his involvement with municipal reform, woman suffrage, and especially the cause of labor. He helped organize a general strike there and performed the funeral of five IWW members killed in the course of the strike. His daughter, Anna Louise Strong, later became famous in her own right, living for twelve years in Communist Russia and, as a journalist, chronicling various revolutions throughout the world. Her autobiography, *I Change Worlds* (New York: Garden City

Publishing Company, 1937), is an insightful account of a career that, in a sense, began in Oak Park and a family that once shared in Oak Park's system of values.

130. *Oak Leaves*, 30 November 1907.
131. Quoted in ibid., 7 September 1907.
132. Ibid., 11 May 1912.
133. Reported in ibid., 13 June 1914.
134. Figures reported in ibid., 12 April 1913.
135. Quoted in ibid., 20 July 1907.
136. Quoted in ibid., 31 August 1907.
137. *St. Edmund Parish Monthly*, February, 1911.
138. *St. Edmund Church Souvenir Program*, Silver Jubilee (Oak Park: St. Edmund Church, n.d.). See also the introduction to John J. Code, *A Shock of Sheaves* (Chicago: Thomas More Library, 1943), p. vii, which notes that "there was literally no room for him in Oak Park. The first mass was said in a barn."
139. *St. Edmund Parish Monthly*, various issues, but especially July through October 1914.
140. *Oak Leaves*, 15 July 1916.
141. For example, Father Code was not a part of the Pastors' Union, did not preach at union vespers in the summer, and did not appear at affairs such as a symposium on "Has Your Church A Special Message for the Age?" When Oak Park pastors spoke of "the churches" of Oak Park it was often clear that this did not mean St. Edmund. Among the clergy of Oak Park, Father Code seemed to be a minority of one.
142. *St. Edmund Parish Monthly*, February 1915 and June 1916.
143. *Oak Leaves*, 29 January 1910.
144. Ibid., 26 February 1910.
145. Ibid., 15 April 1911.
146. Ibid., 4 March 1911.
147. The total vote was 1,059 for and 3,027 against, while the vote in the southernmost precincts was 578 for and 617 against. Ibid., 8 April 1911.
148. Ibid., 27 March 1915.
149. Ibid., 1 January 1916.
150. Ibid., 1 March 1913.
151. Ibid., 7 June 1913.

CHAPTER FIVE

1. That the ward divisions had more than political significance was emphasized by the fact that the city newspaper contained separate sections devoted to news from the third and fourth wards (South Evanston) and from the sixth ward (North Evanston).
2. Quoted in the *Evanston Index*, 19 February 1898.
3. Ibid., 16 July 1898.

4. Ibid., 30 July 1898.
5. Ibid., 6 May 1899.
6. Quoted in ibid., 13 August 1898.
7. Ibid.
8. During most of this period the *Index* had competition from the *Evanston Press*, and for a brief time the two were joined by a third paper, the *Evanston News*. In 1915 a merger created the *Evanston News-Index* and the *Press* went out of business.
9. The nature of the *Index* as a newspaper was certainly one of the contributing factors in giving Evanston a different tone from Oak Park. *Oak Leaves* was printed with a magazine format and each week carried a cover photograph of a person or persons identified with some positive aspect of community life. It carried only local news, and as a matter of stated policy did not print even local news that it felt was detrimental to community morale. By contrast the *Index* had an appearance much more like the metropolitan press. It frequently carried front-page stories about crime, insanity, suicide, and other forms of social maladjustment. It did not restrict itself to local affairs, and even at one point had a full-page summary of metropolitan, national, and international news. It carried notices and reviews of Chicago theaters and other cultural events. Toward the end of the period it even became a daily paper. At the least, these things seemed to say that the *Index* thought of itself as a city newspaper. Whether they in any sense represented a conscious attempt to encourage the people of Evanston to think of their community as a city can, of course, only be a matter of speculation.
10. *Evanston Index*, 26 January 1895.
11. Ibid., 21 June 1902.
12. Ibid., various issues of 1913.
13. Ibid., 31 March 1894.
14. Ibid., 26 January 1895.
15. Ibid., 9 February 1895.
16. Ibid., 16 March and 6 April 1895.
17. Ibid., 20 April 1895.
18. The report of the meeting and Grover's speech appeared in ibid., 11 January 1902.
19. Ibid., 25 February 1899.
20. Ibid., 19 August 1911.
21. *Evanston News-Index*, 16 August 1915. Note once again the raising of the threat of annexation as connected to the resistance to change. The repeated attempt to establish a linkage between annexation and an intolerance for urbanization was in stark contrast to Oak Park, where "citification" was only a more subtle form of annexation.
22. Ibid., 20 August 1915.
23. *Evanston Index*, 12 January 1907.
24. *Evanston News-Index*, 11 May 1915.
25. *Evanston Index*, 19 January 1907.

26. Ibid., 14 January 1911.
27. Ibid., 6 June 1908.
28. *Evanston News-Index*, 2 October 1916.
29. Ibid., 8 February 1913.
30. There was one clear exception to this. The *Index* vigorously supported Taft in the Republican primary of 1912. When the Evanston vote went for Roosevelt by about 3 to 1, the *Index* accepted the verdict and maintained a discreet silence throughout the campaign for the presidency.
31. *Evanston News-Index*, 20 November 1915. This edition of the paper contained a full-section insert with the title "St. Mary's Parish Jubilee Edition." This was perhaps another one of the "subtle" ways that the paper announced the emergence of a new Evanston.
32. In 1893, for instance, there was a union meeting of the Scandinavian churches that passed resolutions for temperance, against secret societies, and against support for the World's Fair unless the Sabbath was to be observed. *Evanston Index*, 7 January 1893. These churches also combined to hear speakers or conduct revivals.
33. Ibid., 17 September 1898.
34. Ibid., 27 January 1894.
35. Ibid., 8 April 1899.
36. Ibid., 18 March 1916.
37. The description of how Emmanuel Methodist came to be was part of an article relating to a mortgage burning celebration, ibid., 9 February 1907.
38. Reported in ibid., 26 September 1896.
39. Northwestern's charter, it will be remembered, contained a provision that no alcoholic beverages were to be sold within four miles of the university. This presented several problems, however. The four mile limit extended into Chicago and other areas over which Evanston had no jurisdiction. The enforcement of the provision therefore became something of a complicated matter. In addition, there was continuing litigation over how the four miles were to be measured, whether it was to be as the crow flies or by the shortest available route of transportation. A further complication was the existence of what had come to be known as "blind pigs" both inside and outside the city limits. Blind pigs were situations where liquor was sold clandestinely under the cover of some other business enterprise. Collecting evidence against the "blind pigs" and prosecuting them sometimes proved to be a formidable task. Constant harassment seemed to be the most effective means of controlling the situation. For these reasons temperance was by no means a dead issue in Evanston.
40. *Evanston Index*, 9 December 1899.
41. Ibid., 30 December 1904.
42. Ibid., 26 November 1904.
43. Ibid., 26 November 1910. Headline: "Seven Pastors Fail to Draw."
44. Ibid., 1 January 1910.
45. Ibid., 8 January 1910.

46. Ibid., 18 November 1911. It may be appropriate to note at this point that the 1910 census figures showed white people of native parentage to be in the minority in Evanston. The total population was listed as 24,978. Of those, 10,165 were whites of native parentage, 1,160 were blacks, 7,912 were whites of foreign parentage and 5,700 were foreign-born whites.

47. Ibid., 31 January and 7 February 1914.

48. Ibid., 1 January 1898.

49. Ibid., 27 February 1904.

50. Ibid., 7 March 1908.

51. Ibid., 18 March 1916.

52. Ibid., 26 August 1893.

53. Ibid., 26 March 1898.

54. Ibid., 18 September 1909.

55. Ibid., 4 February 1911.

56. "This is not an earth whose regeneration may be expected day after tomorrow according to my optimistic prophecies, but a lost world . . . helpless and hopeless save through some demonstration in history of an essential redemption and salvation," B. Fay Mills quoted in McLoughlin, *Modern Revivalism*, p. 345.

57. This was not common for the *Index*. There were long periods when sermons were not reported at all. At other times the minister, for instance, of First Congregational would have his sermon printed each week. Only for a few years during the period was there an attempt to present a cross section of sermons on a regular basis.

58. Ibid., 9 January 1904.

59. Ibid., 16 January 1904

60. Ibid., 6 February 1904.

61. Ibid., 25 June 1904.

62. Ibid., 10 September 1904.

63. Rev. Benjamin Greene (First Baptist), quoted in ibid., 21 May 1904.

64. Dr. Timothy Frost (First Methodist), quoted in ibid., 19 November 1904.

65. Ibid., 1 July 1899.

66. Ibid., 23 December 1904.

67. Rev. John Mills preaching at First Presbyterian, quoted in ibid., 26 July 1902.

68. Ibid., 7 May 1904.

69. Rev. Frank Bristol, First Methodist, quoted in ibid., 13 February 1897.

70. Ibid., 4 November 1899. Evanston, like Oak Park, had an ordinance relating to the sale of cigarettes within the village. There is no indication of any activity to strengthen the ordinances. In spite of the strong interest in the issue shown by some of the churches at various times, the WCTU seems to have been the primary organization involved in monitoring the situation. They complained at various times that the ordinances were not being enforced.

71. Quoted in ibid., 22 February 1908.

72. Ibid., 12 May 1905.

73. Ibid.

74. On more than one occasion ministers who publicly aligned themselves with the Prohibition Party were gently or condescendingly criticized. Their commitment to temperance principles was applauded, but their political judgment was held up to ridicule. It was suggested that they would be better off leaving politics to someone else. On another occasion Rev. McElveen (First Congregational) was taken to task for unkind remarks he was alleged to have made about the Republican candidate for vice president. It was suggested that preachers had best stay out of politics and that one might question whether such remarks, which were sure to turn people away from the church, were even a wise policy from the perspective of the church. That was admitted, however, to be a concern of the church and not the public. Ibid., 26 September and 3 October 1908.
75. Ibid., 13 October 1905.
76. *Evanston Press*, 10 January 1914.
77. *Evanston Index*, 25 November 1911. The Drama Club was not primarily concerned to monitor the negative effects of theater, but rather to encourage and promote the dramatic arts and to raise the quality of theatrical productions.
78. Ibid., 10 and 17 January 1914.
79. *Evanston News-Index*, 21 April 1915.
80. Ibid., 24 September and 27 October 1915. Earlier in the year the paper had even offered its space for readers to present their opinions of various movies and thus bring the pressure of public opinion to bear on theater owners. Such active concern for the moral welfare of the community all but vanished as the evils of censorship superseded the evils of films in the mind of the editors.
81. *Evanston Index*, 13 January 1912.
82. *Evanston News-Index*, 21 September 1915.
83. Ibid., 22 November 1915.
84. *Evanston Index*, 9 January 1897.
85. There seems to have been little difficulty in attracting staff and leadership from the community, but it is difficult to tell how well attended the various programs were. Annual reports did not appear, nor did reports of specific meetings. At the outset the *Index* carried a weekly listing of the activities that were planned for the following week at the settlement, but as time went on even this became irregular.
86. Ibid., 9 January 1909.
87. Ibid., 5 June 1897.
88. The account of the meeting appeared in ibid., 19 September 1896.
89. In the meantime, still another offshoot of the Salvation Army had established a relationship to Evanston. Herbert Booth, the third son of William Booth, had split from both the Salvation Army and the Volunteers of America. In 1902 he came to live in Evanston, from which point he intended to start an organization of his own. Herbert Booth's arrival was, however, the extent of his press notices in Evanston. Ibid., 1 November 1902.
90. Ibid., 14 May 1904.
91. Ibid., 17 September 1904.

92. Ibid., 6 January 1905.
93. Hopkins, *The Rise of the Social Gospel in American Protestantism*, p. 282. Additional information on Stelzle's life and thought may also be found here.
94. *Evanston Index*, 12 March 1904.
95. Ibid., 16 April 1904.
96. It was not stated at the time precisely what precipitated the accusation against Boyd, but if he spoke in Evanston the way he was to speak in Chicago three years later, it is not difficult to understand why he might have come under attack. Portions of a speech delivered in February of 1907 were reprinted locally. In it he referred to blacks as "backward" and "defective." He said that the white man is, and will always remain, the master of black people, and that the "ultimate solution of the Negro question will be his segregation." Quoted in ibid., 16 February 1907.
97. Ibid., 23 April 1904.
98. Ibid.
99. Ibid., 30 April 1904.
100. Ibid., 10 November 1894.
101. Ibid., 16 August 1902.
102. Ibid., 7 and 8 June 1915.
103. Ibid., 29 August 1903.
104. Ibid., 8 March 1902.
105. Ibid., 8 March 1902.
106. The statement made in the other community newspaper was not as vehement, but it did implicitly challenge the church's leadership on the issue of temperance. "The *Press* is sure that public sentiment in Evanston is now just as strong against the illicit sale of liquor as it has ever been. Conditions are now not nearly as bad as they were in 1896 when the *Press* took upon itself the idea of exposing them. . . . *However the moral ideas of Evanston may change*, the selfish interest of this city will never change so as to permit the free sale of liquor in Evanston." *Evanston Press*, 8 March 1902 (my emphasis). Thus the *Press* noted that temperance was perhaps no longer firmly tied to Christian morality, but was tied only to Evanston's "selfish interests."
107. *Evanston Index*, 28 October 1899.
108. Ibid., 19 March 1898.
109. Ibid., 10 December 1898.
110. Ibid., 1 April 1899.
111. Ibid., 6 October 1894.
112. Ibid., 23 April 1904.
113. Ibid., 28 May 1910.
114. Ibid., 19 September 1908.
115. Ibid., 3 and 10 July 1909.
116. Ibid., 10 April 1897.
117. Ibid., 4 February 1899.
118. Ibid., 19 February 1898.
119. Ibid., 4 January 1902.

120. Ibid., 18 January 1902.
121. Ibid., 25 January 1902.
122. Ibid., 1 and 8 February 1902.
123. Ibid., 25 January 1902.
124. President Harris, quoted in ibid., 1 August 1908. At the time of the controversy the *Evanston Press* posed "A Question for 'higher' mathematicians: How many members of the faculty of Northwestern University and Garrett Biblical Institute would be left if all should resign who have views, but do not express them, contrary to the printed creed of the Methodist church?" *Evanston Press*, 8 February 1902.
125. *Evanston Index*, 1 February 1902.
126. Ibid.
127. Ibid.
128. Ibid., 22 February 1902.
129. Ibid., 26 April 1902.
130. Ibid., 12 July 1902.
131. Ibid., 8 August 1903.
132. Sketches of McElveen's career appeared in ibid., 14 March 1908 and 10 December 1917 in connection with his arrival and departure.
133. Periodical literature on the Emmanuel movement in 1908-1909 was extensive. A few titles may suffice as examples. "Christ, the Sick and Modern Christianity," *Arena*, May 1908: "The Emmanuel Movement and the Church," *Independent*, 26 November 1908; "New Crusade: Religious Therapeutics," *Current Literature*, March 1908; "Spiritual Unrest," *American Mercury*, December 1908.
134. *Evanston Index*, 2 and 23 January 1909.
135. For the classic statement of this see George M. Beard, *American Nervousness* (New York: G. P. Putnam's Sons, 1881).
136. *Evanston News-Index*, 4 March 1915.
137. *Evanston Index*, 22 June 1895.
138. Ibid., 1 December 1906.
139. Ibid., 5 December 1903.
140. Ibid., 17 and 24 December 1910.
141. Ibid., 18 and 25 May 1912.
142. Ibid., 24 August 1912.
143. *Evanston Press*, 7 February 1914.
144. *Evanston News-Index*, 13 February 1915.
145. Ibid., 15 February 1915.
146. Ibid., 23 February 1915.
147. Ibid., 3 May 1915.
148. Ibid., 10 May 1915.
149. Ibid.
150. Ibid., 17 May 1915.
151. Ibid., 24 May 1915.
152. Ibid., 1 June 1915.
153. Ibid., 3 June 1915.

154. Ibid., 27 May 1915.
155. Ibid., 2 June 1915.
156. Ibid., 3 June 1915.
157. Ibid., 12 June 1915.
158. Ibid., 28 May 1915.
159. Ibid., 15 June 1915.
160. Both Burnham and Taft were known as Evanstonians, not just as occasional or accidental residents of the area. Burnham was a member of many local organizations including the prestigious Evanston Club. Taft lectured to both church and secular groups in Evanston on the art of the fair.
161. A discussion of the World's Parliament of Religions may be found in Paul Carter, *The Spiritual Crisis of the Gilded Age* (Dekalb: Northern Illinois University Press, 1971), pp. 209-17.
162. *Evanston News-Index*, 9 October 1916.

Bibliography

Background Sources

Abell, Aaron I. *The Urban Impact on American Protestantism, 1865-1900*. Hamden, Conn.: Archon, 1962.

Andreas, A. T. *History of Cook County, Illinois*. Chicago: Andreas, 1884.

Arnold, Isaac N. *William B. Ogden and Early Days in Chicago*. Fergus Historical Series, no. 17. Chicago: Fergus Printing Co., 1882.

Baker, R. S. "Spiritual Unrest." *American Mercury* 67 (December 1908): 192-205.

Balestier, J. N. *The Annals of Chicago: A Lecture Delivered before the Chicago Lyceum, January 21, 1840*. Chicago: Edward H. Rudd, 1840.

Beard, George M. *American Nervousness*. New York: G. P. Putnam's Sons, 1881.

Billington, Ray. *Westward Expansion: A History of the American Frontier*. 3rd ed. New York: Macmillan Co., 1967.

Boorstin, Daniel. *The Americans: The National Experience*. New York: Random House, Vintage Books, 1967.

Carroll, Peter N. *Puritanism and the Wilderness*. New York: Columbia University Press, 1969.

Carter, Paul. *The Spiritual Crisis of the Gilded Age*. DeKalb: Northern Illinois University Press, 1971.

_____. *The Decline and Revival of the Social Gospel*. Ithaca: Cornell University Press, 1956.

Chicago Inter-Ocean, 16 March 1889.

Chicago Tribune, 30 March 1873; 9 October 1903.

Cross, Whitney R. *The Burned-over District*. Ithaca: Cornell University Press, 1950.

Cutten, B. "The Emmanuel Movement and the Church." *Independent* 65 (26 November 1908): 1228-30.

Dana, C. *The Garden of the World, or the Great West*. Boston: Wentworth and Company, 1856.

Davis, Allen F. *Spearheads for Reform: The Social Settlements and the Progressive Movement*. New York: Oxford University Press, 1967.

Dreiser, Theodore. *The Titan*. New York: New American Library, 1965.

Duncan, Hugh Dalziel. *Culture and Democracy*. Totowa, New Jersey: Bedminster Press, 1965.

Earhart, Mary. *Frances Willard: Prayers to Politics*. Chicago: University of Chicago Press, 1944.

Eggleston, Edward. *The Hoosier Schoolmaster*. New York: Grosset and Dunlap, 1913.

Fletcher, Henry J. "The Doom of the Small Town." *Forum* 19 (April 1895): 214-23.

Flower, B. O. "Christ, the Sick, and Modern Christianity." *Arena* 39 (May 1908): 557-64.

Frederick, Harold. *The Damnation of Theron Ware*. New York: Holt, Rinehart, and Winston, 1958.

Hofstadter, Richard. *The Age of Reform*. New York: Random House, Vintage Books, 1955.

Hopkins, Charles Howard. *The Rise of the Social Gospel in American Protestantism*. New Haven: Yale University Press, 1967.

Howe, Edgar Watson, *The Story of a Country Town*. New York: New American Library, 1964.

Isaac, Rhys. "Order and Growth, Authority and Meaning in Colonial New England." *American Historical Review* 76 (June 1971): 728-37.

Kraditor, Aileen. *The Ideas of the Woman Suffrage Movement, 1890-1920*. New York: Doubleday and Company, Anchor Books, 1971.

Lewis, R. W. B. *The American Adam*. Chicago: University of Chicago Press, 1958.

Lockridge, Kenneth A. *A New England Town: The First Hundred Years*. New York: W. W. Norton and Company, 1970.

Mann, Arthur, ed. *The Progressive Era*. New York: Holt, Rinehart, and Winston, 1963.

Marty, Martin E. *Righteous Empire: The Protestant Experience in America*. New York: Dial Press, 1970.

Marx, Leo. *The Machine in the Garden*. New York: Oxford University Press, 1967.

May, Henry F. *The End of American Innocence*. Chicago: Quadrangle Books, 1964.

_____. *Protestant Churches in Industrial America*. New York: Harper and Row, Harper Torchbooks, 1967.

McLoughlin, William G. *Modern Revivalism*. New York: Ronald Press, 1959.

Miller, Perry. *Errand into the Wilderness*. New York: Harper and Row, 1964.

Miller, Perry, and Thomas Johnson. *The Puritans*. 2 vols. New York: American Book Company, 1938.

Miyakawa, T. Scott. *Protestants and Pioneers*. Chicago: University of Chicago Press, 1964.

Morgan, Edmund S. *Visible Saints*. Ithaca: Cornell University Press, 1971.

Mowry, George. *Theodore Roosevelt and the Progressive Movement*. New York: Hill and Wang, 1960.

Nash, Roderick, ed. *The Call of the Wild, 1900-1916*. New York: George Braziller, 1970.

"New Crusade on Behalf of Religious Therapeutics." *Current Literature* 44 (March 1908): 289-92.

Noble, David W. *Historians Against History*. Minneapolis: University of Minnesota Press, 1965.

Nye, Russel B. *Midwestern Progressive Politics*. East Lansing: Michigan State University Press, 1951.

Pierce, Bessie Louise. *As Others See Chicago*. Chicago: University of Chicago Press, 1933.

_____. *History of Chicago*. 3 vols. New York: Alfred A. Knopf, 1937.

Porter, Jeremiah. "The Earliest Religious History of Chicago." Address read before Chicago Historical Society in 1859, reprinted in Fergus Historical Series, no. 14. Chicago: Fergus Printing Company, 1881.

Powell, Sumner Chilton. *Puritan Village: The Formation of a New England Town*. Middletown: Wesleyan University Press, 1963.

Quandt, Jean B. *From the Small Town to the Great Community*. New Brunswick: Rutgers University Press, 1970.

Smith, Henry Nash. *Virgin Land: The American West as Symbol and Myth*. New York: Random House, Vintage Books, 1950.

Smith, Page. *As a City upon a Hill: The Town in American History*. New York: Alfred A. Knopf, 1966.

Strauss, Anselm. *Images of the American City*. Glencoe: Free Press of Glencoe, 1961.

Strauss, Anselm. *Mirrors and Masks: The Search for Identity*. Glencoe: Free Press of Glencoe, 1959.

Strong, Josiah. *The Challenge of the City*. New York: Young People's Missionary Movement, 1907.

Timberlake, James H. *Prohibition and the Progressive Movement*. Cambridge: Harvard University Press, 1963.

Wade, Richard C., and Harold M. Mayer. *Chicago: Growth of a Metropolis*. Chicago: University of Chicago Press, 1969.

Walzer, Michael. *The Revolution of the Saints*. Cambridge: Harvard University Press, 1965.

Weisenburger, Francis P. *Triumph of Faith*. Richmond: William Byrd Press, 1962.

_____. *Ordeal of Faith*. New York: Philosophical Library, 1959.

Wentworth, John. "Early Chicago." Fergus Historical Series, no. 8. Chicago: Fergus Printing Co., 1876.

Wiebe, Robert H. *The Search for Order*. New York: Hill and Wang, 1969.

Zuckerman, Michael. *Peaceable Kingdoms: New England Towns in the Eighteenth Century*. New York: Random House, Vintage Books, 1972.

Oak Park and Evanston Sources

Amacker, Arthur. Oak Park, Illinois. Interview, 3 May 1973.

Barton, William E. *Autobiography*. Indianapolis: Bobbs-Merrill Company, 1932.

Code, John J. *A Shock of Sheaves*. Chicago: Thomas More Library, 1943.

Cook, May Estelle. *Little Old Oak Park*. Privately printed, 1961.

Evanston Index, 1873-1915, later called *Evanston News-Index*, 1915-1918.

Evanston Press, 1872-1915.

First Congregational Church, Oak Park. *Golden Jubilee Booklet*, 1913.

_____. *Church Bulletin*, 1900-1920.

_____. *The Red Book*, 1924.

Foster, Clyde D. *Evanston's Yesterdays*. Evanston: n.p., 1956.

French, Frederick E. *Old Evanston and Fifty Years After*. Privately printed, n.d., Evanston Public Library.

Furbeck, Elizabeth Porter. "Personal Reminiscences of Pioneer Life." Typed copy of speech delivered before the Society of Pioneers of Chicago, 25 May 1898, Oak Park Public Library.

Gale, Edwin O. *Reminiscences of Early Chicago and Vicinity*. Chicago: Fleming H. Revell Company, 1902.

_____. *Reminiscences of Oak Park, Galewood, and Vicinity*. N.p., 1898.

Grace Church. *Grace Church Items*, 1899-1924.

Halley, William. *Pictorial Oak Park*. Oak Park, Halley, 1898.

Heald, Robert. River Forest, Illinois. Interview, 20 October 1972.

Hoagland, Gertrude Fox, *An Historical Survey of Oak Park, Illinois*. Compiled under Federal W.P.A. Project #9516, 1937.

Humphrey, Dr. Simon James. *James Wilmarth Scoville: A Memorial*. N.p., n.d., Oak Park Public Library.

Hurd, Harvey B., and Robert D. Sheppard, eds. *History of Evanston*. Volume 2 of *Historical Encyclopedia of Illinois*, edited by Newton Bateman. 2 vols. Chicago: Munsell Publishing Company, 1906.

June, Frank H., and George R. Hemingway, *Glimpses of Oak Park*. Introduction entitled "The Secret Charm of Oak Park" by William E. Barton. June and Hemingway, 1912.

LeGacy, Arthur Evans. "Improvers and Preservers: A History of Oak Park, Illinois." Ph.D. dissertation, University of Chicago, 1967.

Lewis, John. *Chapters in Oak Park History*. Privately printed, n.d.

Lunt, Cornelia Gray. *Sketches of Childhood and Girlhood*. Evanston: privately printed, 1925.

Oak Leaves, 1902-1918.

Oak Park Reporter, 1899-1902.

Reeling, Viola Crouch. *Evanston: Its Land and Its People*. Evanston: Fort Dearborn Chapter, Daughters of the American Revolution, 1928.

St. Edmund Church. *Parish Monthly*, 1910-1918.

_____. *Souvenir Program, Silver Jubilee*. N.d.

St. John, Robert. *This Was My World*. Garden City: Doubleday and Company, 1953.

Sanford, Marcelline Hemingway. *At the Hemingways: A Family Portrait*. Boston: Atlantic Monthly Press, Little, Brown and Company, 1961.

Strong, Anna Louise. *I Change Worlds*. New York: Garden City Publishing Company, 1937.

The Vindicator, 13 January 1883.

Willard, Frances. *A Classic Town: The Story of Evanston*. Chicago: Women's Temperance Publishing Association, 1891.

Index

Addams, Jane, 152-53, 153, 200
African-Americans
  in Evanston, 185-86, 256n
  See also Racism
African Methodist Episcopal Church
  in Evanston, 185-86
Ahlstrom, Sydney, ix
Anderson, Sherwood
  Winesburg, Ohio, 53
Anti-Saloon League, 147-49
  See also Temperance
Apartment buildings, 179
Armstrong, Reverend, 249n
*As a City Upon a Hill: The Town in American
  History*, 17-18, 236-37n, 237n
Austin, Henry W., 35, 36, 40, 139, 239n,
  240n
Automobiles, 89-90

Baldwin, H. P., 119
Baldwin, Jesse, 63
Balestier, Joseph, 7, 27-28
Baptists, 94-95
  in Evanston, 184
  in Oak Park, 248n
Barclay, Philander, 119
Barton, William E., 29, 40, 63, 85, 216,
  249n, 251n
  on labor, 154-55
  as local leader, 246n
  on morality, 110, 111, 116
  on movies, 120-21, 123, 124
  on Oak Park as model community, 67-68
  on Oak Park's development, 57, 59

on religion, 75, 89, 93, 95
and revivalism, 129, 130, 133-34
"The Secret Charm of Oak Park," 61-62
and temperance, 148
on urbanization, 83
Bates, Mayor, 207-8
Beecher, Edward, 216
Beecher, Henry Ward, 1
Bell, Bernard I., 162-63
Blacks
  See African-Americans
Blanchard, R. K., 42
Blount, Anna, 149-50
Booth, Ballington, 202
Booth, Herbert, 257n
Booth, Maud, 202
Botsford, Jabez, 42
Boyd, John, 165, 188
  accused of racism, 204, 258n
  on biblical infallibility, 214
  on corporations, 195
  and racial discrimination, 204-5
  sermon by, 193
  on Spanish-American War, 171
  and temperance, 205-7
  and Volunteers of America, 202
Brainard, Captain, 46
Brauer, Jerald C., ix
Bristol, F. M., 188, 214
Brooklyn
  annexation by New York City, 28
Brown, Mr. (YMCA state secretary), 107,
  249n
Brown, Andrew J., 42
Brown, E. L., 46, 47

Chicago Studies in the History of American Religion

Editors

JERALD C. BRAUER & MARTIN E. MARTY

(continued, over)

11. Kountz, Peter. *Thomas Merton as Writer and Monk: A Cultural Study, 1915-1951*

12. Lagerquist, L. DeAne. *In America the Men Milk the Cows: Factors of Gender, Ethnicity, and Religion in the Americanization of Norwegian-American Women*

13. Markwell, Bernard Kent. *The Anglican Left: Radical Social Reformers in the Church of England and the Protestant Episcopal Church, 1846-1954*

14. Morris, William Sparkes. *The Young Jonathan Edwards: A Reconstruction*

15. Pellauer, Mary D. *Toward a Tradition of Feminist Theology: The Religious Social Thought of Elizabeth Cady Stanton, Susan B. Anthony, and Anna Howard Shaw*

16. Potash, P. Jeffrey. *Vermont's Burned-Over District: Patterns of Community Development and Religious Activity, 1761-1850*

17. Queen, Edward L., II. *In the South the Baptists are the Center of Gravity: Southern Baptists and Social Change, 1930-1980*

18. Schmidt, Jean Miller. *Souls or the Social Order: The Two-Party System in American Protestantism*

19. Shaw, Stephen J. *The Catholic Parish as a Way-Station of Ethnicity and Americanization: Chicago's Germans and Italians, 1903-1939*

20. Shepard, Robert S. *God's People in the Ivory Tower: Religion in the Early American University*

21. Snyder, Stephen H. *Lyman Beecher and his Children: The Transformation of a Religious Tradition*